AMERICAN MAGNITUDE

AMERICAN MAGNITUDE

HEMISPHERIC VISION AND PUBLIC FEELING IN THE UNITED STATES

Christa J. Olson

THE OHIO STATE UNIVERSITY PRESS
COLUMBUS

Copyright © 2021 by The Ohio State University.
All rights reserved.

Library of Congress Cataloging-in-Publication data available online at https://catalog.loc.gov
Identifiers: ISBN 9780814214831 (cloth) | ISBN 0814214835 (cloth) | ISBN 9780814281673 (ebook) | ISBN 0814281672 (ebook) | ISBN 9780814258118 (paper) | ISBN 0814258115 (paper)

Cover design by Susan Zucker
Composition by Stuart Rodriguez
Type set in Minion Pro

For Anthony and Sarah and the great joy of friendship

CONTENTS

List of Illustrations		ix
Acknowledgments		xi
INTRODUCTION	A Glance at the Map	1
CHAPTER 1	Acquiescing to Accumulation	27
CHAPTER 2	The Andes on Display	69
CHAPTER 3	Of Cities on Hills	101
CHAPTER 4	Animating Interests	141
CHAPTER 5	Size Matters	180
Bibliography		195
Index		217

ILLUSTRATIONS

FIGURE 0.1	P. Haas, lithographer, "Map of the Western Coast of America with the Intended Track of the Steamers from New York to the Isthmus of Panama and from Panama Along the Western Coast northerly as far as California and southerly as far as Conception"	xvi
FIGURE 0.2	Martin Waldseemüller, "Universalis Cosmographia Secundum Ptholomaei Traditionem et Americi Vespucii Alioru[m]que Lustrationes [St. Dié]"	3
FIGURE 1.1	Nathaniel Currier, lithographer, *The Soldier's Return*	53
FIGURE 1.2	Henry R. Robinson, lithographer, *Battle of Buena Vista. View of the Battle-Ground and Battle of "The Angostura" Fought near Buena Vista, Mexico February 23rd 1847 (Looking S. West)*	54
FIGURE 1.3	J. Butler and C. Lewis, lithographers, *Death of Lieut. Col. Henry Clay Jr. of the Second Regiment Kentucky Volunteers at the Battle of Buena Vista. Feby 23rd 1847*	55
FIGURE 1.4	Nathaniel Currier, lithographer, and John Cameron, artist, *"A Little More Grape, Capt. Bragg"*	56
FIGURE 1.5	Nathaniel Currier, lithographer, *The Gallant Charge of the Kentucky Cavalry Under Col. Marshall at the Battle of Buena Vista Febr 23d 1847*	57

FIGURE 1.6	Charles Risso, lithographer, after a daguerreotype by J. H. William Smith, *Rough and Ready as He Is*	59
FIGURE 2.1	Frederic Edwin Church, *Cotopaxi*, 1855	73
FIGURE 2.2	Frederic Edwin Church, *Cotopaxi*, 1862	74
FIGURE 2.3	Frederic Edwin Church, *View of Cotopaxi*, 1867	75
FIGURE 2.4	Frederic Edwin Church, *Heart of the Andes*, 1859	77
FIGURE 2.5	Frederic Edwin Church, detail from *Heart of the Andes*, 1859	79
FIGURE 3.1	"Lost City in the Clouds Found After Centuries"	128
FIGURE 3.2	Hiram Bingham, "An Architectural Triumph: Machu Picchu"	131
FIGURE 3.3	H. L. Tucker, "A Picture of the Same Part of the City of Machu Picchu as Shown in the Preceding Illustration, But Photographed the Year Before"	132
FIGURE 3.4	Hiram Bingham, "Intihuatana Hill and the Terraces West of the Sacred Plaza"	132
FIGURE 4.1	José, still from *La Historia de José*	160
FIGURE 4.2	Ramón, still from *La Historia de Ramón*	160

ACKNOWLEDGMENTS

When a project takes longer than expected to finish, as this one did, it goes through many inspirations and picks up lots of debt. *American Magnitude* started while I was in Ecuador in 2005. Then, it was a nagging curiosity about how much Ecuadorian artists were said to have learned from their US counterparts and a skepticism that the learning had gone only one way. By a few years into the tenure track, the project had widened to include artists traveling into other parts of Latin America, but it was still focused on what US image-makers learned when they went south. Around that same time, however, René De los Santos started asking me gentle but persistent questions about my uniformly US-centric perspective. What, he would ask, did Mexicans have to say about this? Ecuadorians? Peruvians? His questions stayed with me—both because he kept asking them and because I didn't have an answer.

For a while, I sidestepped those questions by directing my attention beyond the individual image-makers (Currier, Church, Bingham, and Disney) to the broader contexts in which they worked. Jenny Rice's scholarship on public feeling and conversations with Kate Vieira helped me recognize that I was interested in how large groups of people acquiesced to shared visions of themselves. That realization offered ways forward but few answers. I was nearly tenured, I had a lot of archival material and some bright ideas, but I didn't really have an argument or a theoretical frame beyond the vague assertion that something was happening with magnitude and nationalism.

Enter sensation. Around that time, three things happened: Debbie Hawhee's work on sensory rhetorics came my way; Jenell Johnson, my perennial writing partner, began writing about "visceral publics;" and my advisees, particularly Stephanie Larson, dove deeply into theories of affect, feeling, and embodiment. While my four-month-old son napped in the tent, I sat by a campfire at Split Rock State Park and wrote out—longhand—an affect-heavy theoretical framework for the book. Affect itself eventually faded, but embodied looking and circulating feeling stayed in the book's foreground.

What eventually became the book's titular "public feeling" was born as I watched Donald Trump become president of the United States. I should not have been surprised at the visceral racism, xenophobia, sexism, and nationalism that 2016 laid bare, but I was. I began to see American magnitude in new light. I could no longer think of white supremacy and settler colonial presumption as merely informing American magnitude. They were, I finally recognized, constitutive of it. Alongside events in the news, René's persistent questions and conversations with advisees Chris Earle and Anthony Black made it urgent for this book to more critically and thoroughly address racialization, colonialism, and persistent resistance. They also shifted the book's theoretical and material archives in important ways—though it took a while (including a nudge from Reviewer #2) for those changes to fully emerge.

Around the same time, institutional and national service started taking significantly more of my time. On the one hand, that labor inevitably slowed my writing. On the other, it gave this project time to grow and led me into essential conversations. In particular, frequent discussions with colleagues about racism and white supremacy culture at the University of Wisconsin–Madison and in rhetorical studies, my work on the Rhetoric Society of America (RSA) Board of Directors (and helping plan the 2018 RSA conference), and rhetorical studies' confrontation with its own racism during and after summer 2019 all left their mark on this book's theories, arguments, and presumptions. Kirt Wilson and I rarely talked about our scholarship, but his leadership in RSA and our frequent conversations about the society shaped this book and my investments. Anjali Vats, Ersula Ore, Jessica Enoch, Vanessa Beasley, and Lisa Flores—through their scholarship, our shared RSA work, and the occasional back channel—likewise helped *American Magnitude* come into itself.

My final work on *American Magnitude* happened during COVID-19. I had planned to submit the manuscript for review in late March 2020 but was running a bit behind. When the pandemic hit, writing came to a screeching halt. Taralee Cyphers at The Ohio State University Press (OSUP) was immensely patient with the delay even when I was not. Thanks to the kindness of colleagues—who read almost-final drafts, ignored the many balls I was dropping, and offered encouraging words—the manuscript did eventually get to OSUP.

Caroline Gottschalk Druschke, Morris Young, and Mary Fiorenza, as well as Kassia Shaw and James Ryan (the assistant directors of UW–Madison's English 201 program), deserve special mention for keeping me afloat. Krista Kennedy, Amy Wan, and Jenell Johnson made space to read drafts even in the midst of untenable COVID schedules. The Badasses in Mid Rank, dedicated to the pursuit of "Phil," provided invaluable moral support. When, a few months later, two anonymous reviewers offered powerful, challenging feedback on the manuscript, all those same colleagues again made it possible for me to revise—frantically and intensely—during early fall 2020.

Finishing a manuscript in the middle of 2020's isolation and anxiety amplified for me what I already knew: Writing is communal and writers are interdependent. This book, and I, owe a great deal to a great many people. I have named many in the previous paragraphs, but that narrative couldn't include mention of everyone who deserves thanks.

This book could not exist without archives and libraries (or without archivists and librarians). Its first tiny kernels came into my hands in the reading room of the Fondo Cultural of the Banco Central and the library of the Universidad Católica in Quito, Ecuador. Travis Weiss did the last on-site research for the book at the Rockefeller Archive Center in Sleepy Hollow, New York. In between, Ida Briar at the Olana New York State Historical Site, Debbie Hamm and colleagues at the Abraham Lincoln Presidential Library, and the staff at Yale University's Sterling Memorial Library, the California State Library, the Library of Congress's Prints and Photographs Division, the Wisconsin Historical Society, and the US National Archives answered my vague inquiries, helped me navigate catalog systems, and generally made the rich material stuff of this book available. E. Brooke Phipps tracked down a few last-minute citations at the National Archives and Emily Bouza managed image permissions. Kendra Smith-Howard and Jan Tredwell allowed me into their homes while I did archival work in upstate New York and New Haven, respectively. I am so grateful to the people who donated letters, pictures, and documents; the people who cataloged and preserved them; and the people who ensure that they are accessible today.

Financial support from the Graduate School and the English Department at the University of Wisconsin–Madison, including funds donated by William and Ethel Gofen, gave me time to write and funded research travel. Spring Sherrod, Julie Palmer, and Carole Kraak taught me how to navigate university systems, ensured that the right people got paid, and provided support, insight, and humor along the way. Department chairs Caroline Levine, Russ Castronovo, and Anja Wanner were and are kind, strong advocates. Caroline and Anja have also become feminist mentors and role models for me. I am constitutionally inclined to say yes—to participate in the work of building the systems that support intellectual and community work. I am grateful to Caroline, Anja, Kirt Wilson, and others who have offered me rewarding opportunities to say yes. I am also grateful to Jenell Johnson, Krista Kennedy, and Amy Wan, who help me think through when to say no.

UW–Madison's intellectual communities sustained and informed this project. I am especially grateful to the students, staff, and faculty in communication arts; Latin American, Caribbean, and Iberian studies; art history; and the composition and rhetoric program. Faculty and graduate students at the University of Illinois also gave a much-needed hearing to some early material. For those interactions and others, I owe particular thanks to colleagues Lauren Kroiz, Allison Prasch, Sara Mckinnon, Rob Asen, Alberto Vargas, Cara Finnegan, Kim Hensley Owens, Janine Solberg, and Debra Hawhee; to former graduate students Nancy Reddy, Stephanie Larson, Rubén Casas, Anthony Black, Neil Simpkins, Leigh Elion, Brandee Easter, Kathleen Daly, Chris Castillo, and Chris Earle; and to current graduate students Tori Peters, Ann Kim, and Meg Marquardt. Susan Hagness provided extraordinary and generous mentorship, encouraging me to look past the next step to the ones beyond it (and Michael Bernard-Donals knew us both well enough to know our unlikely pairing would work). My past and current colleagues at UW–Madison astound me with their generosity. Mary Fiorenza and Brad Hughes provided wise guidance for tackling the everyday work of teaching. Jim Brown, Caroline Gottschalk Druschke, and Kate Vieira each read drafts and offered critique and inspiration. Morris Young is an anchor in my professional life. His kindness, steadfastness, and brilliance have shaped my work well beyond this book, and his Korean chicken has—quite literally—fed it (or, rather, me).

René De los Santos, Abraham Romney, Alejandra Vitale, Adriana Angel, Susan Romano, Karrieann Soto Vega, Christina Cedillo, Rachel Jackson, and José Cortez have all helped me see Américan rhetoric in ways that show up throughout this book and in my scholarship more broadly. As earlier paragraphs suggest, René played an especially crucial role in *American Magnitude*. I am grateful for his intellectual generosity, his kind humor, and his impeccable taste in pocket handkerchiefs.

Among colleagues, two stand out for particular thanks: Amy Wan and Jenell Johnson. From my first days in rhetoric and writing studies, Amy Wan has been a role model for me. I still cannot believe my good fortune that she is not only a savvy reader and clear-eyed critic for my writing but also a conference buddy and friend. This book is better because of Amy's feedback, and I am a better scholar, mentor, and teacher because of Amy's friendship. I am also mindful of the excellent meals and tasty snacks that accompany friendship with Amy.

A shared Minnesotan style and loyalty to #TeamSnow may have sparked my connection with Jenell Johnson, but our friendship is rich with intellectual resonances, shared commitments, and hours spent writing side by side. Every page of this book owes something to Jenell. She read paragraphs and chapters, talked me through flashes of inspiration, and commiserated in the doldrums of writerly exhaustion. Sometimes, she sponsored my 10 a.m. croissant (or scone). Her thinking has rubbed off on me in the best possible ways, and I can only hope that some of her brilliance has too.

My children, Freya and Silas, have been no help at all with my scholarship, and they have only the vaguest idea of what this book is about. I am so proud of them and so grateful for their love. After all, what good is a book if there's no one to change the subject to talk about noodles, the etiquette of stuffed-animal weddings, or the Kratt brothers' most recent adventures?

Almost all of this book happened after kids joined our family. I couldn't have researched or written it without the child care workers and teachers who guided, taught, and cared for Freya and Silas. Andrea Graham, Amy Turkowski, and Beth Loheide at Franklin Elementary; Alix Wallace, Linh Duong, Itzel Saucedo, Sara Hassan, Gabriella Pott, Emma Hutchins, Stephen Baraboo, and Emmaray Einstein at University Avenue Discovery Center; and Annette Wagner, Jolene Eckert, Randi Osborne, Sandy Lomas, and Danielle Wachter at SSM Health Childcare deserve special mention. Nina Chosy joined our pod during summer 2020 and spent hours caring for Freya and Silas during an impossible time. All those teachers—and the aides, assistants, and support staff who work alongside them—made a huge difference for our kids. In the process, they made a huge difference for this book.

Anna Henning, my partner and dearest friend, has been there for every step of this project. She pulled me away from research so that we could hike in Vermont; she took a newborn and a rambunctious three-year-old to the National Zoo while I worked at the National Archives; she read the Machu Picchu chapter when I had lost all sense of direction; she is my daily companion. She also shows me through her own work how writing matters in the world. A book is a nice thing. A life alongside Anna is infinitely better.

My wish for all the writers reading these acknowledgments: that you experience the sort of robust engagement, intellectual generosity, and frequent distraction that has fed my writing, and that whenever you confront exhaustion, uncertainty, anxiety, or impatience you be shielded, as I was, by the goodness of others.

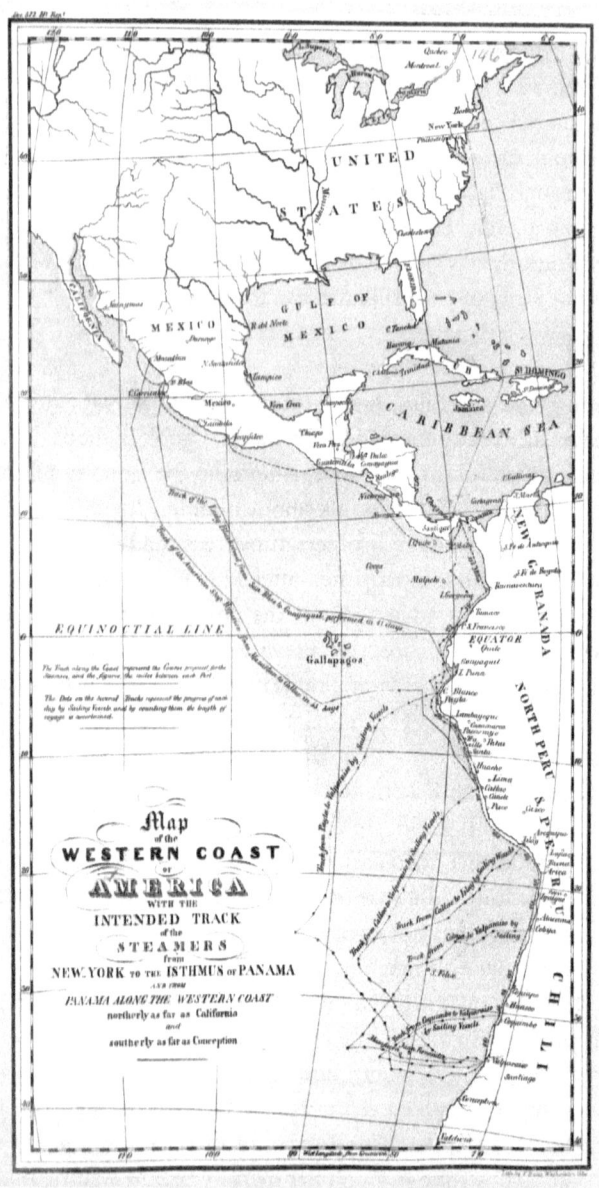

FIGURE 0.1. P. Haas, lithographer, "Map of the Western Coast of America with the Intended Track of the Steamers from New York to the Isthmus of Panama and from Panama Along the Western Coast northerly as far as California and southerly as far as Conception" in A Collection of Maps, Charts, Drawings, Surveys, etc, Published from Time to Time, by Order of the Two Houses of Congress: [United States, Western Hemisphere, and the World]. Washington, DC: United States Congress, 1843. Geography and Map Division, Library of Congress. Call Number: G1200 U5 1843. Digital ID: http://hdl.loc.gov/loc.gmd/g3700m.gct00284.

INTRODUCTION

A Glance at the Map

> "A glance at the map was enough to convince one that sooner or later the United States must extend to the Rio Grande as its natural boundary."[1]
>
> —Gustave Koerner, *Memoirs of Gustave Koerner*

When Gustave Koerner determined so confidently that the United States "must extend to the Rio Grande as its natural boundary," he would have been glancing at a map much like the one before you now (figure 0.1). His contemporaries glanced at similar maps and were equally convinced that the United States must, inevitably, extend to the Pacific Ocean. Some, glancing at the map, were confident that the United States would extend even further south—to the twenty-sixth parallel or beyond. For all these glancers, their sightlines were clear. The outcome was certain. Their country was destined by God to be great.

To gather information with a glance is to rely heavily on what is already known. Glances, in that sense, are tools of presumption and confirmation. Viewers glance to check for what they expect to see.[2] So, I invite you, instead of glancing, to linger on this 1843 map with me and try to grasp the magnitude of presumption at work in those glances some hundred and seventy-five years ago.

---

1. Koerner, *Memoirs*, I:488.
2. A double take, then, is what happens when a glance unexpectedly fails to confirm the expected. In making these claims about "glances," I depart from the phenomenological and theoretical frames for the glance that others have elaborated, in which the glance is a primary means of accumulating information and learning about the world. In my departure, rather than objecting to their approaches, I merely pursue another aspect of a complex phenomenon. Casey, "Attending and Glancing"; Casey, *The World at a Glance*; Zulli, "Capitalizing on the Look."

I have spent my life in a United States that stretches from the Atlantic to the Pacific, from the top of the Great Lakes to the Rio Grande. I can picture the shape of the United States in my sleep and sketch out its boundaries on a blank page without much trouble. But I cannot glance or gaze at this map and tell you that the Rio Bravo must inevitably become the Rio Grande and the southern border of the United States. Yet Koerner and his white settler contemporaries could. Or they thought they could. As I write these words in late 2020, I suspect many of my own contemporaries would agree with Koerner and company. A glance at the map shows some "American" viewers—then and now—what they have already determined to be present: an expansive, grand, inevitable (United States of) America.

This book seeks out the stories that lie behind that glancing confidence and its "assertion of the obviousness of national space."[3] It follows those stories and glances from the early 1800s to the present, showing how, in their accumulation, they picture a great America by drawing on, modifying, and circulating what I term "American magnitude": appeals to grandeur that presume and perpetuate the particular consequence of this place called America. In these stories and through glances, the United States lays claim not only to territory already occupied, inhabited, and storied, but also to a telluric spirit: the constitutive center of a place called America.

There are thirty-some nation-states on the American continent, but more often than not rhetors in the United States habitually, glancingly, claim "America," unmarked, for ourselves.[4] Tracking American magnitude—in stories and glances—illuminates how, across major moments and quotidian activities, the uniquely American Americanness of the United States has come to be common sense. The story of American magnitude is the story of how US Americans—particularly, but not exclusively, white settler US Americans—have come to feel themselves as *the* Americans within a broader American context.[5]

---

3. Rifkin, *Manifesting America*, 5.

4. For much of the sixteenth through eighteenth centuries colonial geographers vacillated between imagining a single American continent, sometimes divided into northern and southern halves, and two distinct American continents, North and South. By the mid-nineteenth century, atlases published in the United States trended toward the two-continent model, while those published in Europe and in Latin America kept to a single continent model. Lewis and Wigen, *The Myth of Continents*, 29–30, 219–20. Even until the mid-twentieth century, however, US proponents of a continental politics continued to assert a single American continent, and popular usage in Latin America still imagines a unitary continent. Lewis and Wigen, *The Myth of Continents*, 32, 220. In this book, I follow the single-continent convention because of its close fit with the rhetorical practices under investigation. Both options, of course, bring new places into being through colonial imagining and colonial action.

5. The presumptive Americanness of the United States makes itself felt in mundane but pervasive ways, including in two problems readers will encounter throughout this book: (1)

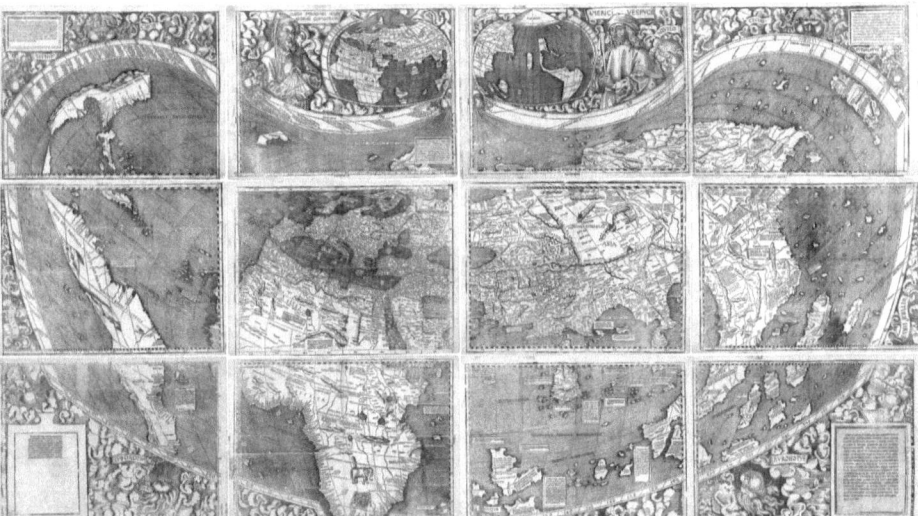

FIGURE 0.2. Martin Waldseemüller, "Universalis Cosmographia Secundum Ptholomaei Traditionem et Americi Vespucii Alioru[m]que Lustrationes [St. Dié]," 1507. One map on twelve sheets, made from original woodcut. Geography and Map Division, Library of Congress. Call Number: G3200 1507 .W3, Digital ID: http://hdl.loc.gov/loc.gmd/g3200.ct000725C.

To begin that pursuit of American magnitude's stories, I open this book with glances at three maps: the one you've already seen and two others. The second map is famous, monumental, and historic: It's the map that names "America." The third map is none of those. It's a simple illustration in a child's book. Our glances at these maps will not show you the inevitable shape of the United States. Instead, they hint at the course and consequence of American magnitude. In them, you just might glimpse the cartographic outlines of the United States gradually becoming *the* consequential site of America.

---

what to call people from the United States and (2) how to distinguish "America," the idea, from "America," the United States of America. Regarding the first: In English, there is no easy way to indicate a person from the United States other than "American." I resist that approach for obvious reasons and instead invite you to trip over "US American." May the awkwardness of the phrase attune you to the presumption behind an unmarked "America." To confront the second problem, I use a combination of italics, brackets, and awkward phrases to ensure clarity about references to "America" (the idea of the continent and its particular telluric character) and the United States of America. To discuss moments when rhetors refer to "America" but mean the United States, I use brackets ([US] American). When I refer to the United States, I either use those two words or, for the adjectival form, "US American." In parallel, "America" and "*America*" always refer to the continent and/or its telluric idea. "América," when it appears, refers to a particularly hispanohablante uptake of the telluric idea. In each case, the disfluency is the point. I invite readers to stumble into awareness of [US] American commonsense.

When America was invented, the United States did not yet exist. I do not mean this merely as a matter of chronology, though it is true that the thirteen British colonies hadn't yet been founded, let alone achieved independence. Instead, I mean that the mapmaker whose famous map so confidently named a continent after one of his colleagues did not yet know that there was a substantial landmass north of the Tropic of Cancer. He drew the Caribbean islands larger than life, placed a long and narrow mass where we would now find South America, and then sketched a petite stretch of "Terra Ulteri Incognita" to the north and west of it. The flag of Castile hovered in between (figure 0.2). For Martin Waldseemüller, "America" was what English speakers today call South America.[6] What would eventually become the unmarked center of America began its existence as an appendage.

More than three hundred years passed between Waldseemüller's 1507 decision to name the "New World" after Amerigo Vespucci and the 1843 "Map of the Western Coast of America." In that time, America took shape and began migrating northward. The "Map of the Western Coast" outlines a shape still familiar today, and it extends "America" from the top of the Great Lakes to midway down Chile's narrow stretch. Though "America" encompasses the whole continent in the 1843 map, the center is already settling. The map imagines steamer routes from New York, across the isthmus of Panama, and south. It preemptively suggests the likelihood of US ports on the California coast—then still part of Mexico. The shape of things to come is palpable. Koerner's glance is corroborated.

Another 175 years passed between the 1843 map and me reading a book about dinosaurs to an eager three-year-old. Over those years, the United States laid rather thorough claim to "America." And so, in 2016, my daughter and I sat down in the middle of America, in a house built on stolen Ho-Chunk land, to read *Giant Dinosaurs of the Jurassic*. The book introduces young readers to the Morrison Formation, a fossil-rich region that stretches north and south along the mountain range that settlers call the Rockies. A map on the first page of the book outlines the Morrison Formation in red. It also, conveniently, marks the borders of the United States. Now, perhaps the shadow of the United States is there to help young readers locate the Morrison Formation in familiar terms, but there is really no reason to mark the United States in this map. The formation pays no attention to political borders—they didn't exist when the dinosaurs died, were covered in mud, and slowly turned to stone. Even if they had, they would have made no difference to fossilization. The shape and extent of the Morrison Formation would be the same no

---

6. Gruesz, "America," 18.

matter what had happened with the US Revolution, the Louisiana Purchase, the annexation of Texas, the Treaty of Guadalupe Hidalgo, or the Gadson Purchase.

The familiar shape of the United States is necessary in *Giant Dinosaurs of the Jurassic* precisely because Gustave Koerner was wrong. "A glance at the map" is not "enough to convince" anyone of the natural shape of the United States.[7] No river or other geographic formation neatly cleaves the continent into nation-sized pieces, let alone the precise shape of the United States. That shape—along with its political, social, and economic implications—needs to be overlaid in order to be legible. And so, there it is, presumed by the mapmakers to be sufficiently consequential to include in a children's book about dinosaurs. A glance at this last map does actually communicate a sense of inevitability about the United States of America. Gustave Koerner's map didn't have the future shape of the continental United States clearly marked out in red lines. His map, like figure 0.1, may well not even have shown the then-accurate borders of the country. Still, given the presumptions of consequence behind his glances, such a lack of clear divisions may have encouraged Koerner's eyes to rove across seemingly empty territory, making space for his own manifest invention.

For, as Edmundo O'Gorman established, America has always been "invented," not inevitable. At first, as Waldseemüller determined, "America" was the territory invaded by Castile and Leon and ultimately brought under Spanish control. In 1823, when US President James Monroe penned his seventh annual message to Congress, "America" could easily refer to the whole "New World," but a particularly American United States was emerging.[8] By 1845, on the eve of the annexation of Texas and the US-Mexico War, when Jane McManus Storm (also known as Cora Montgomery) coined the term "manifest destiny" in John O'Sullivan's *United States Magazine and Democratic Review,* she also named Texas's "American population" among the reasons the former Mexican state truly belonged as part of the United States.[9] And, by 1945, Franklin Delano Roosevelt's Good Neighbor Policy generously (re)extended American consideration to the "other American republics." Each moment of invention—whether it contracted or expanded the geographical boundaries of the United States—added meaning and consequence to "America."

Anibal Quijano, expanding on O'Gorman's study of invention, explains that America is "a geosocial construct" built on four features: "coloniality, eth-

---

7. Koerner, *Memoirs,* I:488.
8. Christa J. Olson, "But in Regard," 267.
9. Storm, "Annexation," 6; Greenberg, *Manifest Manhood,* 20.

nicity, racism, and the concept of newness itself."[10] The "New World" was not found, it was made, with all the universalizing, violent, white supremacist, settler rhetorics of modernity.[11] Conquering territory, drawing boundaries, and establishing control over bodies was, from the beginning, the stuff of making America. This book tracks that colonial, ethnocentric, racist, and innovation-obsessed invention and the claims to particular consequence that accompanied it. It maps how US Americans looking from the United States into the "other" Americas to the south created, sustained, and circulated the United States *as* America through appeals to grandeur, import, and consequence.

American Magnitude focuses on the period of emerging US regional and global power from, roughly, 1845 to 1945. Its objects are visual: prints, paintings, photographs, and films. They are also public: made and circulated by image-makers who repeatedly created pictures with the primary purpose of showing them to large audiences and, more specifically, to *American* audiences. Taking up these objects in context and following them around, *American Magnitude* illuminates the visual processes by which US American image-makers and viewers oriented themselves toward American spaces, American ideas, and Americanness in light of the hemisphere.

One of this book's central assumptions is that, by seeing American scenes, audiences in the United States learned the contours and responsibilities of being American. Scholars in rhetoric and beyond have established the groundwork for that assumption, showing how landscape painting, photography, and tourism, for example, revealed the United States to itself and helped viewers experience themselves as part of the nation.[12] This book extends that view. I argue that becoming American, in its most consequential sense, required looking not only *within* but also *beyond* US borders. It required that US viewers—consistently imagined as white—feel themselves to be particularly American among Americans.

Audiences in the United States learned important elements of their Americanness by encountering American scenes that were not part of the United States of America. They, like Koerner, glanced at what was not the United States and saw their own future. Especially following the US-Mexican war, their glances were turned southward, to the "other American republics" in Latin America. What Gruesz calls a "small question of geographical seman-

---

10. Quijano and Wallerstein, "Americanity as a Concept," 549, 550.

11. Escobar, "Worlds and Knowledges Otherwise"; Mignolo, *The Darker Side of Western Modernity*; Querejazu, "Encountering the Pluriverse."

12. See, for example, Gregory Clark, *Rhetorical Landscapes in America*; Novak, "American Landscape"; Halloran and Clark, "National Park Landscapes"; Finnegan, *Making Photography Matter*; Finnegan, *Picturing Poverty*.

tics," in which "America" becomes a "a synonym for the United States of America," is ultimately quite consequential, and it isn't just a question of semantics.[13] The trophic geographies of "America"—simultaneously symbolic and material—chart the shape and nature of the United States *as* America.[14] And, repeatedly, over centuries, that shape and nature have been felt in terms of magnitude.

Through all that time and into the present, people—unevenly granted or desiring "American" status—have moved over land and across water to establish the shape of the American hemisphere.[15] Sometimes intentionally and sometimes through the sheer fact of existence, their movements have sustained and contested American magnitude. Some of those moving people, usually moving from north to south, have been privileged travelers. They have been invited as guests, they have entered as explorers, and they have invaded, first as conquerors and later as hemispheric police. These travelers have generally presumed their right to move unhindered in American spaces. American magnitude has been their authorizing mode, their tool, and their outcome.

Some of those moving people, going both north-south and south-north, have held more tenuous American status and have not always wanted it. Their movements have often been constrained, but they have also always evaded and exceeded borders. They too have been constrained by, evaded, and exceeded the frameworks of American magnitude. As Lourdes Alberto explains of Latinx Indigenous presence in particular: Despite dismissal and erasure, they are not "liminal subjects occasionally making spectral appearances in the archive" but "integral figures to the formation of the US."[16] Their border crossings and presence contest and enact the United States within America.

The America invented through Quijano's "coloniality, ethnicity, and racism" is built upon Alberto's "integral figures" and integral movements, yet it also seeks to obscure them.[17] Its history includes European imperialism—Spanish, Portuguese, English—and its discontents. Its present includes US imperialism and the continent-wide hegemony of Creole states as well as long

---

13. Gruesz, "America," 17.

14. Druschke, "A Trophic Future"; Druschke, "Against Emergence"; Keeling and Prairie, "Trophic and Tropic Dynamics."

15. I am grateful to Tiara R Na'puti's work on the Marianas for the recognition that water-flows are as important to include as land-flows. See, for example, Na'puti, "Archipelagic Rhetoric," 5–6.

16. Alberto, "Coming Out as Indian," 251.

17. Quijano and Wallerstein, "Americanity as a Concept," 550; Alberto, "Coming Out as Indian," 251.

histories of survivance and direct action.[18] It is lived out not only through policy, diplomacy, and incursion but also through the rich rhetorical storehouses of daily life and common sense.[19] In the United States, as I write, it is palpably present in calls to "Make America Great Again" and also in indignant, horrified assertions that "This is not 'my' America." "Coloniality," Alberto affirms, "is at work globally through Anglophone and Hispanophone empires" in explicit and habitual ways.[20] It is also refused daily in acts large and small. The America created through "coloniaity, ethnicity, and racism" is, likewise, at work and resisted in the wake of the Atlantic slave trade: the forced movement of enslaved Black people into every corner of America; the liberatory movement of fugitives, escapees, and insurgents; the constraints of Jim Crow and mass incarceration; and the breaking out of social movements past and present.[21]

In this book, written in the shadow of coloniality and of the scholars, communities, and activists who counter it, I take up stories about civic image-making that are mostly distinct from, yet always related to, official US policy.[22] "Cultural forms," as Gretchen Murphy explains, can be particularly useful for understanding the public life of imperialism, racism, and coloniality. Across genres, moments, and ideological positions, they "construct narratives that limit or expand readers' sense of social possibility, embodying abstract notions of similarity and difference and harnessing readers' desires to certain visions of group identity."[23] The stories and images that I follow here show how deeply and consistently the magnitude of white settler US Americanness emerged through colonial encounters not only within the boundaries of the United States but also beyond them.

American Magnitude focuses on the movements of those privileged north-south travelers and the pictures they produced, but it does so in order to illuminate how their American celebrations were always in contact with other American stories that were sometimes accounted for, sometimes erased, and sometimes both. I excavate hegemonic, commonsense [US] Americanness as a category of whiteness, as a "universalizing, privileging *process*" that depends on not only delimiting broad constellations of racialized others as constitutive

---

18. Vizenor, *Manifest Manners*; Powell, "Rhetorics of Survivance."
19. Cintrón, "Democracy"; Hallenbeck, "Toward a Posthuman Perspective."
20. Alberto, "Coming Out as Indian," 252.
21. Sharpe, *In the Wake*; Wynter, "Unsettling"; Weheliye, *Habeas Viscus*; Camp, *Closer to Freedom*.
22. For a concise overview of related policy, see Christa J. Olson, "But in Regard."
23. Murphy, *Shadowing the White Man's Burden*, 5.

exteriors but also, I argue, nuanced engagements with American neighbors.[24] Focusing on these hegemonic processes risks privileging the same white, settler US Americanness I aim to destabilize. I take the risk because I believe that majoritarian stories ought not only be contested and contrasted from without but also undermined from within. And, I specifically argue here, if we are to understand how thoroughly the United States' hegemonic American stories depend on the hemisphere—particularly Latin America—we need to take another close, critical look at them.

Euro-American colonialism and imperialism have been consistently "rationalized . . . in racial terms" that link racism and colonialism even as race and Indigeneity are distinct social and political categories.[25] Working in light of that connection, this book investigates American feeling as it has been embodied by white settlers and for white settlers in order to defamiliarize the too often unspoken yet presumed white settler character of the United States of America. Though resistance and rupture thread throughout my analysis, themes of complicity, domination, and acquiescence form its core. I aim to understand the commonsense of [US] American hegemony. In this sense, I take up the challenge offered by Soto Vega and Chávez in their extension of Flores's racial rhetorical criticism.[26] I enact "critical and constant scrutiny" of the "settler colonial heteronormative systems from which most white dominant scholarship arises" and seek to illuminate America as a "[system] of domination entwined with race and ethnicity" and coloniality.[27] This book, then, examines white settler colonial hegemony and racialized US national vision as an act against it. I tell anew the accustomed stories of national belonging—Western expansion, Union, Progress, and Power—and reframe them in terms of their indebtedness to a larger America. The recipient of manifest destiny becomes a bad neighbor, the sublime exception becomes an awkward traveler, the city on a hill becomes a fragile bully desperate for recognition. In the process, this book makes visible how thoroughly US national identity is predicated on imagined relationships with a wider America that is always as much another self as it is an exotic other.[28]

Building from that assertion that US Americanness is imagined and circulated in—often implicit—relation to other Americas, my more specific intervention in "American Magnitude" is this: Through broadly sensory means grounded in vision, rhetors within the United States of America have fre-

---

24. Carillo Rowe and Malhotra, "(Un)Hinging Whiteness," 166.
25. Goldberg, *The Threat of Race*, 3.
26. Flores, "Between Abundance and Marginalization."
27. Soto Vega and Chávez, "Latinx Rhetoric," 319, 320.
28. Christa J. Olson, *Constitutive Visions*, 132.

quently sought to establish the millennial grandeur of their nation by engaging the magnitude of the hemisphere—by making claims to be particularly American among Americans. In the process, they have made American magnitude not a set of policies or a particular political position but a commonplace and a matter of common sense. The remaining pages of this introduction gloss and cohere the disparate pieces of that assertion, defining the hemisphere, magnitude, and finally vision and sensation. I close with a reflection on the consequences of American feeling and a guide to subsequent chapters.

Why the Hemisphere?

Hemispheres are colonial constructs—remember the Spanish flag flying over the New World in Waldseemüller's map? Organized by continents, equators, and meridians, hemispheres may seem to be purely elements of physical reality. But, meridians, continents, and equators, like hemispheres, are imagined objects.[29] And Earth's hemispheres were imagined into being in service of the modern/colonial world.[30] John Carlos Rowe points out that "the Western Hemisphere cannot be disengaged finally from the global processes in which it has been historically involved."[31] The Western Hemisphere may be made of earth and water, but it came into existence through acts of marking. And I do not mean only its adjectives: "Western" or "American." The hemisphere itself—starting from a zero line and ending when it reaches that line again on the other side of the world—was created to serve the needs of European navigation. It came into being to enable conquest and capitalism. Greenwich was chosen as the site of the Prime Meridian in 1884. Prior to that, mapmakers working in Europe would choose a prominent city in their homeland as the zero point for navigation. Each mapmaker's origin site was the point of departure for outward journeys of discovery and acquisition. The "global processes in which [the Western Hemisphere] has been historically involved" since the invention of America are colonial processes, and they shape even land itself.

---

29. The equator is the least "imagined" of the set, of course, since it is possible to measure the precise distance between the north and south poles. That said, as the history of error and dispute over the location of the equator in Ecuador suggests and the lack of an actual line except where painted by humans demonstrates, the line itself is imaginary. While the Coriolis effect does mean that storms spin counterclockwise in the Northern Hemisphere and clockwise in the Southern, there is not some sudden direction change the moment they cross the equatorial line.

30. Mignolo, "The Geopolitics of Knowledge."

31. John Carlos Rowe, "Areas of Concern," 327.

Just as the hemisphere is trophic—intrinsically both a material place and a flow of energy—so are coloniality and decoloniality. They concern, simultaneously, the theft/reclamation of land and epistemic imposition/survivance. Gabriela Raquel Ríos notes that scholars addressing America from the perspective of the Latin American modernity/coloniality research program[32] "see decolonization as primarily discursive and/or epistemological and implicitly 'future'-focused."[33] On the other hand, she points out, theories developed within Indigenous studies treat "decolonization as being primarily about sovereignty; they argue for colonial impact to be acknowledged and *dismantled*."[34] For those scholars, Ríos continues, "colonial impact is seen most prominently as one having to do with territorial claims (e.g. to land, knowledge, representations, etc.) and, as such, as having to do with settler subjects and Indigenous subjects, even on a hemispheric or global level."[35] "Decolonization," then (and by extension colonialism), can seem to be quite different things, depending on the scholarly tradition one builds from. Eve Tuck and K. Wayne Yang's critique of how settlers appropriate and dilute the decolonial has drawn attention to the tensions between notions of decoloniality emphasizing epistemic survivance and those demanding territorial sovereignty.[36] Tuck and Yang do not explicitly engage with the modernity/coloniality group, however. Their more pointed critique is for those scholars who claim to decolonize without engaging in the hard work of unsettling.[37] As Rachel Jackson has demonstrated, drawing a stark distinction between epistemic and territorial decolonization creates a division where there was (and should be) none.[38] The colonization that created and continues to create the Western Hemisphere ravishes both land and ways of life; it aims to obliterate territorial, cultural, and rhetorical sovereignty. It functions simultaneously and inextricably in symbolic and material forms. A decolonial orientation toward the hemisphere, likewise, enacts trophic reclamation and resistance.

In this book, then, I treat the American hemisphere in terms of its ongoing colonial character, excavating the history and consequence of [US] Ameri-

---

32. See, for example, Escobar, "Worlds and Knowledges Otherwise"; Mignolo, "The Geopolitics of Knowledge"; Emma Pérez, *The Decolonial Imaginary*; Quijano, "Coloniality of Power."
33. Ríos, "Mestizaje," 113.
34. Ríos, "Mestizaje," 113.
35. Ríos, "Mestizaje," 113.
36. Tuck and Yang, "Decolonization."
37. Tuck and Yang, "Decolonization."
38. Jackson, "Resisting Relocation"; Jackson and Whitehorse DeLaune, "Decolonizing Community Writing." Ríos also demonstrates this point implicitly in her work on land-based literacies. Ríos, "Cultivating."

can claims to it. Those claims are always, simultaneously, about territory *and* definition. The United States has claimed literal, territorial sovereignty over occupied land, and it has exerted rhetorical sovereignty over the American hemisphere and over America as an episteme. While it works within and upon that reality, *American Magnitude* is not a decolonial text. By defamiliarizing America and making our present circumstances an "option" rather than inevitable, this book may do some work that is decolonial in the epistemic sense.[39] However it is, ultimately, an investigation of [US] American coloniality, not an act of decolonization.[40]

Following US-based image-makers in their travels southward and tracking how the pictures they made circulated persuasively in the United States, I show how viewing American scenes beyond the United States "creates a sense of home" for US viewers "without overly resembling home environments of the overtly familiar."[41] Those of us who benefit from these stories and those of us whose worlds would be elided by them need to know these stories and how they have moved and grown. In them, encounters with other American spaces wield the hemisphere to help white settler audiences in the United States feel their own nation as America.[42] Looking at the American hemisphere from the United States has done constitutive rhetorical work for viewers. Following those pictures through their creation and circulation, then, illuminates one set of processes by which US imperial presumption has circulated through everyday looking and, in the process, has come to be commonsense for many US-based rhetors and their audiences. Delinking the component parts of that common feeling requires exposing it and its rhetorical violence.[43] *American Magnitude* takes up that work by inviting glances and glares at the hemisphere.

The complexity, risk, and explosiveness of the collision between the United States and its southern neighbors has, ultimately, made the American hemisphere as seen from the perspective of the United States. South-facing hemispheric images have helped US rhetors position their country's consequence

---

39. Ríos, "Mestizaje," 113; Mignolo, *The Darker Side*.

40. I am indebted to Dave Tell for the language of "investigation" over "critique." Tell, "Critique and Investigation."

41. Gómez-Barris, "Andean Gateways," 339.

42. Though the cases I examine all invoke American hemispheres and continents, they actually treat only part of the hemisphere. The vast territory and complex histories lying north of the United States are untouched. My justification for this erasure is quite straightforward: Historically, the creation of the United States *as* America has a great deal more to do with southward encounters than northward ones. The powerful sense of difference from what we now call "Latin" America has, paradoxically, driven rhetors in the United States to more consistently engage that region as both constitutive exterior and reflection of self.

43. See Wanzer, "Delinking Rhetoric" for a thorough treatment of what it means to delink rhetorics from their Western/modern/colonial tethers.

in the world, and those images have underwritten narratives of growth, progress, and power at home. The hemisphere, particularly embodied by Latin America, becomes a crucial foil and figure for American magnitude. It undergirds the status and consequentiality of the United States' version of America.

On Magnitude and Megethos

That claim about the hemisphere brings us to this monograph's second titular term: *megethos,* roughly translated as "magnitude." Though my focus, here, is on the tropes of magnitude that infuse American rhetorics, the term itself developed well before European conquistadors imagined a place called "America."

Concern with magnitude as a rhetorical feature first emerged in ancient Greece. As such, its analysis has long been grounded in the most traditional of rhetorical theorizing. However, in recent years magnitude has captured the imagination of rhetoricians seeking to understand how things come to matter in other political and cultural scenes—from feminist activism to conspiracy theories and antifluoridation campaigns.[44] *Megethos,* as I treat it, is affective in nature: compounding and circulating as feelings that inform and exceed the political. My uptake of *megethos* emphasizes three key, interrelated points: its role in establishing import, its close links to the sublime, and its profoundly sensory nature, beginning from vision but extending throughout the body. I introduce each of those elements here, surveying historical and recent theorizing that establishes them. Throughout, I also infuse theories of magnitude with the imperatives of racial rhetorical criticism—noting that American magnitude, to borrow Flores's phrase, is "a practice deeply invested in the cultural, social, and political significance of race."[45] American magnitude is raced and racializing.

Megethos was central to Aristotle's notion of amplification—and thereby to his theorizing on how rhetors do the heavy lifting of persuasion. In the *Rhetoric,* Aristotle's most developed discussion of amplification—and of *megethos*—appears in his treatment of the epideictic. That fact is significant to magnitude's public purpose: From its first theorization, *megethos* has been

---

44. For recent analyses of magnitude see, for example, Hawhee, *Rhetoric in Tooth and Claw*; Jenell Johnson, "A Man's Mouth Is His Castle"; Larson, "Just Let This Sink In"; Christa J. Olson, "American Magnitude"; Peeples, "Toxic Sublime"; Rice, "The Rhetorical Aesthetics of More." Much of the recent surge in attention to magnitude can be traced back to two pieces by Thomas Farrell: "The Weight of Rhetoric" and "Sizing Things Up."

45. Flores, "Between Abundance and Marginalization," 6.

involved in the aspects of rhetorical practice aimed at community formation, witnessing, and sense of shared place.[46] Magnitude is a crucial tool in the discourse of power, and it functions most pervasively in the often dismissed and presumed softer realms of praise, blame, and identity formation.

Amplification, Aristotle explains, "aims to show superiority" and thus is a form of praise grounded in the size-comparative trope of *megethos*.[47] Well adapted to the epideictic, amplification is suited less to argument and proof than to "cloth[ing its subjects] with greatness [*megethos*] and beauty."[48] It signals what is important by setting its subject above its peers in size, worth, or virtue. Epideictic, amplification, and *megethos*, in other words, are crucial modes for place-claiming on the affective level. And *megethos* serves epideictic discourse so well in part because it is less a matter of rational deliberation and policy formation than of felt importance. As contemporary rhetorical scholars have established, the once-maligned epideictic is, in fact, ubiquitous, forceful, and essential to analysis of public rhetorics. Attending to it allows rhetoricians to recognize affective community formation as part of the pervasive work of rhetoric.[49] Because it indexes what matters and evokes powerful feeling, *megethos* plays a central role in epideictic constitutive processes happening around and beyond more traditionally political public discourse. The link to racial rhetorical criticism, then, should be obvious and inevitable. "We cannot ignore race," Flores reminds us, because when we are tracking "questions of impact, influence, or circulation" and "questions of affect and materiality" we are always also talking about raced modes and raced bodies.[50] In the context of America, the superior "us" constituted by the invocation of magnitude is always racialized by histories of colonization, settlement, enslavement, migration, and border-drawing. Racialization and differentiation infuse the stuff, the import, of American magnitude.

And establishing importance has long been the primary purpose of appealing to magnitude. In his influential textbook, *On Types of Style,* the Greek rhetorician Hermogenes of Tarsus (second century CE), established "grandeur" (*megethos*) as one of seven governing divisions of style—how a speech produces its effects through tone and structure. Grandeur's task, for Hermogenes, was to impress the importance of a topic on hearers.[51] Two millennia

---

46. LaWare, "Encountering Visions of Aztlan."
47. Aristotle, *On Rhetoric*, 1.9.39.
48. Aristotle, *On Rhetoric*, 1.9.40.
49. Aristotle, *On Rhetoric*, 1.3.3; see, for example, Condit, "The Functions of Epideictic"; Hartelius and Asenas, "Citational Epideixis"; LaWare, "Encountering Visions of Aztlan."
50. Flores, "Between Abundance and Marginalization," 7.
51. Wooten, *Hermogenes' On Types of Style*, 29.

later, when Thomas Farrell brought the attention of contemporary rhetorical theorists back to magnitude, he likewise focused on *megethos* as an index of importance. "Magnitude," Farrell notes, is "essential to the most important concerns of traditional rhetoric: namely, whether an audience may care about any topic sufficiently to attend to it, to engage it, and to act upon it; what consequences will weigh most heavily upon their prospective deliberation; what priorities will finally tip the balance in their judgment; and what appetitive attachments will need to be overcome for rational reflection to be feasible."[52] For Farrell, *megethos* directs attention to those "core attachments" that are, "finally, not an outcome of how we reason but of who we are."[53]

Latin America has not often been treated as a "core attachment" of the United States and, for the most part, has been absent from explicit considerations of US American identity. And yet, as this book argues through pan-historiographic means, a sense of the broader hemisphere has often served to "tip the balance" of American magnitude. Jonathan Balzotti and Richard Crosby argue that *megethos* can function to "[establish] the subject's superiority by virtue of the way it outsizes other subjects."[54] America, as the white, settler United States, "outsizes" its neighbors and stands apart from them. It is made great [again]. But historically and today, that exceptionally great [US] America is always in conversation with its neighbors—drawing from them, relying on them, and asking them to bear the burdens of *megethos*.

Attending to, engaging, and acting upon Latin America as partially constitutive of American magnitude has always involved appetitive attachments to whiteness and coloniality. Trans-American racialization and coloniality are "core attachments" for the United States as America. They pervade not only "how we reason but . . . who we are."[55] In that trans-American production of import, the "weight of rhetoric" is freighted with what David Theo Goldberg calls the "weight" of race.[56] It is constitutive of "who we are" and, as such, is at the heart of American magnitude. Magnitude is "rhetorically invented and construed" in racialized terms. Its racist weight consistently shapes the "things" that are made to "matter."[57] As this attention to racialization suggests, engaging *megethos* does not simply allow rhetors to register an audience's commitments and so arrange reasoned discourse to sway it. Instead, centering

---

52. Farrell, "The Weight of Rhetoric," 472.
53. Farrell, "The Weight of Rhetoric," 472.
54. Balzotti and Crosby, "Diocletian's Victory Column," 330.
55. Farrell, "The Weight of Rhetoric," 472; Flores, "Between Abundance and Marginalization."
56. Farrell, "The Weight of Rhetoric"; Goldberg, *The Threat of Race*.
57. Farrell, "The Weight of Rhetoric," 469, 470.

megethos likewise centers an approach to rhetoric in which the rational and nonrational are intertwined and sensation is primary. *Megethos* is a matter of public feeling and American *megethos* is a matter of American public feeling. It appears and circulates in those words and images that picture identity and place it firmly in a great (United States of) America.

Theories of *megethos* well predating rhetoric's recent re-recognition of bodies and sensation drew attention to the sensory force of magnitude by linking it to the sublime. *Megethos* figured prominently as a matter of moral and visceral elevation in Longinus's *On the Sublime,* for example, where height of eloquence led to both virtue and *ekstasis.*[58] *Megethos* and *hypsos* (height, sublimity), O'Gorman suggests, were thoroughly intertwined. Both were matters of physical impression—earth-rending, heavenly forms—that moved meaning beyond logical apprehension into representation (in *megethos*) and ecstasy (in *hypsos*).[59] O'Gorman notes that for Longinus, *hypsos* and *megethos* lift audiences beyond reason and logos.[60] The eighteenth century rhetorician Hugh Blair likewise understood *megethos* in terms of the sublime, effectively treating them as synonyms.[61] Both, he suggested, are crucial for understanding the highest "causes of the pleasure which we receive from" objects and from writing.[62]

This link between *megethos,* the sublime, and persuasive force again cannot be separated from colonialism and racialization—and not just within the frame of American *megethos.* Given how foundational the sublime—as a form of megethos—has been to US American self-definition, this recognition is crucial for our present purposes. Spivak notes Immanuel Kant's "special inscription of a judgement programmed in nature, needing culture, but not produced by culture" that left "man in the raw"—a category encompassing Blackness and Indigeneity—perpetually unable to apprehend sublimity.[63] Wittenberg, likewise, notes that Edmund Burke and Immanuel Kant were explicit in reserving sublimity for white, Euro-American colonizers.[64] As Shapiro explains, Blackness and the colonized Black body appear consistently in Burke's and Kant's theories as uniquely impervious to the sublime. Likewise, theories of the sublime placed it in constant (negative) relation to Indigeneity.

---

58. O'Gorman, "Longinus's Sublime Rhetoric," 74. Both the date and author of *On the Sublime* are matters of scholarly debate. I follow O'Gorman in simply referring to the author as "Longinus" 85 n.2.

59. O'Gorman, "Longinus's Sublime Rhetoric," 77.

60. O'Gorman, "Longinus's Sublime Rhetoric," 77.

61. Blair, *Lectures,* 55.

62. Blair, *Lectures,* 53.

63. Spivak, *A Critique,* 12, 13.

64. Wittenberg, "Alan Paton's Sublime."

The American sublime and, by extension, American magnitude, were thereby constituted by the exclusion of Blackness and Indigeneity. In America, sublimity is a colonial project where whiteness and the imperative of settlement surge over and exceed the always receding, always deferring colonized other. "The vast racial sublime that separates much of white and black America," Shapiro explains, "is arguably a legacy of an earlier war on ethnic [sic] Americans . . . [and] the violence that took place on the western frontier."[65] Shapiro's focus here is on the conquest and colonization of Native nations, but his point also readily applies to the past and present of the US frontier with Mexico. Throughout the racialized, colonizing history of the sublime, apprehension of magnitude becomes, as Wittenberg explains, "the touchstone for this 'universal,' rational, educated European subject" and "a marker of civilization."[66] Claiming magnitude via sublimity means that the magnitude of the United States as America is always premised on whiteness and coloniality.

The lines connecting *megethos,* sublimity, racialization, and colonization also point us toward *feeling.* Kant's theory of the sublime, as Spivak explains, asserted that sublimity emerged out of a painful disconnect between sensation and rationality.[67] For Kant, vision was the primary sensation involved in the sublime: the "aesthetical estimation" of nature as seen in visual art.[68] In this sense, magnitude is a bodily effect frequently initiated through *differentiating* sight—the ability to distinguish the sublime from the terrible or the merely beautiful.[69] Proper American sight required such differentiating capacity—the ability to see the American hemisphere from a stance that, by definition, was always only available to those privileged viewers looking north to south and perceiving the hemisphere from just the right (white, settler) body.

Hugh Blair, whose influence in the nineteenth-century United States has been widely discussed among rhetoricians, noted early in his lecture on criticism that "all the rules of genuine Criticism I have shewn to be ultimately founded on feeling."[70] Blair used his discussion of Grandeur and the sublime to illuminate the significant force of that feeling, writing, "It is not easy to describe, in words, the precise impression which great and sublime objects make upon us, when we behold them; but every one has a conception of it."[71]

---

65. Shapiro, *The Political Sublime,* 46.
66. Wittenberg, "Alan Paton's Sublime," 5, 6.
67. Spivak, *A Critique,* 10.
68. Qtd. in Spivak, *A Critique,* 10.
69. Spivak, *A Critique,* 10; Wittenberg, "Alan Paton's Sublime," 5–6.
70. On Blair's influence, see, for example, Agnew, "The Civic Function of Taste"; Broaddus, "Authoring Elitism"; Carr, "The Circulation"; Horner, *Nineteenth-Century Scottish Rhetoric*; Holmes, "Say What?"; Nan Johnson, *Nineteenth-Century Rhetoric.* Blair, *Lectures,* 46.
71. Blair, *Lectures,* 55.

Despite his apparent universalism ("every one"), Blair ultimately invoked the mind as the source of that "impression" and made clear that gender, race, and nationality had everything to do with the capacity for refined perception.[72] Again, rational man was uniquely able to perceive sublimity. The sensory experience of that rational man, particularly visual experience, was primary in Blair's understanding of sublimity. For him, encountering Grandeur required that the "objects themselves" be "presented to the eye," particularly a trained eye.[73] Grandeur and the sublime appeared in those aspects of nature "to which the eye can see no limits."[74] Grandeur could be apprehended, first and foremost, by *looking* up to the heights and down to the depths. The educated white man seeing capaciously and well.

American magnitude is created and circulated through vision as a pervasive sense. Writing more recently and without Blair's investment in the rational, white male viewer, Finnegan likewise notes that magnitude is grounded in the visual: "Magnitude says . . . 'Hey, look at this! This is important!'"[75] Pictures enact magnitude through their "ability to confer visibility, significance, and weight."[76] *Looking* thus serves as an essential means of encountering magnitude. But magnitude does not stop at the eyes. With *megethos*, sight is a starting place for feeling, not an end. Blair's visual examples rippled from sight into the rest of the body. The sublime arises whenever "great power and force [are] exerted" on the senses.[77] It is found in the shake of an earthquake, the heat of a forest fire or burning city, the buffeting of wind, and the flash and rumble of an impending storm. In this sense, initiating *megethos* through sight marks vision as a matter of fleshy encounters—sight comes from and returns to the body as a sensory organ. When it comes to establishing import, it matters that viewers are out of breath, panting, when they stop to gaze up at a summit or that the smell of death sends them staggering before they can visually apprehend a battlefield strewn with bodies—just two of the many sensation-filled scenes of American magnitude that populate subsequent chapters.[78] Vision, in *megethos*, is a sensation itself and a gateway to sensation. It invites, extends, and substantiates the feeling of magnitude.

---

72. Holmes, "Say What?," 204, 205.
73. Blair, *Lectures*, 55.
74. Blair, *Lectures*, 56.
75. Farrell, qtd. in Finnegan, *Making Photography Matter*, 130.
76. Finnegan, *Making Photography Matter*, 130.
77. Blair, *Lectures*, 57.
78. Frederic Church, qtd. in Navas Sanz de Santamaría and Church, *The Journey*, 97; Crooker to Crooker, April 27, 1847.

This wholly sensory notion of *megethos* has deep roots. Longinus suggested, for example, that "weight, grandeur, and urgency . . . are very largely produced . . . by the use of 'visualizations' [*phantasiai*] . . . [or what others call] 'image productions' [*eidolopoiias*]."[79] Both O'Gorman and Hawhee take up this aspect of Longinus's sublime to entangle *megethos* with the visual and the visceral. Hawhee notes that "*megethos* is one of the concepts that adds to rhetoric a crucial aesthetic dimension, in the ancient sense of sense *perception*."[80] O'Gorman puts it more physically: Audiences are "dragged away from demonstrative arguments and are astounded by the image, by the dazzle."[81] Working from Hawhee and Farrell, Rice likewise asserts that "*megethos* operates through the human body as an excitable entity, an entity aroused by the sensation of more."[82] In all these cases, magnitude overflows matters of cognitive response; it rushes through a seeing-feeling body, overwhelming and reshaping it. In this book, then, seeing America leads to the production of American feelings.

Feeling American

US Americanness may be officially codified in constitutional language and the various "papers" of citizenship, immigration, and naturalization law, but its everyday life is largely a matter of feeling (even if sometimes feelings about papers) and looking.[83] It is told and contested in stories; it is experienced in affiliation, affection, and rejection; and it is seen—or not—in faces, landscapes, and pictures.[84] Looking American grows from and encompasses all those sensory activities. In "Looking White and Middle Class," Brenton J. Malin relates how, in the early twentieth century, two of the biggest US providers of stereoscope images began to produce materials designed to educate and enculturate viewers through virtual travel. Malin argues that, whatever scenes the stereoscopes might have provided, the advertising and promotional materials made clear that their underlying purpose was to shape the viewer. "Looking white and middle-class" was a matter of one's visual comportment as

---

79. Qtd. in Hawhee, *Rhetoric in Tooth and Claw*, 55.
80. Hawhee, *Rhetoric in Tooth and Claw*, 56; emphasis added.
81. Ned O'Gorman, "Longinus's Sublime Rhetoric," 73.
82. Rice, "The Rhetorical Aesthetics of More," 33.
83. Vieira, *American by Paper*.
84. Trans-American scholarship in literary studies has made this case robustly in its calls to study nationalism and imperialism as carried within narrative and other cultural forms. See, for example, Kaplan, *The Anarchy of Empire*; Murphy, *Shadowing the White Man's Burden*; Sadowski-Smith, *Border Fictions*.

much as it was a matter of one's own self-presentation.[85] Likewise, in the pictures and stories presented here, Americanness is located in the act of viewing—properly, under the right conditions, with the right feelings, as the right sort of person—not in being seen. Viewing Americans might occasionally be invited to emulate a subject depicted in this book—Henry Clay Jr. nobly sacrificing his life for his country or Hiram Bingham standing atop an Incan ruin. Such invitations, however, are incidental to the larger rhetorical project of American magnitude that I track across a hundred-plus years. Again and again, [US] American viewers are invited to stand in the shoes of the picture-maker, learning to view American scenes through the picture-maker's eyes and, by doing so, embody their own American magnitude.[86]

The soldiers, reporters, artists, scientists, and entertainers whose pictures fill the pages of *American Magnitude* made claims to hemispheric vision through embodied access to American places. They made and then circulated American pictures for [US] American audiences, aiming to inculcate a distinct feeling of Americanness within those US viewers. Vision and embodiment were directly and constitutively connected, both in the creation of the pictures and in their circulation.

For all that sensation is presently de rigueur in the humanities, it can be easy to forget that vision is a sense (that it is embodied). Perhaps because the "pictorial turn" preceded the "affective turn," or perhaps because the legacy of positivism has turned vision into a matter of disembodied cognition, recent work on sensation, embodiment, and feeling has tended to treat every sense *except* vision. Within rhetorical studies, "visual rhetoric" and "sensory rhetorics" have largely gone in separate directions.[87] But understanding the force of vision requires that critical work on visual rhetoric track its embodied origins and outcomes. *American Magnitude* assays that work, offering a thoroughly embodied visual rhetoric.

Visual rhetoric has most frequently treated pictures in terms of interpretation.[88] In those analyses, viewers are said to engage explicit or latent cognitive resources—ideologies, semiotics, icons, image vernaculars, topoi—to process what they see.[89] They understand, make meaning of, or draw connections among pictures, in other words, by engaging information presumed

---

85. Malin, "Looking White and Middle-Class."
86. Jack, "A Pedagogy of Sight."
87. Hawhee, "Looking into Aristotle's Eyes" is a notable exception.
88. Work on circulation is an important exception here, though interpretation does still play a role in those analyses. See, for example, Finnegan and Kang, "'Sighting' the Public"; Lester Olson, "Pictorial Representations"; Gries, *Still Life with Rhetoric*.
89. See, for example, Cloud, "To Veil the Threat of Terror"; Lester Olson, *Emblems*; Finnegan, "Recognizing Lincoln"; Christa J. Olson, *Constitutive Visions*.

to reside in their minds. Analysis and criticism in this vein tends to presume a thinking, largely disembodied viewer. But viewers are also feelers. "We do not see with our eyes alone," Janet Vertesi notes. "Learning to see requires both bodily skills and instrumental techniques."[90] Likewise, in *Listening to Images*, Tina Campt reminds us that seeing is a multisensory act.[91] Acknowledging this multisensory nature of sight requires eschewing interpretation as the primary paradigm for visual encounters. Campt connects sound and sight specifically, but her "challenge" to "the equation of vision with knowledge" resonates beyond any particular pairing of senses.[92] Campt proposes "listening to images" as a means for gaining "access to the affective registers through which these images enunciate alternate accounts of their subjects." Her specific purpose is to treat identification photographs not (only) as "site[s] of social reproduction" but as displaying "instances of rupture and refusal." Even when not listening for "rupture and refusal," however, visual rhetoricians have reason to seek access to the affective registers of both seeing and things seen.[93] Embodied, feeling vision is, ultimately, crucial to its rhetorical force.

The pictures at the core of this book were, unquestionably, interpreted in their moments. I occasionally do the same from a greater temporal distance. But it matters much more for the purposes of this book that the pictures were felt.[94] The people who created them moved across land and water, climbed mountains, held brushes, and immersed negatives in developing solution. They dealt with pain, hunger, loneliness, and nerves. The people who later encountered the pictures, likewise, felt them. They stood in front of them, held them in their hands, strained their eyes to see in gaslight, glanced down at them, and jostled up against other viewers. They felt sorrow, nostalgia, excitement, and longing. And, repeatedly, those individual feelings were explicitly

---

90. Vertesi, *Seeing Like a Rover*, 9.
91. Campt, *Listening to Images*.
92. Campt, *Listening to Images*, 6.
93. Campt, *Listening to Images*, 5.
94. Here and throughout the manuscript, I use "felt" and "feeling" as intentionally ambiguous words that index sensation, embodiment, affect, and emotion. This choice allows me to avoid the theoretical logjam of affect. Like many others (e.g., Rice, Hawhee, Berlant, and Cvetkovich), I am interested in "acknowledging the somatic or sensory nature of feelings as experiences that aren't just cognitive concepts or constructions" and that sometimes—but not always—trespass the boundaries of knowledge. Like vision, "feeling" indexes elements both conceptual ("I have a feeling about this") and physical ("This feels hot") and, indeed, marks their blurring. How often does "having a feeling" involve an internal stomach churn, external touch, and lingering memory all at once? Feeling thus provides an imprecise yet generative means to address the effects *and* material of sensation. I am ultimately, however, less interested in theorizing the exact nature of feeling than I am in the ways that seeing American magnitude activated US public feeling. Cvetkovich, *Depression*, 4. See also Hawhee, "Rhetoric's Sensorium," 12; Berlant, *Cruel Optimism*; Rice, *Distant Publics*.

and implicitly connected to American feelings. They responded with swelling patriotism, anxious concern for a communal future, and urgent desire to share their viewing experience with others who would see as they did. Hemispheric vision, in other words, is a form of communal proprioception. It entails a multisensory awareness of position within America that has both internal and external consequences.

Such awareness of position—especially with regard to American feelings—is always racialized. José Muñoz, in "Feeling Brown," explains that in the United States, the "performance of whiteness primarily transpires on an affective register."[95] And that performance of whiteness is also, often, a performance of US Americanness. "Standard models of United States citizenship are based on a national affect" and just as English-only movements declare a national language, "there is an unofficial, but no less powerfully entrenched, national affect."[96] Bernadette Calafell notes that such "official national affect" is "connected to white middle-class subjectivities and citizenship."[97] "Feeling American" has often been a matter of "feeling white." Looking American, likewise, functions affectively as a practice of white viewership—with implications for the viewer's own sense of position and the places, peoples, and scenes being viewed. Glancing at a map and seeing the future shape of the United States as an inevitable conclusion is but one example among many.

While Muñoz and Calafell each center Brownness, not whiteness, their arguments invite parallel attention to the pernicious, pervasive work of the normative. Muñoz challenges his readers to recognize the "sparse affective landscape of Anglo North America," arguing that "the affective performance of normative whiteness is minimalist to the point of emotional impoverishment."[98] Sparse though that normative landscape may be—especially when applied, as it is throughout this book, to white masculinity—it is still thoroughly affective. It is constituted by feelings. And, perhaps ironically, given Muñoz's assessment, magnitude is among the most prominent of those feelings. For white, masculine settlers—especially those standing on literal or figural frontiers—American magnitude has been an assertion of gender and national belonging.[99] Importance, grandeur, and centrality have been cultivated as fundamental, constitutive American feelings that must be fed repeatedly and consistently in order to maintain prowess and pride.

---

95. Muñoz, "Feeling Brown," 68.
96. Muñoz, "Feeling Brown," 69.
97. Calafell, "Brownness, Kissing, and US Imperialism," 198.
98. Muñoz, "Feeling Brown," 70.
99. Greenberg, *Manifest Manhood*.

By turning our attention to that gendered and raced voracious appetite for magnitude, I direct what Karma Chávez calls a "textual stare" on normative white bodies.[100] If rhetorical studies has tended to treat "white, cisgender, able-bodied, heterosexual, and male" bodies as abstractions, addressing them only as part of a universalized "acknowledge[ment] that rhetorical practice and training are embodied after all," this project chooses not to take that normative body and its normative affects "on its own terms."[101] Instead, it stares, intensely, at some of the pictures, peoples, and places that perpetuate American magnitude as an essential component of normative (white, masculine, settler) public feeling in the United States.[102] Doing so requires understanding the *public* of "public feeling" as a "visceral public": a public formed through intensity of feeling and a need to monitor bodily borders both literal and symbolic.[103] Not every public—or even every national public—is a visceral public in the specific way Jenell Johnson intended when she developed the term. In the pages ahead, however, I take up "visceral public" as not only naming a particular type of public, but also providing an orientation toward publics as sensory. Johnson, in other words, has identified a feature of publicity as well as a type of public. Publics are always about feeling. They are made of sensation, shared risk, affiliation, and affection. Thinking of publics through the visceral and as spaces of individual and collective feeling enables us to notice how sensations that churn, ripple, tear, and flash as well as those that whisper, brush, flicker, and seep work to form public affiliation, give it staying power, and lend it consequence. *American Magnitude* presumes that American public feeling has always been a visceral concern. "How Americans feel about themselves as Americans" is a matter of enduring rhetorical practice, created and recreated over generations and contexts.[104] It is normative common sense.

Panagia argues that "sensation interrupts common sense."[105] In *American Magnitude,* I assert instead that sensation is the base material of common sense. The image-makers and viewers featured throughout this book would likely have agreed. Nineteenth-century US perspectives on common sense, informed by Blair, presumed that moral and communal values emerged from sensation. Taste—a category of discernment and reflection—"provid[ed] the medium through which individual feelings achiev[ed] collec-

---

100. Chávez, "The Body," 248.
101. Chávez, "The Body," 246, 248.
102. Garland-Thomson, *Staring.*
103. Jenell Johnson, "A Man's Mouth Is His Castle," 2.
104. Doss, *Memorial Mania,* 15.
105. Panagia, *The Political Life,* 2.

tive significance."[106] And such "collective significance," Holmes reminds us, was always raced and gendered.[107] Long after Hugh Blair's direct influence faded, however, common sense remained (and remains) felt. How and what we feel leaves marks on us, and those marks, in turn, mark our public and private orientations. Over time, those sensations become habitual. Like the shape of the United States on a map about dinosaurs, common national sensations become so familiar that they are no longer recognizable as having been created. Yet they remain powerful. America and its magnitude are feelings as much as or more than they are ideas. They always have been.

Approach

The manuscript in your hands proceeds chronologically and geographically. It extends further southward as it progresses from the middle of the nineteenth century to the middle of the twentieth. Taking a pan-historiographic approach, its structure is episodic rather than exhaustive.[108] It highlights moments of hemispheric image-making that fit three criteria, chosen to illuminate both continuity and change in the rhetorical life of American magnitude. Those criteria are that the pictures and image-makers involved (1) are specifically dedicated to cultivating widespread public attention through visual engagement, (2) do their work in moments of significant change in American public feeling within the United States, and (3) offer instances in which US audiences are invited to view their Latin American neighbors as participants in America, rather than exclusively treating them as distant or exotic others. Though the historical moments, media, and locations featured in the case studies vary widely, these criteria ensure consistency across them in the realm where such consistency matters: addressing the question of how American magnitude developed, was sustained, and became consequential over time as a hemispheric feature of American public feeling. Though each case study invites readers to view American magnitude from a particular angle, they work together to show how, across media and moments, hemispheric *megethos* has been a powerful authorizing force for what it feels like to be American among Americans.

This introduction has sketched a conceptual framework for American magnitude. Coming chapters show it in action through four case studies,

---

106. Agnew, "The Civic Function of Taste," 29; See also Broaddus, "Authoring Elitism"; Carr, "The Circulation"; Gregory Clark, "The Oratorical Poetic."
107. Holmes, "Say What?," 204, 205.
108. Hawhee and Olson, "Pan-Historiography."

moving from mid-nineteenth-century printmaking during the US-Mexican War and later nineteenth-century painting in the years surrounding the Civil War to scientific exploration and photography during the early twentieth century and animated film at mid-century. Chapter 1, "Acquiescing to Accumulation," begins from the United States' last extensive, contiguous territorial acquisition: the land wrested from Mexico in the Treaty of Guadalupe Hidalgo following the US-Mexican War of 1846–48.[109] It draws from archival material—lithographs, maps, letters, and newspapers—to investigate how white audiences in the United States simultaneously grew skeptical of the war and accepted as natural the acquisition of Mexican territory. Offering "accumulation" as a crucial supplement to theories of rhetorical circulation and as an index for how magnitude works through gradual processes, I argue that the proliferation and piling up of war-related material over time shifted American terrain and American feeling. Those shifts also set the scene for the notional rather than territorial expansions of American magnitude that form the center of the remaining chapters.

Moving further into the nineteenth century and farther south, while drawing away from actual territorial expansion, chapter 2 tells six stories about Frederic Edwin Church's Andean landscape paintings and their public circulation prior to, during, and immediately following the US Civil War. Those six stories track Church's movement and his pictures'. In the process, they reveal American magnitude itself as a story. The story of American magnitude, this chapter shows, was perpetuated in Church's pictures, but it is troubled by close engagement with his actual travel. Following Church to Colombia and Ecuador and back to New Haven, we follow the contradictions of American normative affect during and after the US Civil War.

Chapter 3, "Of Cities on Hills," uses the "scientific discovery" of Machu Picchu and its presentation in photographs to examine how American magnitude circulated in early twentieth-century popular culture as authorization for the United States' newly expanding sense of its own global consequence. Engaging rhetorical, decolonial, and visual theory, the chapter presents discovery and invention as interconnected matters of revelation, and it theorizes revelation as a crucial stage in establishing magnitude. Working both with archival material from the Yale Peruvian Expedition and published accounts of the "discovery" of Machu Picchu, I show how Hiram Bingham's discovery, invention, and revelation of the ruins renewed the spirit of American explo-

---

109. The "extensive" is important here, even within the continental United States. During the nineteenth century, the United States continued to acquire contiguous territory from foreign powers (e.g., the Gadsden Purchase, the San Juan Islands), and then and now the United States threatens, occupies, and encroaches on land promised by treaty to Native nations.

ration for a new era, claimed Machu Picchu for American magnitude, and reflected the grandeur of Incan civilization onto himself and the United States.

Chapter 4, "Animating Interests," examines the visual strategies of the World War II–era US Office of the Coordinator of Inter-American Affairs (OIAA) in order to illuminate American magnitude as contested and appropriated. Building from OIAA-contracted and Walt Disney Company–produced films as well as contracts, memos, and other archival materials, this chapter turns the gaze of American magnitude back toward the United States. It tracks the US government's anxious desire that Latin Americans not only look *at* the United States but *to* it as a guide and exemplar. The Disney-OIAA material suggests that Latin Americans did often look at and to the United States as the origin site of American magnitude. Just as frequently, however, their looking came askance, prompting distinctly uncomfortable feelings for normative US viewers and turning American magnitude to contrary purposes.

Taken as a whole, *American Magnitude* reveals how integral seeing Latin America has been to the crucial matter of *feeling* American in the United States. Its cases and objects illuminate a long history of visual encounters with the hemisphere that helped US audiences view other American places in the service of US nationalism not so much through political discourse but through ubiquitous, pervasive, and everyday cultural practice and public embodiment. The conclusion brings that long history into the present and imagines a future where its importance subsides. Working across time, *American Magnitude* traces the rhetorical, constitutive work of hemispheric vision as it trains US audiences to feel particularly American among Americans. It ends by imagining a United States of America otherwise.

CHAPTER 1

Acquiescing to Accumulation

This chapter was originally going to track American magnitude through mid-nineteenth-century printmaking and lithographs, showing how they celebrated manifest destiny and forcefully projected US territory into Mexico. The archives had other ideas. The objects they held hopelessly complicated the story of American magnitude that I expected to tell. And so, this chapter engages the varied documents and artifacts that together brought the US-Mexican War before the eyes of audiences in the United States in the mid-1840s. In the process, it shows how American magnitude functions across multiple registers—not only patriotic bombast but also unlooked-for, creeping realization. That which will eventually become grandiose, this chapter demonstrates, sometimes begins in the most quotidian of ways: a letter, a footstep, a packet of seeds. I therefore begin this first case study chapter by bringing before your eyes a file folder full of yellowing letters from the collections at the Abraham Lincoln Presidential Library and Archive. Sitting before such folders was where I first realized that accumulation—quiet, slow, regular—was an essential component of and a crucial starting place for American magnitude.

Between May 1847 and April 1848, brothers John and Frederick Snyder kept up a steady correspondence while Fred was with the US Army in Mexico and John remained at home in Belleville, Illinois. Fred's experience of the US-Mexican War was, ultimately, unexceptional. He was a second lieutenant in an Illinois volunteer company that arrived in Mexico late in the war and was stationed in the occupied north. The soldiers in Fred's regiment did not participate in any battles or see any significant conflict after early spring 1847. Fred's letters report small skirmishes with Mexican guerrilleros, but his regiment otherwise drilled in vain.

The archive of letters that the Snyder brothers left behind, however, is remarkable. It encapsulates the lively, expansive, cross-genre conversation taking place in the United States during the 1846–48 war with Mexico. Perhaps because his family ran the Belleville post office and so had a professional relationship with letter-writing, John Snyder amassed an unusually robust collection of war letters that includes examples from both sides of the conversation.

The conversation between John and Fred ranges widely, and it covers topics common in soldiers' letters. The brothers shared anecdotes from daily life, reported on their health and others', and speculated about when they would see one another again. Woven into those discussions of life in Reynoso, Mexico, and Belleville, Illinois, is also a record of the many forms, genres, and sources of information about the war that passed through both men's hands. That record shows not just that soldiers, their families, and their compatriots across the United States documented the war, but that such documentation was conscious, reflexive, and weighty. Even today, its materiality drags on the pages that describe it, heavy with feeling and freighted with desire for connection. That desire and the objects that carried it, I argue, are evidence of American magnitude in formation. While it would be impossible to draw a straight line from any single letter or artifact to any particular nationalist opinion, their concatenation is the very stuff of American public feeling.[1]

The urgent need to maintain ties despite distance comes across most palpably in Fred's letters as he asks, repeatedly, for news from home. The opening paragraphs of every letter Fred wrote list how many letters and newspapers he had received since he last wrote. He repeatedly comments, "I make it a point to answer every letter or paper that I receive from you," establishing a habit of connection that he urged his brother to emulate.[2] Fred also kept careful track of every letter sent and received in a ledger he maintained separately from his correspondence.[3] He likewise proposed a scheme to ensure that he received news from their other brother, William, who was on the Santa Fe Trail with another regiment of Illinois volunteers. Fred asked John to forward all of Wil-

---

1. This assertion is nearly impossible to prove. Yet anyone who has sat in an archive, reading a stack of letters between strangers, and been overwhelmed by the emotions and affiliations within them, can attest to it. See, for example, Cifor, "Affecting Relations"; Clyde, "The (Unexpected) Emotional Impact"; Powell, "Dreaming Charles Eastman."
2. Snyder to Snyder, July 4, 1847, 4.
3. Snyder to Snyder, July 1, 1847.

liam's letters to Reynoso as soon as the family in Belleville had read them, and he requested that John send William all of his letters from Mexico.[4]

But it wasn't just family news that Fred craved. In multiple letters he pled with John to send newspapers. On July 1, 1847, he wrote, "Now, I want you John to send me every paper you can lay your hands on; I don't care how old or what politics. Send me one every day of your life and be sure to put them in a letter envelope, and direct them as below or I will never get them. Let me know all the news you can."[5] He repeated the request in at least four subsequent letters over the next two months.[6] Fred's requests for newspapers seem only vaguely related to a desire to keep up with current news. In his letters, he was more likely to comment on personal relationships—births, deaths, illnesses, and marriages—than on politics. Instead, reading the papers from home ensured that he was wrapped in his community's concerns and goings on.

John, at home in familiar territory, was less desperate for general news than was his brother, but he still took his duty as a correspondent seriously. John's anxiety for Fred's health and safety infuses both his letters and Fred's responses to them. In each letter, John asked after small details of Fred's experience and worked hard to keep Fred tightly bound to family life in Illinois—once even sending Fred a piece of wedding cake from the marriage of a family friend. The cake did not survive the trip, and Fred described the letter, on arrival, as having been so ravaged by mice that the paper itself was chewed to bits. The humor and affection between the brothers is palpable, even a hundred and fifty years later.

John's letters also reveal the larger scene of war material that proliferated back home in the United States. In one letter, he described the celebration that Belleville had planned for soldiers of the First and Second Illinois regiments returning from Mexico after the battle of Buena Vista. He explained, "We are going to give our boys a great dinner on the 28th and at night the town will be illuminated. I have got three large transparencies for the occasion. One represents Bragg's battery and Old Taylor riding up to him and saying 'A little more grape Cap. Bragg.' The other represents Santa Anna on his mule with only one leg and the third is a full length portrait of 'Old Rough & Ready.'"[7] In another

---

4. Snyder to Snyder, August 10, 1847.
5. Snyder to Snyder, July 1, 1847.
6. Snyder to Snyder, July 4, 1847; Snyder to Snyder, July 27, 1847, 27; Snyder to Snyder, August 10, 1847, 1; Snyder to Snyder, August 16, 1847.
7. Snyder to Snyder, July 15, 1847. The "transparencies" that John describes were common means of public celebration during the war. Scenes and portraits were painted on large pieces of cloth that were then hung before windows and illuminated with candles or lamps. Local businesses would sponsor such transparencies for celebratory public events, often described

letter, John mentioned having received a daguerreotype of their brother William, made during a brief stop at Fort Leavenworth. John reported as well on news that traveled by word of mouth (e.g., the arrival of a war-injured friend in St. Louis) and local responses to war news (e.g., "We have just heard (today) of the victory of our arms at Cera Gorda [sic]. In the reception of the news, the citizens held a meeting passed resolutions, and fired the six pounder &c.").[8] Far from the battlefield, John's world was rife with news, representations, and personal experiences of it. War came home in reams of paper, in images and pictures, in injured and weakened bodies, and in cannon blasts.

The Snyders, in other words, were immersed in a vibrant and varied rhetorical ecology of war documentation.[9] They participated in creating it, they moved it over space and time, and they held onto it tightly. Pictures, papers, letters, even pieces of cake made the journey from Mexico to the United States and back again. And though the Snyder brothers' correspondence is particularly robust and frequent, its concerns and the wide range of materials it invokes are common in US-Mexican War–era archives. News of the war was widely available in the United States, and it spread quickly. City streets were flooded with it and so were isolated farmsteads on the edge of the frontier. Not every person in the United States read the news, sent a family member to war, or saw a picture of "Old Rough and Ready" at Buena Vista, of course, but those without a material connection of one sort or another were in the minority.[10] Whether they approved or disapproved of the war, whether they followed the news with glee or anxiety, audiences in the United States tracked

---

as illuminations. It's worth noting that the scenes and portraits included in these transparencies echoed those reproduced in lithographs, though no transparencies from the era survive today, so we cannot say whether the transparencies were actually copied from lithographs. Certainly, though, the idea that there were particular scenes worth reproducing did circulate, and relatively quickly. General Scott's army routed Santa Anna at Cerro Gordo on April 17, 1847. According to another of John's letters, Belleville, Illinois, heard the news of that victory on May 6, though John does not relay the story of Santa Anna's missing leg at that time. The news of Santa Anna's hasty retreat (without his artificial leg and leaving behind a plate of soup) first came in a report by George Wilkins Kendall of the Picayune, published in the New York *Herald* on May 10 and May 15. By July 15—two months later—however, the image of Santa Anna fleeing on a mule was common enough knowledge in southern Illinois and northern Mexico that John could mention it without explanation. Snyder to Snyder, May 6, 1847; Amon Carter Museum of Western Art et al., *Eyewitness to War*, 42 n.55.

    8. Snyder to Snyder, May 6, 1847.
    9. Edbauer, "Unframing Models of Public Distribution."
    10. Lithographic portraits of General Taylor were popular fare, and one produced after Buena Vista was particularly well received and widely circulated. Newspapers in Missouri, Indiana, Maryland, Mississippi, Louisiana, New York, and beyond announced its publication and weighed in on its accuracy.

its progress closely across media and modes. The war's implications—its aims, its triumphs, its costs—were before their eyes.

All told, the US-Mexican War was an almost obsessively documented war. People in the United States saw, heard, and read about the war on a near-daily basis. They bought newspapers and lithographs, heard sermons and speeches, retrieved letters from the post office, stopped on the street to hear news bulletins read aloud, held pictures and papers in their hands, and embraced the messengers carrying them. War documentation was simultaneously a symbolic matter of discourse, sign, and image and a material matter of objects, pictures, and bodies. For those living through it, there was no doubting the magnitude of the war. For them and for those looking back now, there is also no doubting the magnitude of its material.

Despite all that physical material, however, in the United States today the US-Mexican War is, for most, a "forgotten war." Most US audiences know little or nothing about the it. Uncertain where to place it temporally, they might well collapse it with the Spanish-American war or confuse it with the Mexican Revolution. While they may vaguely understand that the United States' southwest was once Mexico's north, the fact that it was the spoil of a war of conquest that was begun with its annexation in mind is largely missing from dominant US public memory. This is curious, given how crucial the territorial spoils of the war were to the continental claims of American magnitude and manifest destiny at the time.

This "forgotten" war that cost the lives of an inordinate percentage of its participants, produced an unprecedented flurry of attention, and then faded out of dominant memory offers, perhaps paradoxically, a perfect case study of how shared experiences and circulating material gain consequence in public life. It aids us in theorizing magnitude in general and American magnitude in particular. Understanding how an intensely experienced and material-rich war could be forgotten draws our attention to the dregs and drips of material that accumulate into public feeling, persuading and constituting national sentiments that can later be summoned to serve new ends. It introduces, as well, a crucial but underrecognized aspect of magnitude: that every experience of sublime awe and presumption of inevitable grandeur is undergirded by seemingly insignificant moments and actions. Magnitude may sometimes come as a surprise or become abruptly palpable, but those sudden moments rely on processes of accumulation such as those I outline in this chapter. Accumulation is the practical sibling in magnitude's drama-prone family.

Prior to the US-Mexican War, large majorities in the United States were enthusiastically expansionist. They expected their country to span the continent and justified such expansion using arguments of racial superiority and manifest destiny.[11] The war troubled that confidence, though it persisted. If the United States was destined to stretch from sea to shining sea and be a beacon of democracy in the hemisphere, the fact that accomplishing that continental dream required aggressive war with an American "sister republic" was a problem. National feelings of destiny couldn't abide the specific history of the war. The nation's magnitude may be inevitable and destined, but the road to reach that destiny was uncomfortable in places and difficult to square with the story the United States wanted to tell about themselves.

While the benefits of forgetfulness are clear, then, the fact that it was possible raises interesting questions. How did so many conversations, so many bodies, so many newspapers, so many pictures—so much public documentation—disappear so thoroughly from public memory? The answer, of course, is magnitude. In "The Weight of Rhetoric," Farrell offers a brief "glossary" of magnitude's topoi built around contrasting pairs (essential/accidental, spectacular/routine, significant/trivial, etc.), reminding his reader that magnitude is always a matter of relation.[12] Farrell is clear, though, that those relations are ambiguous and complex. Sometimes, one set of objects, experiences, or memories must be made insignificant in order for the desired story of significance to take hold. Other times, the trivial accumulates into significance. In this case, I argue, both functions of magnitude are at work: The stuff of the US-Mexican War accumulated into something other—something grander—than the war itself. All that stuff became and gave way to public feeling about the size, shape, and rightness of the United States of America. Over the course of the war, accumulating documents helped US publics encounter the US-Mexican War and—whether they approved, disapproved, or were ambivalent to the war itself—eventually acquiesce to the territorial accumulation it entailed. That happened, I will show, not through concrete memories of the war's particulars but through the accumulation of feelings that were raised by their personal connections to it. Ultimately, the sensations of American magnitude generated by war documentation stuck not to the war itself, but to public feeling about the nation.

That sense of magnitude relied on three sorts of "accumulation" that overlap one another in this chapter: the accumulation of territory, the accumulation of documentary material, and the accumulation of feelings. Though distinct, the three are intimately connected. In particular, as I have suggested already, the third—the accumulation of feelings—helps make sense of the problems otherwise raised by the first and second. The penny pages, cheap

---

11. Greenberg, *A Wicked War*; Greenberg, *Manifest Manhood*; Murphy, *Hemispheric Imaginings*.
12. Farrell, "The Weight of Rhetoric," 471.

prints, and carefully written letters that carried news of the war were ephemeral; the war itself became a source of shame for many; but the feelings that the war mustered were enduring. Those accumulated feelings of national import ultimately became attached to territory. In the process, they helped naturalize and incorporate some Mexican land into US territory and leave other Mexican land as foreign space.

Accumulation was key to that eventual sense of magnitude. Understanding accumulation, however, also requires engaging another now-familiar rhetorical concept: circulation. Rhetors across the United States picked up pieces of US-Mexican War documentation and moved them around, sharing them with family and friends, discussing them in public and private, weighing them as part of political and economic decisions. But that documentation did not simply flow, as our existing theories of circulation would have it.[13] It built up. Its magnitude became significant because that which circulated also stopped. Pictures piled on letters; letters piled on newspaper stories; newspaper stories piled on personal experience. People held, read, sat with, prayed over, and kept all those objects. And when they shared them, they passed them from hand to hand.

Retheorizing circulation to account for this accumulation will help us understand not only the major moments of dispute that prompted rhetors to support US ambitions or take a stand against an unjust war but the slow processes of sedimentation that allowed those same people to look at the Mexican territory gained through the war and see it as an inevitable part of the great United States. Accumulation, in other words, helped provide what Christina Cedillo terms the "ideological basis of empire" during and after the US-Mexican War and what Mark Rifkin analyzes as the "quotidian modes of feeling" that authorize a "sense of ease in the territory claimed by the settler state."[14] Studying accumulation allows us access to the quiet rhetorical practices that led US audiences and rhetors to acquiescence and certainty. Neither patriotic fervor nor antiwar anxiety stirred in the chest of every soldier, let alone every US resident, during the war. Nevertheless, ideas, phrases, and orientations toward what it means to be America (and American) were accumulating in the available documents and in the hands of the people who saw them. That accumulation led gradually and almost imperceptibly to an accepted common sense that made Mexico's North into the United States' Southwest, stretched the significance of the United States of America from ocean to ocean, and forgot the war that made it so.

---

13. Edbauer, "Unframing Models of Public Distribution," 9. Edbauer's subsequent suggestion that *"the elements of the rhetorical situation simply bleed,"* however, is quite apt for the bloody rhetorical ecologies of war.

14. Cedillo, "Unruly Borders," 11; Rifkin, "Settler States of Feeling," 342.

The War between the United States and Mexico

After his election in 1845, James K. Polk confided to his secretary of the navy that there were four "great measures" by which he would assess his presidency. The first two were economic concerns. The third meant acquiring Oregon territory from Britain. The fourth was "the acquisition of California."[15] The annexation of Texas was nearly complete when Polk entered the presidency, and he wanted yet more territory. He was not alone. Powerful voices, especially in the Democratic party, argued that manifest destiny was a benevolent but inexorable force that would inevitably extend the United States across the continent.[16] In the process, it would bring enlightenment to all of humanity. They were generally silent on the fact that reaching California meant incorporating territory that was claimed by Mexico and inhabited as ancestral territories by dozens of distinct Native nations.

When the United States went to war with Mexico in early 1846, some of Polk's political allies—including his treasury secretary—advocated annexing Mexico's entire territory, at least as a protectorate. By late in the war, Secretary of State James Buchanan had joined that camp. Polk, likewise, increasingly hoped to force Mexico into complete submission. Until the very end, he argued that Mexico should cede all territory north of the twenty-sixth parallel.[17] The Treaty of Guadalupe Hidalgo, which ended the war in February 1848, angled the border farther north. That agreement still added more than five hundred thousand square miles to the United States, diminishing Mexico by half. To reach that settlement, the United States and Mexico fought a bloody, lopsided war that devastated Mexico's population and economy and, proportionally speaking, killed more US soldiers than any war in US history other than the Civil War.[18] It took three years and some 40,000 lives to accomplish the measure of Polk's vision.

---

15. Qtd. in Nevins, introduction to *Polk,* xvii. Polk later wrote in his diary (somewhat disingenuously) that he "had not gone to war for conquest," but "we would if practicable obtain California and such other portion of the Mexican territory as would be sufficient to indemnify our claimants on Mexico, and to defray the expenses of the war which that power by her long continued wrongs had forced us to wage." Polk, *Polk,* 91.

16. Greenberg, *Manifest Manhood,* 21, 28–29; Greenberg, *A Wicked War,* 55; Storm, "Annexation."

17. Polk, *Polk,* 118.

18. The Congressional Research Service Report "American War and Military Operations Casualties: Lists and Statistics" lists the death rate for US Soldiers in the Mexican War at 16.8 percent. Greenberg suggests this is likely a low estimate. For comparison, deaths on both sides of the US Civil War—the deadliest war in US history—were somewhere between 20 and 25 percent; on the Union side (a more parallel comparison) they were 16.4 percent. No other war in US history has risen above 2.5 percent mortality for soldiers. Also of note: Nonbattle deaths

Tensions between the United States and Mexico ran high in the years leading up to the war. Texan independence chafed at the Mexican governments of the era, and they never fully accepted its sovereignty. When the US Congress agreed to annex Texas in February 1845, its members knew that Mexico would view annexation as an act of aggression. Because Polk wanted even more Mexican territory but could not appear to initiate war, he went through the motions of diplomacy.[19] His diplomacy, however, aimed to give Mexico maximum insult while offering US audiences the appearance of an effort to avoid conflict.[20] When Mexico rebuffed Polk's slight-infused offers, Polk presented the United States as the insulted partner. Economically weak and politically tumultuous, Mexico hoped to avoid war, but its leaders were unlikely to resist provocation for long. Polk was happy to oblige, pressing hard on a sore spot.[21] Rather than annex Texas with its southern border at the Nueces River—a boundary Mexico had grudgingly accepted—Polk claimed the Rio Grande as Texas's southern and western border.[22] Citing defensive needs, he sent troops under General Zachary Taylor into that disputed territory and waited for an aggressive response from Mexico. From Mexico's perspective, the United States had just invaded. Polk claimed that Taylor's troops were on US soil. Both sides blamed the start of hostilities on the other and neither ever declared war: "Each announced that the other had invaded, and therefore that a war existed."[23]

Once war began, it progressed slowly but brutally. General Taylor and, later, General Winfield Scott were overextended and undersupplied. The volunteer regiments that made up the bulk of the US Army were often poorly trained, badly equipped, and undisciplined. Even so, the much larger Mexican Army did not win a single major battle of the war and lost many more soldiers in each battle than did the United States.[24] Constant political turmoil

---

outweighed battle deaths during the war by a factor of more than 6.5 to one. DeBruyne, "American War," 1–2. Greenberg, *A Wicked War*, xvii.

19. For a thorough overview of the multiple conflicts brewing between the United States and Mexico at this time, see Clary, *Eagles and Empire*; Henderson, *A Glorious Defeat*.

20. Historians now agree, though, that the United States could have accomplished the annexation through negotiation and financial pressure, given sufficient inclination. Greenberg, *A Wicked War*, xviii.

21. Greenberg, *A Wicked War*, 78.

22. Clary, *Eagles and Empire*, 68; Greenberg, *A Wicked War*, 67.

23. Clary, *Eagles and Empire*, 100.

24. Mexican record-keeping during the war was inconsistent, making it difficult to know how many Mexican soldiers died and the ratio of battle deaths to noncombat deaths. The *Encyclopedia of the Mexican-American War* notes that estimates of total deaths among soldiers range from 14,700 killed and wounded to as many as 50,000 (125). More striking are the battle disparities. At Palo Alto and Resaca de la Palma (the war's first battles), US forces lost 38 soldiers.

in Mexico made the nation seem unstable to US officials, so after each major victory the US generals assumed they would receive a speedy surrender from Mexico.[25] The arrogance of the United States worked against that goal, and the violence that US soldiers wreaked on Mexican civilians guaranteed that they remained hostile to the invading army. Though leaders in the United States repeatedly proclaimed the war nearly at an end and soldiers reported constant rumors of the same, hostilities ultimately continued for almost eighteen months. The battles ended only after the US Army occupied Mexico City in September 1847. Negotiating a peace took nearly six months more. Altogether, 13,283 US soldiers and at least 25,000 Mexicans (mostly civilians) died in the conflict, and the territorial shape of the continent was permanently changed.[26]

In the United States, early sentiment about the US-Mexican War was marked by the internal politics of the moment. Indeed, many scholars understand the war primarily as a major precipitating factor in the US Civil War.[27] Northern abolitionists and Whig political leaders opposed the war, seeing it as an excuse to extend slave territory. Some Southern Democrats, including Calhoun, worried that tensions over war with Mexico would endanger their "peculiar institution" and so pushed against it. Many Northern Whigs opposed the war as imperialist, but their concerns were racist: They feared annexing Mexico's nonwhite majority would degrade the US national body. Most Democrats, despite their distaste for federal power, favored aggressive expansion and saw US political dominance as an unmitigated blessing for the peoples of the continent.[28] The latter position—with its enthusiastic support for white settlement—was particularly strong in the West. Even Western Democrats concerned about slave state power had supported James Polk for the presidency

---

The Mexicans lost at least 256. At Churubusco and Mexico City (the war's last battles), the US Army had 133 soldiers killed and 865 wounded and 130 killed and 703 wounded, respectively. Mexico's killed and wounded reached 4,297 at Churubusco and 2,200 at Mexico City (126). Tucker et al., *The Encyclopedia of the Mexican-American War*, vol. 1, A–L:126; Clary, *Eagles and Empire*, 412; Guardino, *The Dead March*, 1.

25. Polk's initial funding request to Congress only funded a few months of war—he believed the United States would quickly force Mexico to capitulate. He likewise at first requested only one-year commitments from volunteer soldiers, a decision that left the generals with poorly trained and constantly rotating forces (and a problem population of former soldiers that hung around the occupied territory and made trouble). Clary, *Eagles and Empire*, 100, 118, 144. Polk presumed from the beginning that Mexico would be easily bullied into selling California to the United States. Greenberg, *A Wicked War*, 76.

26. Greenberg, *A Wicked War*, xvii.

27. Greenberg, *A Wicked War*, 268–69; Guardino, *The Dead March*, 3.

28. Greenberg, *A Wicked War*, 44; Schroeder, *Mr. Polk's War*, 33–34.

thanks to his full-throated advocacy for annexing further Western territory. The confluence of all these conflicting arguments and goals meant that the war—before it commenced and as it progressed—was discussed in political and editorial contexts using explicit terms of national responsibility and identity.

The US Army during the US-Mexican War was really two armies under separate hierarchies at the regimental level—one "regular" and the other volunteer. These two groups were often hostile to one another. Each embodied a host of contradictions. The regular army was heavily made up of immigrants who joined because they had few other options for making a living. Most soldiers in the regular army came from the Eastern United States. Compared with the volunteers, they were better trained, better disciplined, and generally had more skilled officers. They rarely participated in the looting, murder, drunkenness, and rape for which the volunteers became notorious. However, that discipline came at the expense of dignity: Enlisted men in the regular army were subjected to violent and degrading punishments and their personal freedom was constrained. For this reason, soldiers in the regular army were viewed with suspicion and disgust by many US civilians (and by soldiers in the volunteer army). Their servile status was presented as at odds with the essential nature of the ideal white American man.[29]

Most volunteers, on the other hand, were from the South and West. The first rounds of volunteers were more likely to be native born than soldiers in the regular army and came from the class of pioneers and yeoman farmers so prized in the self-image of the republic. These volunteers rankled at the discipline expected of them in the army and often refused to be fully pliant to the demands of their officers.[30] Their letters sometimes include explicit reflection on the incompatibility of army service and republican spirit.[31] The officers for the volunteer army were often elected by their men, which made the relationship more quasi-democratic but also left the officers unwilling or unable to restrain their soldiers' impulses.[32] For their misbehavior, recalcitrance, and often unreliable response to danger, the volunteers earned a bad reputation with the regular army leadership.[33] Their lack of discipline, unfamiliarity with best practices for camp life, and uneven access to supplies also meant that the volunteers died of noncombat-related causes at a much higher rate than did

---

29. Foos, *A Short, Offhand, Killing Affair*, 13, 22–25, 33.

30. Winders, "Will the Regiment Stand It?," 70.

31. Johannsen, *To the Halls of the Montezumas*, 40–41; See, for example, Conze, Letter; Engelmann, "The Second Illinois," 426.

32. Foos, *A Short, Offhand, Killing Affair*, 32.

33. Foos, *A Short, Offhand, Killing Affair*, 57, 89, 93; Johannsen, *To the Halls of the Montezumas*, 41.

their peers in the regular army.³⁴ Still, at least nominally and at first, volunteers joined the fight out of patriotism and a desire to show valor; regulars sought employment and income alongside glory and adventure.³⁵

At the start of the war, General Taylor and his army progressed from Matamoros on the Rio Grande south to Monterrey in north-central Mexico and eventually further into the mountains at Saltillo. Another force under General Wool, composed largely of volunteer regiments, headed west along the Rio Grande and then to San Antonio before turning south toward Parras. They met Taylor's army just south of Saltillo and together fought a costly battle at Buena Vista, claiming victory only because of Mexican general Santa Anna's unexpected retreat after heavy losses. Taylor's army eventually pulled back to Monterrey and the scene of war shifted to central Mexico under General Scott.³⁶

In the spring of 1847, Scott began his march toward Mexico City at the coastal city of Vera Cruz. After heavy bombardment, Vera Cruz surrendered to Scott on March 28, 1847, and the army moved inland, winning a major victory at Cerro Gordo on April 17 and 18 and then encountering little formal resistance as it crossed into the central highlands and took up positions in Jalapa, Perote, and Puebla.³⁷ There, Scott paused for four months to replenish supplies and reinforce his army.³⁸ In late August 1847, the US Army began its final push, skirting around Lake Chalco and approaching the City of Mexico from the south. They met and routed the Mexican Army at Contreras and Churubusco on August 19 and 20. After a pause for further negotiations with Santa Anna, they eked out a victory in an unnecessary assault on the Molino del Rey on September 8 and then took one of Mexico City's main defenses, the castle of Chapultepec, on September 13. From there, they assaulted the city itself and, after two days of bloody hand-to-hand fighting, forced its surrender. The US Army occupied Mexico City until the following summer. They were not viewed with affection by the Mexican people.

---

34. Foos, *A Short, Offhand, Killing Affair*, 90; Johannsen, *To the Halls of the Montezumas*, 42.

35. Later rounds of volunteers were often recruited/coerced from debtor's prison, taverns, and work gangs, making their motivations somewhat less nationalist in nature. Foos, *A Short, Offhand, Killing Affair*, 61–81.

36. There was significant tension between Scott and Taylor, an animosity that Polk abetted in his fear that the two Whig generals lacked loyalty to his Democratic administration. For fuller accounts of those personal and political rivalries, see Clary, *Eagles and Empire*, 252–54; Greenberg, *A Wicked War*, 143–44; Wheelan, *Invading Mexico*, 294–95.

37. Reilly and Witten, *War with Mexico!*, 135.

38. Reilly and Witten, *War with Mexico!*, 143.

During the six months between the end of outright battle and the end of the war, US diplomat Nicolas Trist negotiated with the Mexican government, much of the time without backing from the Polk administration. Polk recalled Trist to Washington in November 1847, thinking to force a more advantageous settlement. Trist ignored the summons and continued to negotiate, aided by General Scott.[39] Ultimately, though many Democrats argued for permanent occupation, the president dreamed of the Sierra Madre line, and his cabinet had settled on the twenty-sixth parallel, Trist's Treaty of Guadalupe Hidalgo offered a border that followed the Rio Grande northwest to the existing Mexican provincial border of New Mexico at El Paso and then tracked New Mexico's provincial border west and north to follow the Gila and Colorado Rivers until they reached the Gulf of California, leaving Baja California to Mexico and creating essentially the border we know today.[40] US public sentiment against the war constrained Polk to the lesser prize offered by Trist. He took it grudgingly. The United States had California. Mexico lost 50 percent of its territory in exchange for fifteen million dollars. Mexican citizens remaining on the wrong side of the new border were left to fend for themselves.

From the beginning of the war, the comings and goings of the US Army, political machinations in Washington and in Mexico, and the exploits and crimes of the soldiers were before the eyes of US audiences as never before. That visibility came thanks not only to war interest but also to technological change. The mid-1800s saw a sudden growth in the sheer amount of news available in the United States.[41] As the population grew (and grew increasingly urban), demand for information skyrocketed. At the beginning of the century, there were just a few hundred mercantile and political newspapers in the United States. In the 1830s and '40s, the "penny papers" entered the scene, using sensational stories and local news to garner a popular, working class audience. Between 1828 and 1840, the circulation of newspapers doubled, reaching 148 million copies annually. By 1860, there were three thousand newspapers pub-

---

39. Greenberg, *A Wicked War*, 238–39; Reilly and Witten, *War with Mexico!*, 219.

40. The Gadsden Purchase of 1853–54 added just under thirty thousand square miles to the United States in what became Arizona and New Mexico, settling a point of dispute that remained following the Treaty of Guadalupe Hidalgo and firmly establishing the present-day boundary of the United States.

41. Stewart, "Artists and Printmakers," 4. "The events of the war coincided with two very important developments in American cultural history: the rise of lithography and the advent of popular journalism. The Mexican War became the first event of its kind to be photographed, the first to be reported by war correspondents for mass circulation newspapers, and the first to be extensively recorded in lithographs intended for a broad audience."

lished in the United States. Literacy among white people had long been relatively high in the United States, but the mid-nineteenth century saw greater awareness of reading as a mass practice and a common presumption of access to reading material.[42]

Penny paper editors knew that providing quick, accurate accounts of the war would draw readers. They sent the world's first war correspondents to cover the activities of the US Army in Mexico.[43] Most of the professional correspondents on the front were employed by New Orleans newspapers, but their columns were reprinted across the country, and they gained national followings. Their eyewitness stories of battle and camp life were presented as the most reliable accounts of the war, and those accounts arrived quickly thanks to the courier systems that the correspondents developed. In addition to those professional correspondents, many soldiers also wrote for newspapers. Some were former journalists who had joined volunteer regiments and sent reports back to their one-time employers. Other soldiers sent letters to the editors of their hometown newspapers for publication. Still others had their private correspondence published with or without their permission.

The 1840s saw telegraph wires strung between major East Coast cities, and news reports could travel quickly along them. At the time of the war, the telegraph did not reach far enough to allow direct transmission from the battlefront or even from New Orleans to the East Coast. It did, however, speed communication outward from major East Coast cities once news arrived there. Miles of telegraph wire were added to the system during the war in response to growing public demand.[44]

Though pictures could not be easily reproduced in newspapers in the mid-1840s, illustrations of the news still appeared consistently and widely throughout the war. Lithography had served commercial needs in the United States since early in the century, but it took a new public turn just prior to the war and exploded during it. Lithographers played a significant role in helping US audiences visualize the conflict. Nathaniel Currier, who would later partner with James Merritt Ives to become the famous duo, opened his lithography shop in 1835. He almost immediately began illustrating current events—disasters like New York's Great Fire or shipwrecks.[45] "With the outbreak of the

---

42. Brandt, *The Rise of Writing*; Henkin, *The Postal Age*; Soltow and Stevens, *The Rise of Literacy*.

43. Though firsthand accounts of war had been published and circulated for centuries, the innovation of the Mexican War was to have professional journalists hired by specific newspapers writing reports and transmitting them directly to their employer.

44. Stewart, "Artist and Printmakers," 5.

45. Shepley, "By Which Melancholy Occurrence."

Mexican War," Stewart notes, "Currier almost single-handedly created a market for popular prints of its events" and hired newsboys to hawk them in the streets.[46] By the end of the war, Currier had published seventy lithographs with war themes, and his shop was just one of around twenty-five publishing similar scenes.

Though Currier was particularly adept at collaborating with newspapers to distribute prints and nearly half of the lithographs made on US-Mexican War themes were published in New York, war lithographs were printed in cities from Philadelphia to New Orleans, Boston to Cincinnati.[47] Likewise, newspapers regularly reported on new lithographs that crossed their desks, circulating descriptions of the prints to readers who would never see them in person. In December 1847, the *New York Herald* announced that the war would be the subject of its "Annual Pictorial Herald" and listed thirty-six engravings "which are copied from sketches taken on the spot by competent artists and may be relied on for accuracy."[48] Newspaper reports of celebrations—either of particular battles or of patriotic holidays—make clear that publishers commonly sponsored illuminated transparencies that gave large-scale tribute to the war's heroes and major battles.[49] Broadly speaking, the idea that newspapers and pictures could work alongside one another was firmly established during the war and had powerful effects on visual culture and the economy. The mass distribution of visual news became possible and profitable.

The postal service likewise contributed to the rapid accumulation of US-Mexican War documents. Starting in the 1830s, the US Post Office took advantage of growing rail and steamship networks to distribute mail—including newspapers—across the rapidly expanding country.[50] Between 1840 and 1860, the total number of letters carried each year by the US Postal Service quintupled from around 27 million to around 161 million. That meant that, per capita, US residents sent or received 5.15 letters per year (up from 1.61).[51] However, David Henkin notes, "These figures do not tell the whole story.... What changed was not simply the volume of correspondence or the number of correspondents but the expectation of contact and the perception of access."[52] The war attracted volunteers from across the country, so families from Wisconsin

---

46. Stewart, "Artists and Printmakers," 17.
47. Stewart, "Artists and Printmakers," 19, 16.
48. "The Annual Pictorial Herald."
49. See, for example, stories about illuminations in Philadelphia and New York: "The Illumination"; "The Illumination in Philadelphia"; "From the New York Sun."
50. Harter, *World Railways of the Nineteenth Century*, 41; Romanski, "The Fast Mail."
51. Henkin, *The Postal Age*, 3.
52. Henkin, *The Postal Age*, 3.

to Florida, Massachusetts to Kentucky read and shared letters from soldiers. And they knew about and expected such communication. The readers and viewers of newspapers, lithographs, letters, and telegraphs were a war public. They had reciprocal awareness of the "concatenation of texts" that circulated across the country and accumulated around them.[53]

Theorizing Accumulation

Accumulation is a means to magnitude. Sublimity may be magnitude's most familiar catalyst, but even sublimity comes from somewhere. The volcanos so frequently associated with the sublime (and so central to the story of magnitude developed in the next chapter) are, after all, themselves products of accumulation. And sometimes, instead of bowling viewers over with sudden appearance, magnitude creeps up on them. It insinuates itself into daily life until, eventually, it becomes integral. Accumulation "makes things matter" gradually, incrementally.[54] It covers over some options and lives and clears the path for others, determining what will be treated as significant and what trivial.[55] Frequently, magnitude acquired via accumulation has great staying power. It underwrites the "glance at a map" that so easily and presumptively lays claim to territory, destiny, and import.[56]

Recently, rhetoricians have used theories of circulation—especially Warner's—to better understand the force of rhetoric's subtle and indirect processes. Edbauer foregrounds circulation as providing a "framework of *affective ecologies* that recontextualizes rhetorics in their temporal, historical, and lived fluxes."[57] Tracing how pictures move and move us, Cara Finnegan and Jiyeon Kang use "circulation" to emphasize that images are "always in the process of making," and Laurie Gries illuminates "*how* things become rhetorical as they circulate and transform with time and space and contribute to collective life."[58] Circulation draws attention to the movement of claims, ideas, pictures, and images. It highlights their processual and protean nature and locates rhetoricity not in artifacts but in their flow. Tracking circulation has allowed

---

53. Warner, "Publics and Counterpublics," 62.
54. Farrell, "Sizing Things Up," 1.
55. Black feminist scholars working on the legacies of anti-Blackness have repeatedly theorized such processes of covering-over. Spillers, "Mama's Baby, Papa's Maybe"; Hartman, "Venus in Two Acts"; Sharpe, *In the Wake*.
56. Koerner, *Memoirs*, I:488.
57. Edbauer, "Unframing Models of Public Distribution," 9.
58. Finnegan and Kang, "'Sighting' the Public," 395; Gries, *Still Life with Rhetoric*, 3.

rhetoricians to identify influence without resorting to static rhetor+audience frameworks. It hasn't, however, accounted for the tiny pauses and particulates that, I argue, are equally essential to rhetoricity and its force.[59]

Accumulation is circulation's necessary counterpart. Where circulation tracks how arguments move affectively and effectively among social milieus, accumulation identifies their aggregation—their moves toward magnitude. The buildup of material over time—as slowdowns in the rhetorical river drop arguments and objects out of the flow—precipitates new actions, beliefs, and orientations. Such accumulation is sometimes so subtle and slow that its sediments cannot even be identified as "new." But tracking accumulation accounts for the rhetorical particulates that gather around everyday lives and, over time, shape their terrain in dramatic ways. As Jenny Rice explains, "coherence is nothing but accumulation—a sticking together until something feels whole."[60] And, I add, until that something feels consequential. A crucial aspect of rhetoric, then, accumulation draws attention to the stuff that sticks around and creates significance. Just as silt builds up at the mouth of a river or toxins concentrate exponentially as you go up the food chain, accumulation accounts for the material sediments that lend circulation staying power and that make circulation matter.

For rhetoricians, questions about what drops out, where it lands, and what happens when it does ought to be as crucial as the flow itself. Letters sent from Mexico did not simply circulate. They paused in their circulation—in a parent's hands, on the desk of a local newspaper editor, in the grasp of an enemy scout—and those pauses left ideas, feelings, and impressions behind. Both the paper and the feelings that remained behind accumulated and built up in people's lives. Accrue enough of those objects, pile them up, and even the most mundane information becomes consequential. Magnitude emerges from the accretion of the seemingly trivial.

Tracking rhetorical accumulation as a function of magnitude draws our analytical attention to overlapping paradigms that I label "proliferation," "sedimentation," and "precipitation." The first marks sheer amounts of material, the second the crucial matter of buildup, and the third the possibility of transformative interaction among elements. The next paragraphs offer brief overviews of each paradigm; the next sections elaborate each more fully in light of US-Mexican War documents.

---

59. See, for example, Edbauer, "Unframing Models of Public Distribution"; Gries, *Still Life with Rhetoric*, 7; Lester Olson, "Pictorial Representations."

60. Rice, "The Rhetorical Aesthetics of More," 40.

Proliferation

A surge of production, a flurry of news, or an uptick in arguments all signal that an issue has gained public import. Existing theories of circulation tend to account at least partially for this aspect of accumulation. Warner describes publics as "concatenations of texts over time."[61] Lester Olson's "re-circulation" tracks how images move across multiple objects, transforming themselves (and their objects) along the way.[62] Gries follows the multiple pictures that repurpose, respond to, and reject an image and so move it forward. Rice emphasizes the "Rhetorical Aesthetics of More."[63]

Olson's "re-circulation," Gries's "iconographic tracking," and my own previous work on topoi, however, all understand proliferation in terms of an individual image or idea that circulates, transforms, and becomes multiple.[64] They appear in new contexts, serve new purposes, and take new material forms, gaining consequentiality in the process. The proliferation I highlight here is messier, but it is equally essential and perhaps more ubiquitous. Frequently, proliferating objects share themes and consistent concerns, but are not tied together by a single image or commonplace.

Attending to proliferation helps account for the material that builds up as an event takes shape. Even if we cannot determine with certainty what any individual person saw, heard, or held in their hands, we can account for the amount of material that collected and so track its consequentiality. Encountering those piles of material allows access to the rowdy, complicated world of publicity. We cannot fall into simple sender-receiver models in this context, nor grant any object singular persuasive power. Instead, we must locate the consequences of rhetoricity in the messy mass itself.

Sedimentation

But proliferation alone is insufficient for treating the mess and mass. As materials multiply and move, they also pause and pile up. The values and feelings that infuse those materials pile up too. They sediment. Everyday life is rife with eddies and snags where persuasive bits catch and accumulate like silt on a river bottom, eventually reforming its pathways.

---

61. Warner, "Publics and Counterpublics," 62.
62. Lester Olson, "Pictorial Representations," 3.
63. Rice, "The Rhetorical Aesthetics of More."
64. Gries, *Still Life with Rhetoric*; Lester Olson, "Pictorial Representations"; Christa J. Olson, *Constitutive Visions*.

The proliferating news sources associated with the US-Mexican War add up to a great deal of material—mostly paper and ink. And as the Snyder brothers' letters remind us, circulation had an aim: being dropped into the hands of readers, viewers, and loved ones. Letters were unfolded and read, stuck on walls or stuffed in boots, refolded and forwarded on, carefully tucked into keepsake boxes and saved for more than a century. Understanding the persuasive effects of those accumulating materials requires considering the objects as sediments—small pieces that have their own materiality and that gain force and significance in concert with masses of other small pieces. It requires, as well, attention to the sedimentation of feelings, ideas, and experiences that accompany the accumulation of objects.

Sediments (objects, ideas, feelings) build up within publics and within individual lives. Even when no single thing seems to spark change—letters are full of mundane insights, newspaper stories report thrilling but distant events, pictures show scenes that could be any battle, anywhere—they are agglutinative, sticking to us and to each other. Piling up, they become momentous. They reinforce some pathways and foreclose others.

Precipitation

"Precipitate" is both a verb and a noun. "Precipitate," the verb, has causal and catalytic force: One event precipitates another. "Precipitate," the noun, points us to the solid things that emerge from interaction. As a feature of rhetorical accumulation, precipitation involves both verbal and nominal elements. It directs attention to the interplay between accumulating stuff and changing inclinations. It links gradually accrued affective inclinations to abrupt shifts in public behavior. Dramatic announcements and creeping loss of enthusiasm are both matters of precipitation.

It is easy for rhetoricians to track the precipitation of dramatic persuasion. Abraham Lincoln was elected to the US House of Representatives obsessed with tariffs. His first speech on the floor, however, was a stinging renunciation of the US-Mexican War. We can track the accumulating factors that precipitated that dramatic shift by reading Lincoln's letters and knowing that while en route to DC he heard his hero, Henry Clay, speak against the war. What mattered to Lincoln changed abruptly and consequentially.

But accumulating material also precipitated more subtle changes in the United States during the war. Though they grew increasingly uncomfortable with the war, US publics eventually incorporated large swaths of northern Mexico into their sense of the nation and envisioned a clear distinction between Mexican territory south of the Rio Grande and US territory north and west of it. Despite that ultimate acquiescence, though, "one glance at a map" and a long look at the accumulated material of the war make clear that its acceptance as natural, inevitable, and right was, ultimately, a matter of both subtle and dramatic precipitation.

Together, proliferation, sedimentation, and precipitation tie the flux and flow of circulation to the stuff and feelings carried along by it. They show how accumulation builds toward magnitude. Circulation, after all, means little without the material being carried or the people and places it encounters. Circulation does little without accumulation. Letters left Fred Snyder's tent or arrived there. Captain Bragg's battery at the battle of Buena Vista determined life or death for soldiers and then appeared on canvas and paper back home as communities celebrated US victory. A mouse-eaten letter, rough sketches of battlefields, and tired feet all made their way across northern Mexico's desert, across the United States, and into homes. These places, objects, and bodies circulated and paused. As they accumulated in those places of pause, they cohered into public feeling about the war and about American magnitude.

"You Must Write": Urgent Proliferation

Audiences in the United States were hungry for war news. The New York *Sun* announced that between regular editions and extras it was printing nearly seventy thousand copies per day early in the war.[65] Likewise, war produced a powerful desire for images that only lithography—with its relative ease of production and adaptation to commercial use—was technologically able to satiate.[66] Public demand for information meant proliferating sources, proliferating genres, proliferating means of circulation. During the war, war news was what mattered. Its magnitude was unquestioned even as pretty much everything else about the war was up for debate. Though the importance of the war would eventually fade, the in-the-moment presumption of magnitude was responsible for the sheer quantity of material that today takes up space in archives across the United States.

Despite the objections of their officers, soldiers wrote incessantly, sharing their accounts of battles, complaining about conditions, and critiquing their

---

65. Reilly and Witten, *War with Mexico!,* 2.
66. Stewart, "Artists and Printmakers," 5.

leaders. Early in the war, a correspondent writing to the *National Intelligencer* noted, "The complaints, sufferings, and achievements of the Army of Occupation have been given to the public by almost as many pens as there are bayonets among its numbers."[67] An officer in General Taylor's camp fumed, "The papers from the United States are now arriving . . . [and] it would appear that almost every camp follower, whatever his capacity or means of information, has believed that his own circumstantial report of transactions here, was a sacred debt he owed his country and the world."[68] This officer's annoyed comment tellingly links soldiers' public writing and its reception to a feeling of patriotic obligation. Even in the midst of official annoyance, there was a sense of national pride involved in the production of eyewitness accounts and in the urge to document. Indeed, the secretary of the navy boasted, "Nothing is more remarkable or more indicative of the intelligence and education of our people, than the fact that newspapers have been established in every town of importance which has been captured from the enemy."[69] Despite his enthusiasm for occupation newspapers, Secretary Mason likely frowned on the reports US soldiers sent back home. Still, the same democratic spirit of free speech and free press infused them. And it wasn't just the information carried by these papers that produced pride (or frustration), it was also their sheer number—the piling up of accounts and presses—that sparked commentary.

So, writing carried a sense of national obligation and democratic accomplishment. It also, however, served a powerful constitutive purpose. Writing bound communities together across distance; it sustained those "core attachments" that Farrell places at the root of magnitude.[70] That purpose is most palpably present not in public letters but in the private exchanges of ordinary soldiers writing to their families and friends.[71] Soldiers were far from home, in a strange land, and having new experiences. They wrote to share those experiences; they also begged and cajoled their interlocutors into response.

---

67. "Army of the Centre. Letter from a Correspondent of the National Intelligencer."
68. Qtd. in Stewart, "Artists and Printmakers," 6.
69. Qtd. in Reilly and Witten, *War with Mexico!*, 192.
70. Farrell, "The Weight of Rhetoric," 472.
71. This study draws primarily on letters collected in the Wisconsin State Historical Society and the Abraham Lincoln Presidential Library, supplementing them with letters that were collected and published. That choice of archives means this analysis is heavily inclined toward the experiences of volunteers. While published collections include some soldiers from the regular army, they tend to come from officers whose family ties or later fame made publishers willing to print their letters. While the letters reviewed here do not represent the experience of every soldier, their remarkable consistency and wide range is striking enough to suggest they are reasonably representative.

The sheer mass of letters written and requested by soldiers speaks eloquently to the depth of that need for connection.

Though not every US resident would have exchanged letters with a soldier during the war, enough did to create a critical mass of experience. The approximately twenty-seven thousand "regulars" and seventy-three thousand volunteers were drawn from a US population of around 20 million people (3 million of whom were enslaved). Roughly one out of every two hundred people in the United States fought in the war. Volunteers came from across the country, so their letters also moved across the country.[72] Those letters placed physical and emotional demands on writers and recipients. As they built up in postal bags and family chests, they shaped both individual and common experiences of the war.

Like Fred Snyder, soldiers frequently began and ended their letters with meta-discussion on correspondence. They and their interlocutors consistently called on each other to write. They listed the letters they'd received, explained how many letters they'd sent, and—often—remonstrated with each other to write more often. Sometimes, commentary on writing would take up a large proportion of a letter. This intense focus on correspondence suggests that letters did sustaining, world-making work for their writers and their recipients.

The soldiers writing letters were bound by enlistment contracts rather than prison bars. Even so, the urgency with which they admonish parents, siblings, and spouses to write resonates with the adamant need for connection that Chris Earle identifies in prison writing.[73] For Earle, the desperate call for correspondence reveals "not only that we are vulnerable . . . to the address and claims of others . . . but also that we are vulnerable to the address or to communication itself."[74] Soldiers at the edge of battle are by nature exposed. They too experience fundamental precarity and risk of annihilation, and for them, too, those experiences become tied to written connection.[75] Fear of death or injury generates desire for contact: one last word from or to home. But just as

---

72. Twenty-two of the twenty-eight states in the Union at the start of the war sent volunteers to the front. Companies were formed in Alabama, Arkansas, Florida, Georgia, Illinois, Indiana, Kentucky, Louisiana, Maryland and DC, Massachusetts, Michigan, Mississippi, Missouri, New Jersey, New York, North Carolina, Ohio, Pennsylvania, South Carolina, Tennessee, Texas, and Virginia as well as the territory of Iowa and the Anglo population of upper California. All but one of the states that didn't muster a volunteer regiment were in the Northeast, where antiwar sentiment was strongest. The residents of those states, however, were not isolated from news of the war. They simply received it in different form (including antiwar sermons). Schroeder, *Mr. Polk's War*, 35–37.

73. Earle, "Dispossessed."

74. Earle, "Dispossessed," 58.

75. Given that the regular army was often an option of last resort for enlisted men, a site of significant control and corporeal punishment, viewed by many citizens as a servile profession

often, the letters evince what Earle describes as vulnerability to communication itself. The soldiers want letters for letters' sake, letters to help them remain who they were and to ensure that they are safely ensconced in the heart of the community they have left. "It does seem as though you might write," remarks Adolph Engelmann. "You must let me hear from you," pleads Turner Crooker. "Please tell [Cam] he must write to me," urges John Nevin King.[76]

Such calls for more writing were frequently accompanied by explicit descriptions of how letters sustained connections to home. King chided his sister, "You know what pleasure it used to give you to hear from Pittsburgh when in Lick Creek, and then think of my situation in a far and distant land surrounded by trials and suffering, subject to soldiers and many miles even from the most distant relation. Now when you receive this [indecipherable] think how well please [sic] I would be to hear from you and all about [indecipherable] children and many of my old friends and acquaintances."[77] Even more than simply means of staying in touch, letters from home served as means of sustaining soldiers' whole sense of themselves. As Adolph Engelmann explained to his parents after being injured at the battle of Buena Vista, "Even though these letters may imply that I may be on the home road when you receive them, answer by all means at weekly intervals until I tell you I am leaving here, for should my wound trouble me and compel me to stay indefinitely I will need your letters more than ever."[78] No matter what, he urged, "I insist that you continue writing."[79] Lindorf Ozburn, a soldier on the Santa Fe trail, explained to his wife, "In conclusion I would say Diza my only request at present to write often to me and get all the friends of the boys to write for you do not know the anxiety they have to hear from home."[80] And Crooker exhorted his mother, "You cannot Imagine [mms torn] g[ood] it does us to hear from our homes. Do write."[81] Soldiers feared being forgotten, cut off. They feared social death, not just physical death. The war mattered to these men, of course. But frequently, their letters suggest that the visceral connections of community and the everyday, rather than abstract, experience of the nation

---

not worthy of free men, it may actually be appropriate to draw closer parallels between prison and the regular army at the time of the war.

76. Engelmann, "Second Illinois," 393; Crooker to Crooker, April 8,1847; King to King, February 3, 1847.

77. King to Dunstan, November 28, 1846.

78. Engelmann, "Second Illinois," 448.

79. Engelmann, "Second Illinois," 452.

80. Ozburn to Ozburn, July 14, 1847. Ozburn's letters are interesting in part because both his orthography and language suggest that he was not comfortable with writing and probably hadn't done much prior to departing home. Yet he, too, felt compelled to write letters.

81. Crooker to Crooker, April 8, 1847.

was what mattered. Even in the midst of war, the need to belong outstripped the specific histories of battles won or lost.

Early in the war, Frances Webster, the wife of a US Army officer fighting in Mexico, suggested that the same emotional need that soldiers expressed might also be experienced by families back home, writing, "Mail is the barometer by which my spirits are elevated or depressed; if it comes without the expected letter from you (and once a week at least I look for one) I am completely disconsolate."[82] Private letters were not simply tools for exchanging news, they were a form of sustenance. They were proof of life and a means for sustaining it. Receiving them, in quantity, was essential and constitutive.

Letters did vital work for their authors and recipients. They crafted, articulated, and authenticated the bonds of relationship across distance. Their proliferation mattered for individual soldiers and for the networks of family and friends they brought into being and sustained. Repeated letters traveling back and forth tied Illinois farmers to their fields and families, they linked career army men to the nation of civilians, they made the war fightable not through grand patriotism but through the desperate hope that someone on the other end of the letter-writing relationship was living their everyday life on familiar terrain. Mundane accounts of quotidian experience (and queries after the same from home) forged a meaningful, material connection between Mexican territory and a US homeland, between the personal experience of the war and the public experience of national growth.

Sediments of the Mundane and Exceptional

Sedimentation creates new terrain. It adds depth, reroutes familiar passageways, and makes solid ground where there once was none. In this sense, sedimentation is materially generative rather than cartographic. Cartography maps claims onto existing topographies. Sedimentation makes topos, makes land.[83] Sedimentation happens at the pace of flowing water and blowing wind. Though sometimes a flood will rapidly carve a new channel and block the old, sedimentation is usually a matter of slow, subtle accumulation. By the time there is a landmass visible and consequential, it will seem to have always been there. Noting sedimentation within the frame of magnitude thus directs attention to where the presumption of grandeur comes from. It tracks, in

---

82. Qtd. in Henkin, *The Postal Age*, 4.
83. Olson, "Democratic Hemisphere."

other words, what had to build up in order for Koerner and his compatriots to "glance at the map" and see the inevitable United States.

The US-Mexican War arrived in the United States slowly. Though news from the front traveled quickly by nineteenth-century standards, it still came at a delay. News of victory arrived days or weeks after the battle. News of death came from the lists of dead and wounded that journalists on the front painstakingly gathered, from a friend's letter sharing the news, from—eventually—an official letter of condolence. Families received letters at a delay of weeks or months. Lithographers read news in the papers, selected scenes, prepared stones, and made prints. A lag of a few weeks following the first newspaper stories was inevitable; some pictures took much longer.

But it wasn't just travel time and distance that made the war arrive slowly. It came, as all things do, at life pace. Soldiers writing home to family and friends narrated their experience one day at a time because that's how they lived it. Their readers followed along, traveling mile by mile down the Mississippi, across the gulf, and into Mexico. Newspapers, likewise, by necessity appeared one issue or special edition at a time. Lithographs captured the war battle by battle, heroic sacrifice by enemy surrender because that is the pace at which they occurred. Today we can encounter the war as a whole, crossing months and leagues by leaps and bounds. The war's original actors and audiences had to live it in real time. Some future rhetorician may look back at early twenty-first-century climate collapse and political upheaval and wonder how their ancestors lived such magnitude so mundanely. The answer is the same for them and us: Major moments and mundane particulars accumulated slowly, sedimenting.

In objective terms, the annexation of Mexico's north was a matter of cartography. Following the Treaty of Guadalupe Hidalgo, maps had to be redrawn and border markers established to instantiate a new claim on already existing land. But if the border shift involved abrupt cartographic action, US audiences encountered the land and made sense of it over a much longer period. The changed maps were preceded by millions of footsteps, hundreds of encampments, and dozens of sketches. Those footsteps, camps, and sketches were carried to and across the United States in newspaper articles, lithographs, and letters. Audiences back home read words and looked at pictures. Slowly the land they presented emerged into view.

The abrupt cartographic change wrought by the Treaty of Guadalupe Hidalgo posed fundamental problems for US manifest destiny. It risked putting the lie to Polk's protestations that conquest was not his purpose.[84] Audi-

---

84. Polk, *Polk,* 91.

ences in the United States needed to have acquiesced, in advance and over time, to that sudden enlargement. They needed to see it as inevitable and natural. The sediments of the war helped provide the grounds for that acceptance of vast but also limited territory. Footsteps and letters, wagon trains and lithographs had already brought the land before the eyes of US publics. Those materials brought into being borders more subtle, sentimental, and solid than the invisible treaty line.

Racism, xenophobia, ethnocentrism, and greed were, obviously, primary drivers of white settler willingness to claim some (but not all) Mexican land in order to accomplish the greatness of the United States. Conquest still, however, needed the slow accretion of feeling to naturalize, sanitize, and make it acceptable. The feelings normally associated with war—horror, anger, triumph, pain—are not immediately well suited to the production of normalcy. We know, however, that sustained shifts away from what is normal can create a new normal. And, of course, most people in the United States—unlike their counterparts in northern and central Mexico—did not live in the midst of battle. Even with all the violence and the disproportionate death, the "new normal" for US audiences during the war was one of anxiety and waiting, interspersed with eruptions of joy or sorrow. Early twenty-first-century readers in the United States may well be able to commiserate. The media that carried the US-Mexican War into the hands of readers and viewers in the United States brought its costs, its territory, and its acquisitions slowly into focus, giving them time to adjust to the feel of new American spaces.

Lithographs were particularly engaged in situating the war's progress within a clear and acceptable national frame. They told a sanitized, though still violent, story of the war. War was a matter of heroic victories, ordered regiments, and noble death. Even the most accurate of prints valorized moments of grandeur and conquest.[85] There were certainly exceptions, but the major lithography firms specialized in a popular nationalism that pictured the US Army confronting a foe that was far from its equal yet stalwart enough to be a worthy opponent. Though the early prints in Currier's archive showed scenes of violence and conquest, it is worth remembering that in the following decades Currier—joined by Merritt Ives—became a preeminent narrator of American normalcy. Prints celebrating iconic figures and momentary heroes as well as those picturing ordinary soldiers' return to their sweethearts quite explicitly position the war within a hortatory national normal in which the United States is both grand and benign (figure 1.1).

---

85. Scholarship on US-Mexican War lithographs has tended to focus on matters of correctness and fact (as well as artistic quality) and leave aside their consistent persuasive purpose. See, for example, Roth, "Journalism," 103; Stewart, "Artists and Printmakers," 7.

ACQUIESCING TO ACCUMULATION • 53

FIGURE 1.1. Nathaniel Currier, lithographer, *The Soldier's Return*, 1847. Hand-colored lithograph. Prints and Photographs Division, Library of Congress. Reproduction Number: LC-DIG-pga-09841.

Just as printmakers' images of human heroes helped incorporate soldiers into normal American life, they also helped incorporate the land those soldiers fought on into American normalcy. Topography—real or imagined, accurate or flawed—figures prominently in US-Mexican War–era lithographs. Prints depicting the battle of Buena Vista (February 1847) are representative in this regard, so I will linger with several of them.

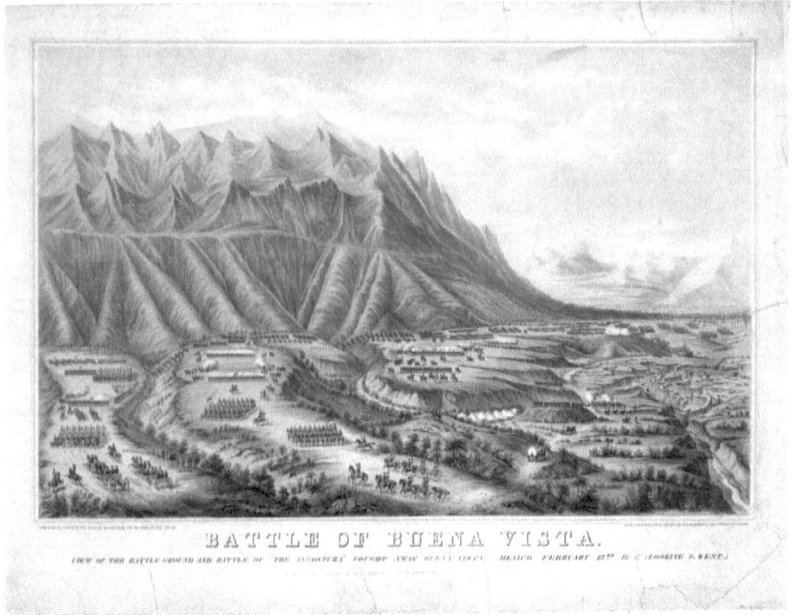

FIGURE 1.2. Henry R. Robinson, lithographer, *Battle of Buena Vista. View of the Battle-Ground and Battle of "The Angostura" Fought near Buena Vista, Mexico February 23rd 1847 (Looking S. West)*, 1847. Prints and Photographs Division, Library of Congress. Reproduction Number: LC-DIG-pga-02525.

The most topographically complete lithograph of the battle was published in early September 1847, during the final push toward Mexico City. This largely accurate (though simplified) view of the battleground was taken from a sketch made on-site by Major Joseph H. Eaton, one of Taylor's officers, transformed into a lithograph by Frances Flora Bond Palmer, and published by Henry R. Robinson (figure 1.2). Its publication was announced in New York newspapers and celebrated for its "evident truthfulness" and "appearance of life." The *New York Herald* concluded, "The picture is well worth having" for US audiences wanting to celebrate their nation's victories.[86]

Alongside the bird's-eye view of prints like Robinson's, Buena Vista inspired a number of lithographs showing crucial moments of the battle. Several recognizable officers lost their lives there, and they were quickly memorialized in lithographs. Lieutenant Colonel Henry Clay Jr.—heir of the nation's leading Whig—was most frequently represented. He sparked romantic nationalist sentiment when, mortally wounded, he reportedly urged his men, "Leave me, take care of yourselves. Take these pistols to my father and tell him, I have

---

86. "Fine Arts—View of the Battle of Buena Vista."

FIGURE 1.3. J. Butler and C. Lewis, lithographers, *Death of Lieut. Col. Henry Clay Jr. of the Second Regiment Kentucky Volunteers at the Battle of Buena Vista. Feby 23rd 1847.* "Leave me, take care of yourselves. Take these Pistols to my father and tell him, I have done all I can with them and now return them to him," 1847. Prints and Photographs Division, Library of Congress. Reproduction Number: LC-DIG-pga-05510.

done all I can with them and now return them to him."[87] His death was featured in at least four different prints, most of which explicitly reference his last words (figure 1.3). Colonel John Hardin of the Illinois volunteers also died at Buena Vista. He had represented Illinois in Congress but chose to go to war in 1846 rather than campaign for reelection. Hardin was Abraham Lincoln's main political rival, and his death likely paved the way for Lincoln's rise.[88] In the moment, though, he was remembered both in Illinois and in lithographs as a hero who put country above ambition. In a less mortal scene, one of the most famous and widely reproduced sayings of the war came out of Buena Vista. General Taylor's apocryphal instruction to Captain Braxton Bragg for "a little more grape" was featured across the country on lithographs, transparencies, and even tobacco packages (figure 1.4).

---

87. Butler and Lewis, *Death of Lieut. Col. Henry Clay Jr.*
88. Greenberg, *A Wicked War*, 86–90.

FIGURE 1.4. Nathaniel Currier, lithographer, and John Cameron, artist, *"A Little More Grape, Capt. Bragg"—General Taylor at the Battle of Buena Vista, Feby 23d, 1847*. Hand-colored lithograph. Prints and Photographs Division, Library of Congress. Reproduction Number: LC-DIG-pga-09337.

All these prints stage moments of death and bravery on Mexican territory but in American terms. Butler and Lewis's print *Death of Lieut. Col. Henry Clay Jr.* (figure 1.3) does this quite explicitly. It surrounds Clay and his compatriots with undergrowth and palms; threateningly racialized Mexican soldiers encroach from the left. The US flag waves proudly over the tableau, though, and its pole is planted firmly in the ground behind Clay. Through its paean to heroism, the lithograph claims that small piece of Mexican territory for the United States. An etching and aquatint of the same scene, produced by Matteson and Sadd some years later, adapts the details of the picture but leaves the flag flying above the fray at the center. The Kellogg brothers' lithograph of Clay's death scene replaces the flying US flag with a captured, limp Mexican flag. The effect is parallel, though. Clay's last sight is a symbol of the nation he has helped conquer. His last words, "I have done all I can with them," describe his pistols and remind audiences that his death helped ensure US victory on Mexican soil. In these scenes, viewers found a patriotic man to emulate. But they also saw their nation pictured—gallant, proud, and filled with masculine vigor. They saw, as well, the inevitable diminishment of Mexico in the face of US destiny.

FIGURE 1.5. Nathaniel Currier, lithographer, *The Gallant Charge of the Kentucky Cavalry Under Col. Marshall at the Battle of Buena Vista Febr 23d 1847*. Hand-colored lithograph. Prints and Photographs Division, Library of Congress. Reproduction Number: LC-DIG-pga-08747.

Likewise, in scenes of hand-to-hand combat—as in Currier's print *The Gallant Charge of the Kentucky Cavalry Under Col. Marshall*—US soldiers lean forward, driving ahead and encroaching on the space of their Mexican counterparts (figure 1.5). The Mexican line almost invariably falls back, disorganized at the onslaught of sharply ordered US ranks. Even in these static prints, the Mexican soldiers appear to shrink as their attackers bear down on them. Another Currier print, *Flight of the Mexican Army*, shows the retreating forces spread out over undulating hills, their backs turned to the viewer as they leave behind the broken bodies of their compatriots.

Frequently, lithographers placed US soldiers slightly higher than Mexican forces and surveyed the attack from a vantage point just above and behind the US position. The scene of Buena Vista in Carl Nebel and George Wilkins Kendall's definitive visual history of the war, for example, positions viewers some twenty feet off the ground, just behind General Taylor's threatened command position. Below, Captain Bragg rushes forward with his battery to defend the general. Meanwhile, the soldiers in Captain John P. O'Brien's battery stand firm against the Mexican bombardment, giving their lives to allow Taylor's reinforcements time to arrive. The Mexican army, though a serious threat at this moment in the battle, blends into the terrain, a smudge of darkness at the base of the mountains.

On first glance, these pictures seem primarily to provide viewers in the United States with a bird's-eye view of the territory they're conquering. But even in those rare moments when the territory is accurately depicted, it is the movement of the United States within and across that territory that takes center stage. A well-received lithograph of Taylor "at Buena Vista" reinforces this point (figure 1.6). Taylor himself is shaded and textured to appear as lifelike as possible. He stands out from the page, shown "as he is." The ground at Taylor's feet is just slightly less detailed. Bare ground, spent shot balls, rocks, and a scattering of flora provide him a place to stand. As the scene moves away from Taylor, though, it fades into nothingness—a line here, a smudge there. Off in the distance, vaguely in the direction of Taylor's gaze, a stone fort rises on a hill. If Taylor is "as he is" and "at Buena Vista," though, the background is anything but. There were no buildings, let alone a fort, at Buena Vista. In this print, the particulars of the territory matter far less than the feelings evoked by the rough-and-ready man (and men) who triumphed on it. Conquered territory is generic. The conquering American is particular.

In all these prints, the sedimenting image of US dominance is offered in simultaneously human and topographical terms. US soldiers take over Mexican territory by literally taking up the prints' symbolic space. Seeing the prints or reading about them, viewers were exposed to Mexican territory and offered a feel for the power and prowess of the US Army. Even as US publics debated the war's ethics by either decrying or minimizing its status as a war of conquest, lithographs seemed bent on building up a sense of glorious conquest and accumulating feelings of national pride.

When categorizing war prints, Stewart draws a distinction between the relative accuracy of some topographical prints and the wholly inaccurate prints that, Stewart suggests, were "designed to appeal to widely held social, racial, or nationalist feelings."[89] However, as my previous analysis suggests, the function of accuracy, topography, and objectivity cannot be separated from racist, nationalist sentiment. The topographically detailed war lithographs that Stewart so celebrates were equally aimed at shoring up nationalist feelings about national territory.[90] Audiences on the streets of New York, Philadelphia, Cincinnati, and beyond were repeatedly invited to oversee Mexico and the progress of the war. Seeing bodily risk and the triumph of arms on the wide fields of Mexico, they were offered a full sensory reminder of their own home-

---

89. Stewart, "Artists and Printmakers," 7.
90. Stewart, "Artists and Printmakers," 7.

FIGURE 1.6. Charles Risso, lithographer, after a daguerreotype by J. H. William Smith, *Rough and Ready as He Is*, 1847. University of Texas at Arlington Special Collections.

land's consequence. Here was magnitude in its more familiar setting—great, overwhelming, and blatant.

But even as these lithographs piled up feelings of victory, heroic sacrifice, and continental dominance, they were not the only Mexican scenes that accumulated for US audiences. While the hortatory enthusiasm of lithograph after lithograph built claims to Mexican territory, such claims were ultimately reshaped and resituated by the more intimate tales told in soldiers' letters from their long marches. Over the course of the war, US publics became increasingly uncomfortable with overtaking the land pictured in lithographs. As they dropped into the hands of family and friends, soldiers' letters provided another way to encounter new territory. They carved out the proper extension of the United States and banked up the foreign soil beyond it. The slow progress and worn boots that populate soldiers' letters make Mexico both distant and proximal. Through them, readers in the United States traveled the extensiveness of their own country and ran up against boundaries of fundamental difference that seemed natural and reasonable. The small-scale, familial intensity of the letters combined with the sweeping topographical claims of lithographs and the constant flow of news reports to allow twin feelings of racial distinction and American cohesion to coexist. Sedimenting together, the sense of continental dominance proffered by lithographs and the stacks of letters that recreated the Mexican desert in US homes slowly built new [US] American land for US audiences out of what had once been Mexican territory. The shape of a particular, great [US] America that extended specifically to (but not beyond) the Rio Grande came gradually into focus.

Private letters walked their readers through an intimate sense of the war, one whose criticisms and celebrations were based less on grand questions of governance and more on the slow accretion of days, miles, and words. Marching through dry desert, scorching heat, and spiny chaparral gave soldiers a close encounter with the American territory so coveted by their political representatives in Washington. For soldiers hailing from places like Wisconsin, Kentucky, Illinois, New York, and Connecticut, the land they traversed mile by mile was new, hostile, and often undesirable. In their letters, they repeatedly compared the soil, timber, and flora of Mexico to those of their homeland, and they usually came up lacking. Emmerson James, an Illinois volunteer, wrote to his parents from Monclova (near the border with Texas), noting, "As for their country it is not worth owning for I have not seen one tree in Mexico that would make rails the soil is nice but you cannot raise any thing unless you have it watered by artificial means for there is no rain here only at certain seasons."[91] Soldiers on the ground—in their letters and diaries—had ample opportunity to gather evidence that countered the imagined unity of the continent offered up from Washington. Even laying aside cultural differences, the land itself, "by no means [felt] like American territory."[92] If "one glance at a map" told Gustave Koerner back home that the Rio Grande should be the national border, soldiers collecting dust on their boots were less sure.[93]

---

91. Emmerson to Emmerson, November 8, 1847.
92. Greenberg, *A Wicked War*, 101.
93. Koerner, *Memoirs*, I:488.

The Illinois volunteers who accompanied General Wool west and south toward Chihuahua and then back east to Buena Vista described Mexico as empty and dry, even dead.[94] On the one hand, this empty land might seem to authorize US occupation just as lithographs' topographic expansiveness made territory available to US gazes. For some writers, it did.[95] But more often, the soldiers' clear desire not to linger undercuts such impulses. Early on in his march, while crossing toward San Antonio, Adolph Engelmann offered the assessment of a settler, noting, "Generally speaking, the land we have seen on our march here cannot compare with our Illinois prairies, it being too sandy. . . . The scarcity of timber will no doubt be the greatest drawback to the development of the agricultural regions."[96] Texas was, for Engelmann, a strange territory: "All plants here have thorns, all animals stings or horns and all men carry weapons and all deceive each other and themselves."[97] Engelmann assumed that the United States would occupy this territory, but his skepticism also suggests that he saw limits to his country's extension.

Once he crossed further into Mexico, Engelmann's sense of the territory's uselessness expanded, moving from a settler's skeptical assessment to outright refusal: "With little exception, what we have seen of Mexico is barren and probably will never be farmed. The country between here and Monclova, except for a few valleys already farmed, would not feed a goat."[98] Two weeks later, he repeated his assessment, telling his parents, "It seems to me as though that part of Mexico through which we came after leaving Santa Rosa is as thickly populated as it ever will be. Except a few mighty fine little valleys every foot of tillable ground is cultivated; the rest is desert, often a day's journey between water and where even a goat could not exist."[99] Though Engelmann's wording might imply a future in which the United States could occupy large portions of Mexico, it is also clear that he imagined both the land itself and the possibility of occupation as fruitless. John Nevin King, in a similarly biting tone, described Mexico as "the valley of life and death, or ants and flies," and then noted, "I have not seen a fence since I left home, that is since I left New Orleans."[100] Engelmann and King were not alone in this sentiment. There is a recurring ambivalence in US soldiers' relationship to Mexican territory,

---

94. Emmerson to Emmerson, November 8, 1847; Ralston to Wheat, March 22, 1848; Crockett to Crockett, January 23, 1847; Harris to Riggins, October 24, 1846; Greenberg, *A Wicked War*, 151.
95. See, for example, Ralston to Wheat, March 22, 1848.
96. Engelmann, "Second Illinois," 377.
97. Engelmann, "Second Illinois," 389.
98. Engelmann, "Second Illinois," 415–16.
99. Engelmann, "Second Illinois," 420.
100. King to King, August 22, 1846.

especially Mexico's north. They were drawn to it and desired it. They were horrified by it and disdained it. It is easy to imagine readers back home holding the letters, reading them, and shaking their heads. As boots accumulated miles on desert roads and letters describing Mexican land accumulated back home, the sense that Mexican territory was destined to become part of their country becomes less and less certain.[101]

Soldiers' letters took their readers slowly across the land, accumulating details about it in the process. They crossed from the United States into Mexico and accounted for the distance between those two nations while simultaneously making Mexican territory proximal to their readers. Working in this vein, soldiers' letters served an ethnographic function deeply tinged by racism. Fred Snyder told John of the Mexican curiosities he would like to send home. Ephraim Smith's praise for the climate of Monterrey was tempered by his assessment of its people and political capacity. He wrote to his wife, "It truly might be an earthly paradise were the inhabitants civilized. They, alas, are lost in the most groveling superstition and ignorance and are under a government that tramples them to the dust."[102] Likewise, James Ralston scoffed to A. Wheat, "Really it is of but little consequence where the [nominal?] boundary shall be fixed—if all the troops were withdrawn east of the Rio Grande, Mexico could not govern the country this side the Sierra Madre—but Americans would set up an independent government and hold the country without resistance. . . . [T]he Mexicans are Indians a little advanced in civilization but effeminate, treacherous, cowardly."[103] This overbearing racism, as in Ralston's comment, frequently led US soldiers to imagine US control further into Mexico. The racist vision of manifest destiny and its "benevolent" influence encouraged soldiers to imagine their nation's greatness in terms of direct governance. Having arrived in the valley of Mexico, Smith, for example, mused, "If I could have my friends around me and a good government I should delight to pass my life in Jalapa."[104] But if a sense of racial superiority made Mexican conquest seem natural and inevitable, it also made national identification nearly impossible. The United States could take the territory, could rule it. But the farther soldiers traveled into Mexico, the more the conquered terrain that built up in letters and lithographs was just that: conquered terrain, distinct and distant,

---

101. It is worth noting that letters written by soldiers who went to California are less bleak. That territory was perceived and described as very much worth taking. And, of course, it was taken.
102. Smith, *To Mexico with Scott*, 69.
103. Ralson to Wheat, March 22, 1848.
104. Smith, *To Mexico with Scott*, 139.

not us and not ours. American magnitude might confer a racist "right" to rule, but it didn't extend naturally into that territory.

Though soldiers' letters marked Mexican land as foreign and inhospitable, it was still territory they traversed and conquered. Alongside reams of other war documentation, they built up a sense of Mexican territory subordinated to US purposes and US decisions. Simultaneously "ours" and "foreign," it could then be divided, marked with a border that already seemed to make sense and that was dictated on US terms. Slowly, the new land that appeared for readers back home became recognizable as undesirable (or desirable). That recognition, in turn, helped the new border seem not a political or military acquisition but a matter of nature. It came into view and became solid for audiences in the United States in part because of the piles of documentation that entered their homes. Maybe they had long held to the Rio Grande as Texas's border. Maybe they had believed all along that California would belong to the United States. But incorporating the physical reality of that line and its proper position into national sentiment required something more. Stationed near Buena Vista before the battle, Adolph Englemann wrote his parents, musing, "With very few exceptions all the Volunteers of this section are mighty tired of this war, and sorry they ever left home. They believed that in 14 days they would be at Matamoros, facing the Mexicans on the battlefield in which case they would gladly have died. Instead we are 1,000 miles from there, 600 miles in the enemy country under a thousand difficulties."[105] Englemann, speaking for his colleagues, felt that they had left the proper boundary line far behind (apparently four hundred miles past Matamoros, in this case). His parents likely agreed—missing their son and wanting him home. Such assessments helped build the border from the other side. If lithographs showed soldiers planting US flags over scenes of death and victory far into Mexican territory, soldiers' letters drew that flag back north, toward home. The eventual borders became less a matter of conquest and more a matter of proper division. The quiet impression that lingers between those hortatory images of victory and the soldiers whose aching feet and thirsty mouths tell them they're too far from home is that the US Army could have conquered it all but instead recognized its proper limits. They came upon and created the inevitable, natural shape of their grand nation. What they brought into being became what had always been: a great United States that spanned the continent east to west but stopped short in its journey southward.

---

105. Englemann, "Second Illinois," 426.

Precipitating Consequential Feelings

As the war progressed, people stuck letters into keepsake boxes, tacked lithographs to their walls, wrote the names of deceased sons into family bibles, set aside newspapers to use as kindling or wadding, tucked daguerreotypes into lockets, and embraced returning soldiers. But paper, ink, bodies, and objects sent home were not the only material sediments of the war. It accumulated feelings as well, and those feelings were material in both their substance and consequences. Grief at the death of a loved one left permanent marks on families and their futures. Long periods of absence, likewise, summoned contradictory feelings for family members who awaited news of their soldier relatives. Pride and shame piled up within communities as tales of victory and misbehavior flooded across the country. The objects and documents of the war facilitated, fostered, and sedimented those feelings. They also precipitated new (or newly concrete) feelings about the shape and nature of the nation. Precipitation, in this sense, is about change: The mixture of objects and sentiments produces something entirely new. One of the US-Mexican War's particularly consequential precipitates was a substantial sense of the national public's proper boundaries.

The precipitates of the war direct attention to the visceral "imbrication of discourse, bodies, borders, and feeling" in publics.[106] But, where recent scholarship on publics measures magnitude in terms of intensity—either the heightened strength of feeling present in Johnson's visceral public or the absence of strong feeling examined in Jenny Rice's *Distant Publics*—accumulation marks something else, namely the public magnitude of repetition and familiarity.[107] Intensity of feeling was certainly palpable in public discussion of the war. Anger, hatred, exhaustion, apathy, and desire permeate newspapers, letters, and lithographs. But relative strength of feeling, like the relative impact of any particular piece of documentation, offers only a partial view of how public feelings surrounding the war worked. The ordinary, recurring materials of the war, as they built up, affected how "America" felt to its citizens.[108] The repetition of varied material over time, combined with the sensations that accompanied that repetition, precipitated newly acceptable public boundaries and the feelings of national confidence necessary to accommodate them.

While there were plenty of opportunities for discomfort and disillusionment with the war, the private ways that it came home for many white audiences in the United States meant that those negative assessments of the war

---

106. Jenell Johnson, "A Man's Mouth Is His Castle," 3.
107. Jenell Johnson, "A Man's Mouth Is His Castle"; Rice, *Distant Publics*.
108. Cvetkovich, *Depression*, 11.

itself were ultimately effaced by the need to make sense of their own community's involvement in it. As Sara Ahmed writes of "happy objects," "To experience an object as being affective or sensational is to be directed not only toward an object, but to 'whatever' is around that object, which includes what is behind the object, the conditions of its arrival."[109] The "conditions of arrival" for war documentation included the growing national discomfort with the war and its prosecution, the macro-level sentiments of American destiny that had initially sparked enthusiasm for the war effort, and equally powerfully, the micro-level, personal feelings of and about family members, friends, and neighbors directly involved in the war. Feelings of familial fidelity, grief at individual loss, concern at needless dangers faced, and pride at specific soldiers' actions built up along with the war's more macro-level sediments. Their entrance into homes and their "[taking] up residence within . . . bodily horizon[s]" had, as Ahmed suggests, constitutive effects. "We come to have our likes," she writes, "which might even establish *what we are like*."[110] That point resonates eloquently alongside Farrell's musing that those "core attachments" that are "not an outcome of how we reason but of who we are" are at the heart of magnitude.[111]

Though the objects of the US-Mexican War were often not happy objects, they were complexly affective ones, laced with the joy of connection, the anxiety of separation, the boredom of camp life, the fear of battle, and the hope for safe return. They instantiated those "core attachments" that tied personal feelings with national identity. And those personal sentiments of distance and proximity, of proper boundaries and national capacity were sticky, whatever their holders' larger sentiments about the war in general. When objects, encounters, public feelings, and national sentiments combined, the result was a fierce sense of "what we are like" that ultimately left aside the particulars of the war as less important than the feelings it generated. The murky material of the war mixed with familiar feelings of American magnitude and produced a precipitate: acquiescence to the precise shape of the nation as inevitable, as destined, and as exceptional.

In his single-term presidency, James K. Polk did more to shape the territorial face of the United States than any other president (with the possible exception of Thomas Jefferson). Yet the major piece of that great triumph was accompa-

---

109. Ahmed, "Happy Objects," 33.
110. Ahmed, "Happy Objects," 32.
111. Farrell, "The Weight of Rhetoric," 469.

nied by ignominy—at the time and in hindsight.[112] The war brought to light violent tendencies and dissolute behaviors in the very men who were supposed to be the pride of the nation. Vanity, ambition, and mismanagement among top officers tarnished the army's repeated victories in battle and shone light on the war's costliness in terms of human life. The "rough and ready" general who rose to the presidency thanks to the celebrity he gained in Mexico died a year into his term, leaving behind no particular legacy. The vast territory gained was marked with a sort of rapacious imperialism that the United States preferred to see as characteristic of the monarchical Old World, not itself. Today, one hundred and seventy-five years after the Treaty of Guadalupe Hidalgo, that territory's boundaries continue to be a source of agony and dispute over what it means for America to be "great."

Any significant, detailed public memory of the US-Mexican War threatened then and still threatens to tarnish the territory and spirit of a grand United States of America. Forgetfulness, comfortably wrapped in the poultice of manifest destiny, became necessary in order to make that territory—much desired, purchased at great cost, occupied in violence—innocuously but grandly [US] American. The sheer material accumulation of documentation—heard and read, seen and shared—played a paradoxical role in that transformation. Its intimacy and detail precipitated a public comfort among white US Americans with their newly gained, ill-gotten continental spread. The detail of personal experience eclipsed the memory of war, allowing them to see instead their personal connections and American destiny. That comfort with particular experience and with the more atmospheric sense of US accomplishment washed out the memory of the war itself. It also precipitated a shift in the practices of national expansion. Newspapers, lithographs, personal letters, political speeches, and soldiers' tales all advanced the conclusion that the United States had reached its southern continental limits at the Rio Grande. There would be no further expansion into Mexico.

By starting from the US-Mexican War, this book's tale of American magnitude begins with a thoroughly territorial question of magnitude: the right and proper size of the nation itself. Rhetorical accumulation, in this case, neatly parallels physical accumulation, but it need not always. Indeed, though the United States continued to aggressively acquire land in subsequent years, the end of the US-Mexican War shifted national attention away from continental territorial accumulation and, in turn, initiated a shift in the terms of American magnitude. With only a few exceptions, subsequent territorial accumulation was either presumed to be a fait accompli (e.g., the conquest of Native lands)

---

112. Greenberg, *A Wicked War*, 268.

or marked with imperial rather than national intentions (e.g., filibustering and the territories claimed following the Spanish-American War). From 1848 forward, the mechanisms of accumulation and enlargement underwritten by American *megethos* more consistently emphasized symbolic-material realms. This is not to say that the symbols of American *megethos* lacked physical import. Even today, they carry material consequences for physical territory (think, for example, of the ecological effects of President Trump's border wall). But following the US-Mexican War, the consequentiality of American magnitude was untethered from the literal physical boundaries of the nation and began to roam the hemisphere.

Scholars often point to the Spanish-American War, fought in 1898 and resulting in the acquisition of Guam, the Philippines, Hawaii, Puerto Rico, and the military base at Guantanamo Bay, as the beginning of US imperialism. To the extent that the Spanish-American War was the first war in US history to result in the acquisition of foreign protectorates never intended to fully enter the sovereignty of the United States (some of which are still colonial holdings today), that denomination makes sense. That understanding, however, obscures the imperial aspects of settler colonialism. Subduing First Nations was a seminal project of the new nation-state.[113] The fact that for nearly one hundred years such expansion resulted in national territory rather than protectorates should not obscure the fact that each territorial acquisition produced new colonized populations living in a paracolonial state.[114] The US-Mexican War was a logical step in that trajectory of settler colonialism. The United States had previously waged wars of aggression and conquest against sovereign peoples. This, however, was the first time the United States wrested territory from a republic it recognized as a fellow nation-state, the first signal that the peaceable American kingdom of the Monroe Doctrine was a convenient fiction. The Spanish-American and US-Mexican wars, often confused with one another, mark points on a continuum of colonial expansion that includes annexation and settler colonization, economic colonialism, and the acquisition of political sway. The US-Mexican War was an unjust war of conquest in which thousands of soldiers died invading the territory of a "sister republic" whose greatest sin had been to stand between the United States and California. As US audiences acquiesced to its accumulations and invested further in American magnitude, they increasingly directed their focus to the

---

113. I use "seminal" here intentionally, the work of Euro-American conquest being both an agricultural and carnal project of "seeding" and a thoroughly masculinist endeavor.
114. Vizenor, *Manifest Manners*.

other end of the continuum and, in the process, precipitated a new orientation toward the American magnitude of the hemisphere.[115]

When all was said and done, the death of comrades, the miles marched, and the battles fought precipitated ambient yet consequential sentiments of American magnitude. The vast documentation of the war accumulated not into memorable stories of battle or tedious memories of camp life, but into a powerful corroboration of national destiny. White, US American audiences took the mess and mass of documentation about the war and made it their own. Eventually, the familiar feeling of a nation that "cannot, that will not, that shall not fail" and whose scope of influence spanned the continent was all that was left of the memory of war.[116] We still live with the legacy of that feeling. It didn't start or end with the US-Mexican War, but that war was crucial in defining its scope. The remaining chapters of *American Magnitude* track that feeling as it spreads southward into Latin America and outward across time.

---

115. This assertion does not mean, however, that US expansionists were done seeking new territory in the Americas. Filibustering, in particular, carried forward in semiprivate form the rapacious desire for new land. Greenberg covers this extensively. Greenberg, *Manifest Manhood*.

116. McGinnis to Beal, February 23, 1847, 2.

CHAPTER 2

The Andes on Display

For a while, Frederic Edwin Church followed me around—at least every time I set foot in an art museum. I would stroll aimlessly around galleries, glance through an opening, and find myself facing a triangular volcano, snow-capped and dramatic. I knew the volcano well, but I would check the placard just to be certain. Every time, it would be one of Church's renderings of the Ecuadorian volcano Cotopaxi.

This can't actually have happened more than two or three times—I don't visit that many museums. But Church completed five full-scale oil paintings of the volcano, so there are versions to go around. At the time, Ecuador was very much on my mind, so Cotopaxi's familiar shape resonated. Seeing it, I would be briefly transported back to Quito, where the volcano looms large on the southern horizon.

My own experience of seeing Church's paintings and feeling pulled into Ecuadorian contexts is exactly the reverse of the experience at the heart of this chapter. I looked at what I knew to be a thoroughly US American painting and found myself drawn southward. But, I argue, the white, Northern, US audiences whose experiences bookend this chapter looked at pictures they understood to be exotic, distant, and foreign and, through them, were drawn toward a sense of the United States. A majority of the people who saw Church's Andean paintings in the third quarter of the nineteenth century had never been to South America and never would. They were looking at a painting by one of their era's most prominent painters, a man understood as offering a particularly powerful American vision. Whether Church was painting the woods and farms of the Hudson River valley, the icebergs of Labrador and Newfoundland, or the tropics and mountains of Colombia and Ecuador, he was painting America.[1] And that American vision, in purpose and content, had designs on values, actions, and attitudes within the United States.[2]

In this chapter, six stories—three set mostly in the United States and three set in South America—also meander into galleries, across continents, and up mountains. Along the way, they sketch out the magnitude of white, Northern US hemispheric vision in the second half of the nineteenth century. The stories I tell for the most part engage "majoritarian" narratives. They are, as Tara Yosso says, "embedded with racialized omissions, distortions, and stereotypes."[3] My purpose in telling them (and then tugging at the counterstories that thread through them) is to defamiliarize the presumption of whiteness and [US] Americanness that suffuses Church's paintings and the stories of magnitude told about and through them.[4] As Richard Delgado explains, "The stories or narratives told by the ingroup remind it of its identity in relation to outgroups, and provide it with a form of shared reality in which its own superior position is seen as natural."[5] The stories that Church told and the stories that were told about his paintings are stories of a particular, white, Yankee [US] Americanness. They echoed narratives that were familiar to Church's contemporaries and then extended them, encompassing the hemisphere. Picking up the strands of expansionism and manifest destiny that accumulated in the previous chapter, these stories carry American magnitude even further south. They had few designs on territory in the political sense, but they nevertheless advanced grand American claims.

I have built this chapter around stories and story theory because doing so highlights the extent to which American magnitude is a story—one told in words, pictures, and bodies. In taking this approach, I am indebted to the rich scholarship on story and counterstory that has emerged in rhetorical studies over the last decade, led by scholars in critical race theory and Indigenous rhetorics.[6] Like most majoritarian stories, the story of American magnitude

---

1. Kelly, *Frederic Edwin Church*, 75; Raab, *Frederic Church*, 93.
2. "Having designs on values, actions, and attitudes" is my paraphrase of Jack Selzer's useful definition of rhetoric as "kinds of communications that have general designs on people's values and actions, attitudes and beliefs." Selzer, "Rhetorical Analysis," 280.
3. Yosso, *Critical Race Counterstories*, 9.
4. Yosso, *Critical Race Counterstories*, 10.
5. Delgado, "Storytelling," 2412.
6. See, for example, Jackson and Whitehorse DeLaune, "Decolonizing Community Writing"; Martinez, "A Plea"; Martinez, *Counterstory*; Powell, "Rhetorics of Survivance"; Powell et al., "Our Story Begins Here."

has often not been recognized as such. When it has been explicitly treated in terms of story, it has been a rather messianic story—a mission or calling. It has been offered as a Truth rather than a tale. American exceptionalism and manifest destiny wend their way over oceans, across continents, and through time and, in the process, they become *the* American stories. Critical race theorists and scholars of Indigenous rhetorics remind us, however, to always treat exceptionalism, destiny, and magnitude as situated stories. That familiar trio of American investments perpetuates a story of domination made everyday and ordinary. They presume to make themselves singular and universal, but they are options among many.[7] And stories, as Romeo García observes, "are a site of culture and rhetoric; they are/they become cultural-rhetoric practices."[8] The stories told in this chapter have been lived out, circulated, and practiced. They have accumulated, in the sense discussed in the previous chapter, and they precipitated one set of US American ambitions and fears in the years just before and following the US Civil War. Telling the story of those stories and taking a cue from Malea Powell, I aim "to hold some of the complex shimmering strands of a constellative, epistemological space long enough to share them with you."[9] And, sharing them with you, I hope, makes them both familiar and unfamiliar—something you have likely known all along and yet, perhaps, had not really considered.

The first of this chapter's stories is about Church's Cotopaxi paintings. It offers the chapter's most literal example of paintings that invited US audiences—ubiquitously imagined as white and Northern—to look at South American scenes and see themselves. The second story introduces an even more dramatic invitation for US audiences to enter into Latin American scenes: Church's "great painting," *The Heart of the Andes*. Leaving the United States and moving backward in time, I then tell three lesser-known stories about Frederic Church—stories that have been of little use to the majoritarian narrative. These stories come from Church's time in the Andes—in 1853 and 1857—and they complicate the tale of American magnitude told through the Cotopaxi series and *Heart of the Andes*. Through stories of Andean altitude literally taking Church's breath away and Kichwa guides determining the limits of his enthusiastic exploration, I grasp at the "shimmering strands" of Church's encounters with a magnitude that was distinct from that of the United States and grapple with his fraught presumption of the "right to look."[10] Then, listen-

---

7. See, for example, Cushman, "Wampum, Sequoyan, and Story"; Delgado, "Storytelling"; Jackson, "Resisting Relocation"; Martinez, "The Responsibility of Privilege"; Powell, "Stories Take Place"; Querejazu, "Encountering the Pluriverse"; Yosso, *Critical Race Counterstories*.

8. García, "Creating Presence," 7.

9. Powell, "Stories Take Place," 384.

10. Powell, "Stories Take Place," 384; Mirzoeff, *The Right to Look*.

ing to stories told about Church's influence on the elite white-mestizo Quiteño art world, I pause briefly on the question of who teaches and who learns in the encounter with landscape. Finally, like Church, I return to the United States in order to reflect on the rise and decline of a great American painter. Together, these stories convene and question American magnitude as it circulated in the decades immediately surrounding the US Civil War—a white, masculine, outward-looking yet inward-focused affair.

Cotopaxi and the US Civil War

Nineteenth-century landscape painting had a mission. It was never merely a reproduction of nature but instead, as Jennifer Raab explains, "offered a powerful means to envision ideology and empire, religious and scientific discourses, political and economic capital."[11] Art historical discussion of Frederic Church's oeuvre frequently lingers on this point. It tracks how the allegorical legacy of Thomas Cole—Church's teacher—appears in Church's paining.[12] It notes Church's appeals to both progress and wilderness as American values.[13] It recounts the profound influence that Alexander von Humboldt's *Cosmos* had on Church.[14] And it positions Church's paintings as intentional, consistent reflections on national concerns.[15] Throughout, such scholarship tracks Church's successes and failures in terms of his paintings' ability to meet those pervading expectations.

In each of my stories about Frederic Church, I take that investment in the larger narrative for granted. Church meant his paintings as indexes to identity, shared belief, and national purpose. He meant, as well, to embody them though gendered performances of exploration, observation, and exertion—a combination of the "restrained" and "martial" masculinities Greenberg identifies as predominant during the years of his travels.[16] Even if Church did not consciously intend each implication I untangle in these pages, his orientation toward painting was rhetorical—it had designs on the values and beliefs of others—and the stories he told in paint and ink were imbued with persuasive

---

11. Raab, "Landscape," 57.
12. See, for example, Kelly, *Frederic Edwin Church*.
13. See, for example, Kelly, *Frederic Edwin Church*.
14. See, for example, Avery, *Church's Great Picture*; Huntington, "Landscapes and Diaries"; Rosenbaum, "Frederic Edwin Church."
15. See, for example, Harvey, *The Civil War and American Art*; Kelly, *Frederic Edwin Church*.
16. Greenberg, *Manifest Manhood*.

FIGURE 2.1. Frederic Edwin Church, *Cotopaxi*, 1855. Oil on canvas. 27 inches x 42 inches. Smithsonian American Art Museum, gift of Mrs. Frank R. McCoy, 1965.12.

purpose beyond their aesthetic beauty.[17] Those stories were also, resolutely, American. They were about the United States and its American scope—even when the scenes they showed were far from US borders. As Navas Sanz de Santamaría puts it, Church inspired a wave of subsequent artistic travel such that "for the Americans of that age any unexplored territory of the Americas might be worthy of the American Dream and the public did not distinguish between its America and that of the South."[18] This presumption in Church's work is palpable in his five oil paintings depicting Cotopaxi. In each, and particularly in their totality, Cotopaxi's snow-capped cone again and again reflects the needs and purposes of the United States.

I am not exaggerating or going out on a critical limb when I claim that Church's paintings of Cotopaxi were always fundamentally about the US national scene. Art historians readily agree that the paintings index US public feeling. In a brief *American Art* essay about the paintings, John Wilmerding describes the first in the series, painted in 1855, as "a telling metaphor of the state of the nation at the midpoint of the 1850s" (figure 2.1).[19] And "the nation"

---

17. Selzer, "Rhetorical Analysis."
18. Navas Sanz de Santamaría and Church, *The Journey*, 20. Greenberg's section "Natural versus National Borders: Redrawing the Map" discusses this inclination in more detail, laying out a more explicitly expansionist approach than I examine here. Greenberg, *Manifest Manhood*, 59–78.
19. Wilmerding, "Church, Cotopaxi, and Country," 17.

FIGURE 2.2. Frederic Edwin Church, *Cotopaxi*, 1862. Oil on canvas. 48 inches x 85 inches. Detroit Institute of Arts, Founders Society Purchase, Robert H. Tannahill Foundation Fund, Gibbs-Williams Fund, et al., 76.89.

whose "state" he invokes is, without question, the United States. Wilmerding sees in the painting a sense of satisfaction, rooted in a moment of "territorial expansion, agricultural and economic prosperity, technological advance, and general self-confidence."[20] He places its tranquility within the "relative stasis between the tensions that had erupted in the Mexican-American War half a decade earlier and that would explode again in the Civil War half a decade later."[21] The painting's pastoral scene, brooded over by the volcano's quiet threat, was a perfect allegory for a nation divided against itself, built on a foundation of incredible violence, yet strangely content in the status quo. Wilmerding does not comment on the strangeness of his own story in which a painting of a volcano on the equatorial line can sit "between" a war fought across the Rio Grande and a war fought across the Mason-Dixon line. It is so natural, so expected, that he cannot recognize it as a story. Of course, Wilmerding presumes, when Church painted an Ecuadorian volcano in 1855, he was also painting the United States.

Seven years later, in the midst of the US Civil War, Church painted Cotopaxi again (figure 2.2). This time, the volcano was roiled by eruption. Smoke

---

20. Wilmerding, "Church, Cotopaxi, and Country," 17.
21. Wilmerding, "Church, Cotopaxi, and Country," 17–18.

FIGURE 2.3. Frederic Edwin Church, *View of Cotopaxi*, 1867. Oil on canvas. 11 inches x 18 inches. Yale University Art Gallery, gift of Miss Annette I. Young in memory of Professor D. Cady Eaton and Mr. Innis Young, 1969.113.2.

billowed from its peak and turned the sky, the sun, and the landscape a fiery red. Church had returned to Ecuador in the interim between these two paintings. And though he did not witness an eruption during his 1857 visit, the surrounding territory still bore the marks of Cotopaxi's eruption a few years earlier, and the cone still smoked. Even so, there is little doubt that Church's explosive 1862 Cotopaxi speaks as much to what Church saw around him in the United States as to what he saw in Ecuador. Eleanor Jones Harvey, discussing Church's painting and the broader artistic response to the US Civil War, notes that volcanoes were prominent symbols of war, violence, and judgment.[22] Frederick Douglass had called slavery a "moral volcano, a burning lake, a hell on earth" and Church—probably unwittingly—echoed him.[23]

Church painted Cotopaxi again in 1867 (figure 2.3). Here, the eruption has subsided but not fully dispersed. Red and black smoke boils out of the cone, drifting to the right, and storm clouds lie low over the land on the far left. But the sky above the volcano is blue and sunlight falls on the white snow beneath its burnt-red peak. A placid—and fictional—lake fills the painting's midground. In the foreground a figure wearing a full skirt and red shawl walks

---

22. Harvey, *The Civil War and American Art*; Harvey, "America's Moral Volcano."
23. Douglass, "The American Apocalypse"; qtd. in Harvey, "America's Moral Volcano."

up a path toward a hut half-hidden by brush. The land between the mountain and the lake is blackened and shadowy. Wisps that might be cloud or smoke rise from it. The painting may not "wave the bloody shirt," but it certainly implies commentary on the slow road to recovery and sectionalism's lingering threat to the nation.

Wilmerding, writing of the 1855 *Cotopaxi*, suggests that it is "emblematic" of Church's "expanding continental vision of America" and reflects, "It is no accident that Church painted Cotopaxi as a natural temple in the hemispheric wilderness at the apogee of neoclassical idealism as national vision."[24] Wilmerding, Harvey, and Church's contemporaries consistently treat it as natural, even inevitable, that his South American paintings would reflect his concern for the state of his homeland. As Wilmerding puts it, reflecting on the difference between the 1855 and 1862 versions, "two cataclysmic events had intervened between the early and later interpretations of Cotopaxi: the Civil War and Charles Darwin's publication of *On the Origin of Species*. While the one rent the civil fabric of the country, the other undermined the spiritual order of nature, and Church could not help responding to both."[25] It is of course true that artists are affected by the major concerns of their day. Their work is inevitably shaped by it. But it is not, in fact, inevitable that Church would choose to paint Cotopaxi in light of US political scenes. He could just as easily have chosen to paint US scenes in order to grapple with US cataclysms. Instead, however, Church chose a volcano in Ecuador, one that he never actually saw erupt, to picture US national upheaval. How could that be "no accident" and something he "could not help" unless he (and his audiences and his more recent interpreters) were taking part in the stories of American magnitude that tied grandeur anywhere in the Americas to the grandeur of the United States? Only a powerful, ubiquitous, and commonsense story could allow US cataclysm to be best and most powerfully reflected on the snowy slopes of an American volcano thousands of miles beyond the nearest US border.

The Story of *The Heart of the Andes* as Spectacular Magnitude

For three weeks in 1859, crowds of New Yorkers packed the exhibition hall at the new Studio Building on West Tenth Street to see Church's massive painting, *The Heart of the Andes* (figure 2.4). Contemporary estimates suggest that more than twelve thousand people viewed the painting during that

---

24. Wilmerding, "Church, Cotopaxi, and Country," 17, 20.
25. Wilmerding, "Church, Cotopaxi, and Country," 21.

FIGURE 2.4. Frederic Edwin Church, *Heart of the Andes*, 1859. Oil on canvas. 66 1/8 inches x 120 3/16 inches. Metropolitan Museum of Art, bequest of Margaret E. Dows, 1909.

initial showing, paying twenty-five cents each for the privilege.[26] On the last day of the exhibition, visitors waited in line for hours before entering a room so packed with people that it was only possible to see the painting from a distance.[27] Visitors were encouraged to bring opera glasses so that they could experience the painting's detail even if they couldn't get close. A pamphlet written for the New York opening by Theodore Winthrop declared Church's work a transformative experience: "Men are better and nobler when they are uplifted by such sublime visions, and the human sympathies stirred by such revelations of the divine cannot die."[28]

After the initial exhibition closed, the painting traveled to England for display and engraving. It was then exhibited again in New York from October through December 1859 and subsequently toured to six other US cities.[29] *Heart of the Andes,* today held by the Metropolitan Museum of Art, quickly became Church's best-known and most-discussed South American painting, placed alongside *Niagara* and *The Icebergs* as his most notable works. Raab writes that *The Icebergs* and *Heart of the Andes* "present resolutely foreign

---

26. Avery, "The Heart of the Andes," 52. For perspective on the size of the crowd, it is useful to know that in 1860, the population of New York City was just over eight hundred thousand people, meaning that somewhere between 1 and 2 percent of the city's population saw the painting at its first exhibition.
27. Avery, "The Heart of the Andes," 52.
28. Winthrop, *A Companion to The Heart of the Andes,* 43.
29. Avery, "The Heart of the Andes," 53.

landscapes but are chronologically flanked by decidedly national pictures: on the one side, *Niagara* (1857), and on the other, *Twilight in the Wilderness* (1860) and *Our Banner in the Sky* (1861). . . . Both *The Heart of the Andes* and *The Icebergs* were, following Fort Sumter, presented with a sense of nationalistic purpose—the latter through its demonstrative first title, *The North,* and the former by appearing with presidential portraits at the Metropolitan Fair. But such patriotic stances had to be invented; they were not inherent in either picture's subject matter."[30] Of course, rhetorically speaking, "patriotic stances" are always invented, not inherent, and as this story will suggest, more than just display context gave *Heart of the Andes* its American magnitude.

The Heart of the Andes offers a composite view of the eponymous range. Rather than recreating an existing scene, the painting draws viewers into an idealized landscape meant to illuminate a larger visual truth about the Andes (and America). Not surprisingly, then, the first element to catch the eye is the massive snow-capped peak in the painting's upper left. Theodore Winthrop began his textual tour of the painting there. In the pamphlet he wrote for the opening, *A Companion to The Heart of the Andes,* Winthrop worked downward from the sky and the peak to the details of the foreground. More commonly, though, and encouraged both by the custom frame Church made for the painting and the other pamphlet made available at the exhibition, visual encounter with *The Heart of the Andes* begins in the foreground. There, viewers enter a scene crowded with lowland vegetation surrounding a roaring cataract. A dirt path carries the eyes into the mid-ground where the land starts to rise, and mountain foothills loom over a village nestled by a lake. Far away yet dominating the painting, the snow-capped peak of fabled Chimborazo emerges brilliant from the cloud-speckled sky. While the painting does not dwarf its viewers as thoroughly as it does the Indigenous pilgrims crouched by a cross in the left foreground (figure 2.5), its sense of vastness—in detail and scope—clearly intended to inspire awe.

Church was a master of spectacle and capitalism. He typically worked with his agent, John McClure, to promote his exhibitions as major events; he frequently painted in ways amendable to subsequent engraving; and he issued advance press releases to prime public interest in his paintings.[31] At the exhibitions of *Heart of the Andes,* Church combined all that with written materials that provided context and framing for the painting. The pamphlets—Winthrop's *Companion* and one by Louis Legrand Noble titled *Church's Painting.*

---

30. Raab, *Frederic Church*, 93.

31. These efforts were wildly successful for *Heart of the Andes*. Raab notes, "Booklets were published about the painting, poems written, sermons given, and a musical score . . . composed in its honor." Raab, "Precisely These Objects," 583.

FIGURE 2.5. Frederic Edwin Church, detail from *Heart of the Andes*, 1859. Oil on canvas. Metropolitan Museum of Art, bequest of Margaret E. Dows, 1909.

The Heart of the Andes—were available for purchase at the entrance to the gallery.[32] Both offered enthusiastic descriptions and analyses of the paintings and, "in the manner of travel guides," led viewers through the scene painted before them.[33] The pamphlets present themselves as erudite traveling partners for the viewing public—literally a "Companion" in Winthrop's case. They interpret the picture and model a proper viewing relationship to it. They also model a proper "American" relationship to the Andes themselves.

Key to that relationship, especially for Winthrop, is the perspective of the outside, exceptional, and masculine viewer. The Andes come into being, Winthrop insists, because of who sees them and gives them meaning. The opening pages of *Companion* chart successive waves of attention paid to the Andes, and the viewers are almost always influential outsiders—the noble, the imperial, the wise. They stand apart, embodying masculine ideals of control, vigor, and dominance that would have been readily recognizable to Winthrop's readers and Church's viewers.[34] "Long ago," Winthrop writes, Incas "watched the

32. Avery, "The Heart of the Andes," 59.
33. Avery, "The Heart of the Andes," 59.
34. Greenberg, *Manifest Manhood*.

snowy Andes."³⁵ They faded, though, and the Andes only came back into being when French scientists arrived to measure the equator in the eighteenth century.³⁶ Then the mountains sank out of sight once more until, Winthrop writes, the great Humboldt "lifted the Andes again . . . told . . . of their grandeur, and invited mankind to recognize it."³⁷ And yet, even that recognition was insufficient. The "transcendent glory" of the Andes "remained only a doubt and a dream, until Mr. Church became its interpreter to the northern world."³⁸ For Winthrop, the Andes rise and fall by the grace of gendered Northern vision. While Noble's pamphlet is less colonial in inclination, for him also Church is the Andes' ideal viewer, and South America is "a field entirely new to all modern artists of note and ability."³⁹

Without the gaze of the artist and his Northern audience, the pamphlets suggest, the Andes—despite their height and heft—become almost nothing, "a doubt and a dream."⁴⁰ Their lesson to those seeing *Heart of the Andes* from New York then becomes quite simple. They are to witness the Andes as "entirely new" in order to learn the larger lessons of American destiny and responsibility.⁴¹ Urging viewers to brave engagement and confident sight, Winthrop writes, "We may safely let ourselves grow, and never fear overgrowth. Why should not men become too large for 'creeds outworn!'"⁴² It's easy to imagine that the Monroe Doctrine's premise of nonintervention is among those creeds now too small to contain the ambitions of US American men.

Viewing *Heart of the Andes* in the terms that Winthrop and Noble provided, US publics could position South American grandeur as mysterious and sublime but also as part of the exceptional vision of the United States. Seeing the distant Andes, they saw their own emerging power. Whatever the viewer's own gendered position, as Americans they were invited to view from a stance of greatness utterly imbued with masculine prowess. And newspaper articles reviewing the exhibition suggest that reporters and critics, at least, took the lesson. A *Chicago Tribune* reviewer echoed Winthrop, declaring, "Since the earliest dawn of discovery and conquest, a charmed bell has been sounding" from South America, and Spanish conquistadors, Catholic fathers, and "the very flower of Eupean [sic] chivalry" pursued it. Church, however, achieved

---

35. Winthrop, *A Companion to The Heart of the Andes*, 3.
36. Winthrop, *A Companion to The Heart of the Andes*, 3.
37. Winthrop, *A Companion to The Heart of the Andes*, 4.
38. Winthrop, *A Companion to The Heart of the Andes*, 4.
39. Noble, *Church's Painting*, 7.
40. Winthrop, *A Companion to The Heart of the Andes*, 6.
41. Noble, *Church's Painting*, 7.
42. Winthrop, *A Companion to The Heart of the Andes*, 6.

it: *Heart of the Andes*'s "great charm is perfect truth."[43] That "truth" was there, waiting for the truly American [white, Northern, masculine] Church to champion it.

And it wasn't just the pamphlet authors and reviewers who framed that sort of intimate, proprietary encounter with the Andes. Church designed a custom frame for the painting that primed viewers for a similar interaction. It managed magnitude in scope and scale, ensuring that viewers stepped into a predetermined perspective on the painting and the American scene it offered. Though the frame itself has been lost, art historian Kevin Avery offers extensive evidence that it was designed to look like a window frame and, thereby, to invite viewers to feel as if they looked directly onto the scene itself, not just a painting of it.[44] Viewing the painting through opera glasses, likewise, encouraged "up close" looking and meant that viewers didn't have the painting's edges in view. Therefore, they "more readily crossed the threshold proffered by Church's frame and imaginatively traveled in the landscape."[45] Avery further reflects, "To approach the ensemble of picture and frame was to be absorbed by it, imaginatively to cross a threshold into a post-Biblical Eden."[46] Though Avery is a late twentieth-century commentator rather than a viewer contemporary to Church, his invocation of a "post-Biblical Eden" is telling—and sufficiently parallel to accounts at the time to be taken as indicative. In a Christian understanding, "Eden," of course, was made by God for the use and dominion of God's chosen people. There can be little doubt that white, US viewers in the nineteenth century saw themselves occupying America as a sacred space made for God's new chosen people. America, wherever it was found, had been granted to US viewers—white, Christian, masculine—so that they might inhabit and have dominion over it.

Whether they discuss the frame or not, newspaper descriptions from *Heart of the Andes*' early expositions repeatedly imagine viewers becoming immersed in its landscape and, simultaneously, stake a claim to that landscape through Church's American genius.[47] The frame's window effect, Noble's and Winthrop's travelogues, and the picture itself, as Rosenbaum suggests, "stimulated a reader/viewer imaginatively to retread Church's own sojourn through the Andes, which itself had been a reiteration of [Alexander von]

---

43. "The Heart of the Andes," January 17, 1861.
44. Avery, "The Heart of the Andes," 58.
45. Avery, "The Heart of the Andes," 59.
46. Avery, "The Heart of the Andes," 58.
47. See, for example, "Mr. Church's New Picture"; "Art Matters"; "Church's 'Heart of the Andes' (Correspondence of the Philadelphia Press)"; Allerton, "Church's 'Heart of the Andes.'"

Humboldt's exploration of the area."[48] The artist carried on Humboldt's work and, through him, viewers also became explorers. A column published in St. Louis takes that tendency farther, making white US American viewers into not only visitors but also symbolic occupiers. In the process, the painting's American claims become more direct and explicit. The column extolled *Heart of the Andes* for how it transported viewers into the painting. Seeing "not his work . . . but the actual scene," a [US] American "we" felt

> that we are alone, that we have shaken off the dust of the bustling, anxious, toiling world, that waterfalls murmur, zephyrs waft fragrant odors, and forests cast cooling shadows for our benefit only.[49]

The isolated space, provided "for our benefit only," was, of course, not actually empty, even in Church's own depiction. Indigenous pilgrims and a village graced the scene. And yet, once captured in oil by the great American painter, the scene became decidedly available to imagined colonization by white US viewers. "Many contemporary critics overlooked this human content entirely," John Leary notes.[50] Instead, they placed themselves into the scene. As another review announced, *Heart of the Andes* "has a relish of our soil; its almost Yankee knowingness, its placid clear, intellectual power, with its delicate sentiment and strong self-reliance, are ours; we delightfully feel that it belongs to us, and that we are of it."[51] It is no mistake, of course, that the critic's list of Yankee characteristics matches closely with that moments' emerging masculine ideals. As Greenberg notes, "When American men looked abroad they saw, first and foremost, reflections of themselves and of the men they chose to be."[52] Yankee exceptionalism, these articles suggest, can be found in any American scene, so long as it is sufficiently weighty and its viewer sufficiently American. Church himself seems to have felt something of this. Raab notes that Church "carved" his signature into a tree in the lower left corner of the painting. She explains, "It is as if a spotlight in the exhibition hall had been trained on this part of the painting. This is a sign of the artist's presence, a version of 'I was here' as well as 'This is mine.'"[53] That "mine" refers ambiguously—to the painting, to the tree, and to the place itself. For the properly American artist and viewer,

---

48. Rosenbaum, "Frederic Edwin Church," 29.
49. "Church's Heart of the Andes," unknown publication.
50. Leary, *A Cultural History of Underdevelopment*, 48.
51. "The Heart of the Andes," *The Atlantic Monthly*, 129.
52. Greenberg, *Manifest Manhood*, 51.
53. Raab, "Precisely These Objects," 582.

in other words, it was a short distance from immersion to claim, from visual encounter to proprietorship.

Interlude: Exploration

Nearly every critic—present or historical—who discusses Frederic Church's travels to South America places them in light of Church's admiration for Alexander von Humboldt. Church owned a dog-eared English translation of *Cosmos,* and his travel was directly inspired by Humboldt's call for artists to depict the tropics. Church hoped to present *Heart of the Andes* to Humboldt, making plans to ship the massive painting to Germany. Humboldt died soon after the painting was completed, however, so Church's scheme went unfulfilled.

As that investment in Humboldt's vision suggests, Church's expedition and his art were "scientific" in an era when the connection between art and science was particularly close. In that vein, Rosenbaum suggests that the most striking feature of Church's art "is not merely his interest in investigating the world around him but, more deeply, Church's underlying aspiration to fuse art and science into a single organic unity."[54] By the end of his painterly career, as Darwin's rise shifted scientific thinking and artistic expression trended increasingly romantic, Church's efforts to precisely reproduce the world positioned him outside the mainstream. But the height of his career coincided with the height of a confluence between the grand visions of art and science. And, at least for a painter inspired by Humboldt, achieving that synthetic grand vision meant looking toward the primordial grandeur of South America and the Andes.

Church was not the only elite white man from the nineteenth-century United States to be fascinated with South America. The wave of independence movements in Latin America in the 1820s and the 1846 English translation of *Cosmos* all conspired to turn US eyes southward. Katherine Manthorne notes that at least four US-sponsored scientific expeditions were active in South America in the years overlapping with Church's travels. "The information and pictorial records they gathered were disseminated in government expedition reports and popular travel accounts to a people hungry for reports of *American* territories by *American* explorers."[55] Nor was Church the first or only US artist to turn southward. George Catlin, Norton Bush, and many others went south on their own or in the company of scientific and commercial ven-

---

54. Rosenbaum, "Frederic Edwin Church," 26.
55. Manthorne, *Creation & Renewal,* 52.

tures.[56] Church, however, was by far the most prominent US artist to make the journey, and his experience serves as a representative anecdote for the larger mid-nineteenth-century urge to look toward South America and generate a pseudoscientific American vision. In that curiously ambitious pre–Civil War moment, elite white masculine rhetors across the United States, as Manthorne explains, "stepped up their exploration of what they increasingly refer to as '*our*' southern continent."[57] Filibusters made literal claims to ownership, and even those with no ambitions to annex territory saw a symbolic claim to all of America as utterly natural. Appeals to scientific magnitude helped authorize both.

So, inspired by Humboldt, inculcated in an attitude of proprietary desire, and seeking new scenes, Church traveled to South America. In April 1853, accompanied by the businessman Cyrus Field, he landed at Sabanilla, on Colombia's Caribbean coast, and ascended the Magdalena River. In June, he was in Bogotá and in August he visited the volcano Popayán. From there, Church traveled southward to Quito. He spent ten days in the Ecuadorian capital and then traveled to the coast. He spent a week in Guayaquil before leaving the South American mainland on October 1. He returned to New York by way of Panama.[58] Four years later, in 1857, Church returned to South America, traveling exclusively in Ecuador. His traveling companion on that second trip was the artist Louis Rémy Mignot. They arrived in and departed from Guayaquil, traveling inland and upward to Quito. Along the way, they visited the cities of the central highlands and lingered to view its prominent peaks—Cayambe, Pichincha, Cotopaxi, Chimborazo, and Sangay. After his travels to South America, Church would quickly be crowned "the very painter Humboldt so longs for in his writings" and also *the* "painter of the tropics."[59]

Even though Andean travels were central to Church's subsequent career and even though scholars writing about Church inevitably linger on his South American paintings, the stories from his actual time in Colombia and Ecuador have been scantily treated. His diary from the first trip was published by a Colombian press as part of an exhibit catalogue.[60] That same publication provides in-depth discussions of his itinerary. Accounts published in the United States tend to treat Church's travels in less detail, and there has been

---

56. Manthorne, *Creation & Renewal*, 52–53.
57. Manthorne, *Creation & Renewal*, 56.
58. Navas Sanz de Santamaría and Church, *The Journey*, 13.
59. W. P. Bayley, qtd. in Kelly, "A Passion for Landscape," 48.
60. Navas Sanz de Santamaría and Church, *The Journey*.

no equivalent attention to Church's 1857 trip.⁶¹ The archives at the Olana New York State Historical Site hold copies and transcripts of a diary that Church wrote during a portion of his 1857 trip. Letters that Church wrote home from both trips are held at the Winterthur Museum in Delaware. Ecuadorian art historians tell us snatches of the story from the Ecuadorian perspective and, in a portion of one book chapter, Franklin Kelly offers a brief discussion of moments from the 1853 trip based on Church's letters.⁶² But mostly, those consequential months in the Andes are storied only visually—in the paintings and sketches that Church made, the critiques published in response, and the scholarship analyzing them a century later. Despite that omission, the available tales from Church's time in the Andes are telling. They illuminate stories that not only push against but fully rupture the majoritarian narratives of American magnitude typically told through and about Church's paintings.⁶³ Though the evidence is patchy and dispersed, cobbling it together results in rather different American pictures. Such "critical imagination," as Royster and Kirsch describe it, allows us to "think between, above, around, and beyond" what is available through traditional scholarly methods in order to "speculate methodically about probabilities, that is, what might likely be true based on what we have in hand."⁶⁴ Focusing on the counterstories that have always been there and have always belied Church's majoritarian narrative means using documents of coloniality and para-coloniality against themselves in order to "tell different stories about them, with them, through them."⁶⁵ The stories of Church's paintings, then, can be "re-made" to tell stories of "accountability," speaking back to Church's moment and to our present investment in the feelings of American magnitude.⁶⁶

The Story of Church and the Andean Climate

Reviews of Church's South American paintings frequently lingered on his depictions of tropical air. In an unpublished essay about Church's 1862 Cotopaxi painting, Noble offered a particularly robust version of a typical analysis. He explained to viewers that "the atmosphere, with the clarity peculiar

---

61. Navas Sanz de Santamaría and Church, *The Journey*, 17. Howat, *Frederic Church* is an exception to this, treating the 1853 and 1857 trips in some detail.
62. Kelly, "A Passion for Landscape."
63. Yosso, *Critical Race Counterstories*, 10.
64. Royster and Kirsch, *Feminist Rhetorical Practices*, 71.
65. Powell, "Dreaming Charles Eastman," 121.
66. Dougherty, "Knowing (Y)Our Story."

to those bright altitudes, reveals far-off objects so distinctly that they appear less remote than in latitudes like ours. Hence the immensity of the scene, & the plainness of things, arise not merely from the supposed elevation of the beholder, but from the exceeding clearness of the air."[67] Church's initial attempts to render high-altitude air failed to please reviewers, but eventually he found his footing and critics began to call particular attention to this feature of his paintings.[68] The "atmosphere" that Church captured with light and shadow took the breath away; it was "an ecstacy indeed."[69] His paintings were "ethereal with the light of heaven" and captured the effects of "indefinite space" and high-altitude air as few other artists could.[70] Mary Allerton, writing for the *New Hampshire Statesman*, gushed, "Surely sky was never bluer than this, nor clouds more bewitching than those which lie all around the snow mountains, or carelessly brush the purple summit of the deep-toned one in the centre: and there, positively—there is a microscopic bit of a rainbow."[71] A review of *The Andes of Ecuador*, a painting where golden light seems to infuse everything, called the painting "amazing in its effects of atmosphere and light."[72] Another ended by exclaiming, "Grandeur, isolation, serenity! Here there is room to breathe."[73] Church, in other words, had become particularly adept at communicating to Northern viewers a sense of tropical atmosphere, especially the rarified air of the higher altitudes.

From the air to the foliage, Church was celebrated for the immediacy and detail of his South American paintings. They were, as we have already heard, "perfect truth."[74] But that simply isn't true.

Though Church was celebrated and critiqued for the scientific detail and near-photo-realism of his paintings, they were not actually realistic reproductions of flora, fauna, or atmosphere. They were idealized, composed, and fictionalized to offer just the right tropical scene that Northern viewers would understand as "real."[75] Navas Sanz de Santamaría blandly notes, among other pictorial adjustments, the "imaginary lake" that Church added to his 1862 (and 1867) paintings of Cotopaxi and the clarity of air he invented along the notoriously humid Rio Magdalena.[76] The fact that Church's tropical visions are pro-

---

67. Noble, "Cotopaxi," 62.
68. Manthorne, *Creation & Renewal*, 16.
69. J. M. S, "Church's Heart of the Andes"; "Heart of the Andes."
70. "The Heart of the Andes," *Evening Post*; "Mr. Church's New Picture"; "Fine Arts."
71. Allerton, "Church's 'Heart of the Andes.'"
72. Qtd. in Kelly, "A Passion for Landscape," 49–50.
73. "The Man about Town."
74. "The Heart of the Andes," January 17, 1861.
75. Navas Sanz de Santamaría and Church, *The Journey*, 54.
76. Navas Sanz de Santamaría and Church, *The Journey*, 43.

jections, imagining a "placidity and tranquility" that "[does] not correspond to the hot, humid and even oppressive atmosphere of the tropics," seems to have mattered little to US audiences.[77] That wasn't the realism they wanted. And Church knew it.

If Church painted the "real" tropics rather than the tropics he actually encountered, what does it matter that he was actually there, encountering the particular intensities of the humid lowlands and oxygen-starved Andean highlands? Of course, most practically, even if he did modify what he saw, he still could not have painted his pictures without being there. Kelly, for example, suggests that time in South America immediately affected Church's style, even before he started painting South American scenes.[78] But of more interest for our purposes is the recognition that the tropical lowlands and highlands posed a magnitude problem for Church. Their intensities challenged him— literally getting under his skin and taking his breath away.[79] And though he interpreted those intensities through US American notions of magnitude and oriented himself toward them through tropes of hegemonic American masculinity, the magnitude of the place itself also exceeded his ability to frame it.

Contrasting the serenity of Church's tropical paintings with Church's own words about his time there, Navas Sanz de Santamaría quotes Church's wry comment about having to "go through a course of sand flies and mosquitoes on the river, besides an extra allowance of heat" in order to reach his intended destinations.[80] Church sometimes described the tropical air as invigorating, but even then he noted its discomforts. Writing home early in his 1853 trip, for example, he exclaimed, "The weather is excessively hot and although I perspire without intermission night and day, I feel perfectly well, indeed, for several years I have never been so well at this time of the year as I am at present."[81] His letters and diary repeatedly invoke virility in the face of climactic and geographic hardship.[82] That did not mean, however, that he refrained from complaining about the heat, cold, rain, insects, and storms. His diary from the 1857 trip includes long interludes reflecting on the discomforts of riding and sleeping in snow and downpours. In their details (biting flies, sucking

---

77. Navas Sanz de Santamaría and Church, *The Journey*, 31.
78. Kelly, *Frederic Edwin Church*, 77.
79. See, for example, Navas Sanz de Santamaría and Church, *The Journey*, 57, 97.
80. Church to his sister, Charlotte, qtd. in Navas Sanz de Santamaría and Church, *The Journey*, 57.
81. Qtd. in Navas Sanz de Santamaría and Church, *The Journey*, 61.
82. Greenberg notes that such assertions of virility being enhanced in the tropics appeared regularly in filibustering literature of the time, often aiming to displace the long-standing racist presumption that the tropics were enervating. Greenberg, *Manifest Manhood*, 66–67.

mud, driving hail) and their scope (pervasive humidity, thin high-altitude air, daunting slopes), the tropics did their best to put Church in his place.

Church's account of trying to summit the Colombian volcano Puracé put these contending magnitudes into illustrative relation. On the one hand, Church, as the letter writer, presented himself as a connoisseur of American magnitude. He was anxious to reach the summit and described himself as particularly vigorous in comparison with his North American companions. When Mr. Gregory's horse gave out, that gentleman "pronounced that it was impossible for him to go a foot" and turned back.[83] Likewise, as the party continued upward and all the horses finally tired too much to carry riders, "the guides were obliged to help Mr. Field along."[84] Church, however, continued on his own feet. He "pushed up" to the first crater, eager for a glimpse. Reaching it, he became the Northern scientist, correcting the shortcomings of local naming. Though it had been called the "first crater," he reported that he "found that it was not a crater, but a blowhole or small opening, perhaps a yard in diameter from whence a sulphurous steam blew out with tremendous force. The sides of the peak had several cavities: from some issued steam, others hot water, underneath the ashes a few inches, was pure sulpher and calcined stone."[85] Church ventured to collect one of those stones and found it "so hot that a specimen . . . dropped from my fingers like a hot iron."[86] Though Church asserted his mastery as scientific viewer, the volcano quickly snatched a bit back.

And, ultimately, the volcano and the wisdom of local guides turned Church fully back. Church described the difficulty of breathing at such heights multiple times during his account of the ascent. Early on he noted, "The air began to be exceedingly rarified and the horses, although strong and accustomed to the ascent, dragged slowly up and were obliged every few steps to stop to recover breath."[87] Then, a few sentences later, he explained, "You can scarcely imagine the strange effect that so rare an atmosphere has upon the body; ten steps will put a strong man out of breath."[88] Even a virile American man had to acknowledge that the volcano's magnitude overcame him. The weather, too, overwhelmed the expedition: "Thick clouds hung about us and the rain, which we had experienced for some time, changed into hail. . . . Everything looked like perfect desolation and a cutting wind chilled us to the very bones in spite

---

83. Qtd. in Navas Sanz de Santamaría and Church, *The Journey*, 97.
84. Qtd. in Navas Sanz de Santamaría and Church, *The Journey*, 97.
85. Qtd. in Navas Sanz de Santamaría and Church, *The Journey*, 97.
86. Qtd. in Navas Sanz de Santamaría and Church, *The Journey*, 97.
87. Qtd. in Navas Sanz de Santamaría and Church, *The Journey*, 97.
88. Qtd. in Navas Sanz de Santamaría and Church, *The Journey*, 97.

of thick clothing."[89] Finally, the exhaustion of the other North Americans and the wisdom of the guides prevailed. Church concluded, "I was very anxious to go to the crater, but the guides were unwilling to undertake it in such bad weather and as the others seemed disposed to return, I reluctantly gave it up, but with the intention of returning the next day if the weather was favorable." Though Church closed his account with a return to mastery and vigor—he jogged down the slope while others rode—his story does not quite erase the ways that Andean magnitude exceeded his frame. The volcano, the weather, and the guides remind us that despite Church's protestations of vigor and his paintings' sense of expansive access, there is some irony in the reviewer's exclamation, "Here there is room to breathe."[90]

Recognizing how frequently the tropics—highland or lowland—taxed, annoyed, or perplexed Church asks us to view his paintings differently than we might otherwise. More to the point, that recognition demands that we acknowledge the storying work those paintings carried out. In that majoritarian story, both Church and his viewers traveled to the tropics but retained their particular Americanness. "For some years past," one critic wrote, "Mr. Church has been helping us to a complete knowledge of the exciting and yet indolent beauty of the tropics. He has learned the passion of those Southern climes, while he has not unlearned the energy of his own."[91] Church, according to Winthrop, was particularly adept at this apprehension of magnitude: "Men of science have sighed over their bewilderment in tropic zones, where every novelty of vegetation is a phenomenon. . . . But Art should . . . be its interpreter to the world."[92] The masculinity of previous men had flagged, perhaps, Winthrop admitted, but not Church's. We know, though, that tropical magnitude did bewilder Church. It left him gasping, itching, sweating, and shivering. Church's paintings might have deputized the Andes in service of American magnitude, but the place itself always had other ideas.

The Story of Sangay

Kichwa assistance—paid and/or conscripted—made Church's travels in the Andes possible. Even just on his three-day expedition to see the volcano Sangay toward the end of his 1857 trip, his diary specifically identifies eight Kichwa assistants: the "peon to drive the horse with the luggage," the "Major Domo"

---

89. Qtd. in Navas Sanz de Santamaría and Church, *The Journey*, 97.
90. "The Man about Town."
91. Winthrop, *A Companion to The Heart of the Andes*, 10.
92. Winthrop, *A Companion to The Heart of the Andes*, 11.

of the hacienda, a guide (Quipo), four Kichwa peons ("our Indians"), and "the old woman" at Ysapan who provided food and a fire after a frigid night.[93] Still other Kichwa people appear, unacknowledged—crowding around the expedition as they pass through a village, preparing food at the hacienda, tending the hacienda's crops, and living in huts visible along the expedition's route. Of all these people, Church was able to name only one: the guide, Quipo, who had "visited Sangai," and so provided essential knowledge.[94] In a story rich with details, the omission of names for the people so integral to his experience may not be surprising, but it is notable. One of those assistants—did Church even know his name at the time?—saved Church from a potentially fatal fall. Yet even he remained a type, a "peon," not a character in the story. The volcano, Sangay, however, was very much a character for Church. And, of more note, Sangay was an active character-subject for Quipo, the four *peones* aiding the expedition, and their Kichwa neighbors throughout the region.

Sangay, "The Giver," is a volcano in the eastern cordillera of the Ecuadorian Andes distinguished by its near-constant volcanic activity. It rumbles and smokes, throwing lava and rocks but not quite shifting over into dramatic eruption. When Church visited the area in 1857, Sangay had been steaming, smoking, rumbling, and spewing lava flows for nearly a hundred and twenty-five years. It continued another seventy-five after Church returned home. Then, after a brief period of rest, Sangay returned to activity in the late 1930s and continues today.

In local, Kichwa story, Sangay is a white-haired grandmother at constant work over her kitchen pots.[95] She is spouse to Chimborazo, the region's highest peak, who stands across the broad valley from her. Taita Chimborazo, it is said, fought with Capac-Urcu (el Altar) over the region's female volcanos—Sangay and Tungurahua. Tungurahua had been married to Capac-Urcu while Sangay was Chimborazo's wife. But Chimborazo seduced Tungurahua and stole her away. When Capac-Urcu came to reclaim his wife, Chimborazo dealt him a heavy blow. Today, Capac-Urcu lies broken and Chimborazo keeps two women.[96]

Since the conquest and the rise of syncretic Christianity in the Andes, Sangay has had overlapping relationships. She remains partnered with Chim-

---

93. Church, "A Trip to the Volcano," 1, 2, 3, 5, 11.
94. Church, "A Trip to the Volcano," 3. The white-mestizo governor of Chimborazo province and Mignot are the only other people referred to by their proper names in the journal.
95. See, for example, elements of Sangay's story in Andrade, *Protestantismo Indígena*, 88–89; Botero, *Indios, Tierra, y Cultura*, 94, 96–97.
96. Botero, *Indios*, 97. Violent, possessive masculinity obviously takes many forms in these stories.

borazo but also sometimes appears as Santa Isabela or abuela Isabela, married to San Carlos. As Isabela, she is celebrated in February when the weather is wet and risk of frost persists at high altitudes. The feast day for abuela Isabela and San Carlos comes at the end of Carnival. Then, Isabela passes through the community to receive offerings intended to ensure rain and send away the frost. As a community member in Achullapas put it, "She (the grandmother) would go off and everyone would know the day would dawn white-frosted, and they would say now the summer is coming, already the saving mother has gone about and sends away the ice and frost, it is time to plant my seeds with care. If we were giving [proper] adoration, the ice would not come."[97] Sangay is, in other words, a force to be reckoned with and respected—a powerful local figure. She sends frosts or protects from them, and even if locals approach her, they do so with caution and respect.

Church did not discuss Sangay's stories in his diary. If he knew them, he obviously preferred a more Western orientation toward mountainous storytelling, one where intrepid men tackled the challenges of nature and emerged victorious. Church, in other words, was interested in conquest. As with his account of scaling Puracé, his story about Sangay prioritized achievement—he outlasted companions, battling cold and thin air to attain the heights. At Sangay, Church aimed to climb as high as he was able and capture a view of the mysterious volcano. The fact that very few people had ever approached Sangay was part of the attraction. Church described his guide, Quipo, as unique among locals in his knowledge of the terrain, and even Humboldt never got close to Sangay. So far as Church knew, Sangay had never been scaled. Though he had no illusions that he would reach the summit, he hoped at least to see the notoriously cloud-covered peak unveiled. He wanted access and accomplishment.

In the handwritten version of Church's Sangay diary, the July 10 entry expresses Church's hope that the clear weather would hold as they moved further into the wilderness. Then he commented, "Still the matter will be settled all all [sic] the great stories of Sangay will be proved—true or untrue."[98] In the elaborated, typescript version of the diary, thought to have been made later in the century, Church wrote instead, "Still the Sangai problem will be settled and the wild stories of the mountain be exposed."[99] It's hard to know what stories Church had heard. Most likely he had originally been intrigued

---

97. Qtd. in Andrade, *Protestantismo Indígena*, 88. "Ella (la abuela) se iba y sabía amanecer blanqueando la helada, decían ya sale el verano, ya la mama salvadora se ha ido y manda las heladas, con cuidado mis granitos. Si nosotros estábamos adorando, no sabía caer la helada."
98. Church, "Sangay Diary 1857," 24.
99. Church, "A Trip to the Volcano," 5.

by Humboldt's ruminations on the mountain's power, but perhaps he had also heard warnings or tales in the days leading up to his attempt. Either way, Church's orientation matters. The stories told about Sangay were not stories to be reflected on and dwelt with—they were to be proved or disproved, settled and exposed. He was, in that sense, the necessary outside observer so heralded by Winthrop and so invited by the canvases he would ultimately paint. However, Church's actual experience with the volcano reveals the cracks in that sense of confidence about his own revelatory powers.

Quipo, the four Kichwa assistants, the woman preparing food at Ysapan, and the local Kichwa residents Church passed on his travels all knew Sangay well. Though Quipo was the only one who had climbed to her slopes, Sangay was a constant presence in the region. Her rumbling and smoking were palpably present—shaking the ground, assaulting the ears, and obscuring the view. And, of course, she was a powerful figure of story.

While Church may have heard some of those stories, he likely didn't hear them directly from his Kichwa guides or from the people he met on the way to Sangay. He barely spoke Spanish and had no Kichwa at all. As they approached Yehubamba, the hacienda where they spent the night before beginning their trek, Church's party passed through a village where locals tried to talk with them. Church wrote, "A babel of tongues ensued as each endeavored to give us information. And with my limited knowledge of Spanish I was not a little confused."[100] Though he eventually understood a portion of the message—changing horses and acquiring a new guide—he certainly wouldn't have learned anything particular about Sangay. The four "Indians" assigned to assist the expedition likewise appear to have managed some communication with Church, but they almost certainly relied on pantomime for much of it. Quipo spoke only Kichwa. Or, at least, that was the impression he gave Church.

The language barrier and Church's lack of local knowledge figure prominently in his journal. Church was entirely reliant on his guides to find the way. He would have been helpless without them. They prepared food, cared for the horses, set up camp, lit fires, and demonstrated how to stay warm. After a slow and risky trek from the "Rancho" at Ysapan toward Sangay, Quipo asserted control of the expedition as a whole. In his diary, Church reported,

> "About 3 o'clock Quipo with a mixture of Indian [sic] and pantomime informed me that but a part of our journey was accomplished. That the weather was unfavorable (it was very cloudy) and that we were in a place

---

100. Church, "Sangay Diary 1857," 7.

where water was convenient and that [there] was none for some distance father [sic] and that it was advisable for us to encamp for the night—I could not gainsay it for he was the guide and spoke Indian [sic] and I was a stranger and spoke English—so I resigned myself to another days travel which I fear will be a long one."[101]

By Church's own account, his acceptance of Quipo's knowledge appears somewhat less than gracious—it's about language and familiarity, not recognition of superior insight—but he had no real choice. Quipo was the one in control. Quipo actually did have the critical insight necessary.

Church never got close to Sangay, but he saw it—briefly. After Quipo stopped the expedition near water and the group had eaten, Church set out alone to see if he could get a glimpse of the volcano in the distance.

> I seized my sketch book and commenced the ascent of the hill behind us. It seemed not very high but the exertion in working through the grass was tremendous and I toiled and toiled while every little eminence which I gained revealed a still more elevated one above but I persevered and was rewarded finally by planting my feet on the summit.[102]

Here, at last, Church claimed a little conquest—a minor summit, distant from Sangay, but a summit nevertheless. He planted his feet there. At first, Sangay was shrouded, so he turned to sketch a mountain in the opposite direction. As he sketched, the clouds cleared, and he turned around. There was Sangay "with its lofty plume of smoke [standing] clear before me. I was startled with the beauty of the effect."[103] This was Church in his element. He described the volcano, smoke, and sky with rich language and careful comments about color, making notes for a painting that he never made. Sangay would not hold still for him, but that actually pleased Church: "I was so delighted with the changing effects that I combined making rapid sketches of the different effects until night overtook me and a chilly dampness warned me to retrace my steps."[104] In this sentence, we see Church as both the confident scientist-artist and the foolish outsider. The equatorial night does, indeed, overtake the land quickly and the sudden chill is not merely inconvenient—it can be dangerous. Church described his descent as "comparatively easy" but also noted his risk: "I could

---

101. Church, "Sangay Diary 1857," 35–36.
102. Church, "Sangay Diary 1857," 38–39.
103. Church, "Sangay Diary 1857," 40–41.
104. Church, "Sangay Diary 1857," 44.

not see where my feet were going."[105] Only the sight of the campfire—kept burning by his guides—ensured his safe return.

The greater insight of the Kichwa-speaking locals kept Church alive, safe, and (mostly) comfortable. They were the ones who knew where to make a favorable campsite.[106] They were the ones who knew precisely where the expedition was in relation to Sangay.[107] They were the ones who knew how to sleep safe and warm under their ponchos, even when rain and snow began falling during the night.[108] They were the ones who knew the right time of year to approach the mountain and recognized July as very much the wrong time.[109] They were the ones who pointed to low food supplies and inclement weather and called an end to the expedition.[110] Church had declared himself the one to prove the stories and give the true, scientific account of the volcano. However, it was five Kichwa men, with their combined cosmological and ecological experience, who could effectively interpret the volcano's stories for an outsider. The irony of this point seems to have been entirely lost on Church, but it shouldn't be lost on us. The widely distributed feelings of sublime, powerful, scientific sight that Church transmitted through his paintings must be set in relation to the knowledge and story of his Kichwa interlocutors. Without them and the magnitude of their interventions, Church would have been literally and figuratively lost.[111]

The Story of Church Bringing Landscape Painting to Ecuador

José Gabriel Navarro, one of Ecuador's first art historians, would have us believe that Frederic Edwin Church single-handedly brought landscape painting to Ecuador. Navarro's account centers on the Salas family—Quito's nineteenth-century painting dynasty. After the death of the Salas painter-patriarch Antonio, Rafael, his most talented son, took over the Salas studio. That studio, Navarro explains, quickly became the destination of choice for foreigners drawn to Ecuador for its awe-inspiring natural beauty and to Quito for its long-standing primacy in the arts.[112] "One day," Navarro writes, "Fred-

---

105. Church, "Sangay Diary 1857," 44, 45.
106. Church, "Sangay Diary 1857," 37.
107. Church, "Sangay Diary 1857," 37.
108. Church, "Sangay Diary 1857," 47–48.
109. Church, "Sangay Diary 1857," 51–52.
110. Church, "Sangay Diary 1857," 51.
111. Not that he realized it.
112. Navarro, *La Pintura En El Ecuador*, 204. Unless noted, all translations are my own.

eric Church came to visit."[113] Church and Salas became friends, and Church accepted the Quiteño painter's hospitality during his ten days in the city in 1853.[114] Each day, after sketching and painting studies in *plein* air, Church would return to Salas's home and share his work, talking animatedly about the experience and his painterly practice.

"Little by little," Navarro explains, "[Salas] was initiated into a love of landscape." Church was shocked that Salas "had never thought to be a landscape painter in a country as beautiful as Ecuador."[115] Intrigued, Salas "decided to try [it] out." And with that, Navarro says, "he became the founder of landscape painting in our country."[116]

A column later, Navarro reemphasizes the story. He describes Salas as "convinced by Church's reasoning" but also as caught emotionally. "With an air of surprise," Salas started looking differently at the world around him. "He started admiring the sketches and studies that Church brought to their conversations each night," and, before long, Salas "started to paint Ecuadorian landscapes." Navarro concludes his treatment of Church's visit by repeating simply, "And that is how landscape was born in Ecuador."[117]

There is no doubt that Salas was one of the first Ecuadorian artists to take up Euro-US-style landscape painting. His students, especially Rafael Troya and Luís Martínez, were among the next century's most celebrated landscape painters. There is also no question that Church influenced Rafael Salas. The timing of Salas's turn to landscape roughly coincides with Church's visit in Quito, and the story of their friendship appears to be correct. Navarro's emphasis on Church's influence, in other words, is reasonable. It is also incomplete.

---

113. Navarro, *La Pintura En El Ecuador*, 204.

114. Kennedy Troya, "La Percepción de Lo Propio," 118–19; Navarro, *La Pintura En El Ecuador*, 204.

115. Navarro, *La Pintura En El Ecuador*, 205.

116. Navarro, *La Pintura En El Ecuador*, 205. "Poco a poco," Navarro writes, "le fue inculcando el amor al paisaje, admirado de que un artista como él, no hubiera jamás pensado en ser paisajista, en un país tan bello como el Ecuador. Salas lo comprendió y decidió abordar este tema, con lo cual se constituyó en el fundador de la pintura paisajística en nuestro país."

117. Navarro, *La Pintura En El Ecuador*, 205. "Con aire sorprendido iba viendo lo que nunca se había fijado, iba admirando día a día las manchas y los croquis que le traía Church cada tarde a la conversación nocturna y que, después le servirían para hacer sus grandes cuadros en donde haría ver las bellezas del trópico a los magnates de New York. Hasta un día él también acompañó a Church a pintar lo que él pintaba. Comenzó a pintar paisajes ecuatorianos y en su taller se hacían los paisajes. componiéndoles como los hacía Courbet en su *atelier* para que saliesen los cuadros que luego se disputaban las gentes de dinero para embellecer sus hogares. Y es así como nació el paisaje en el Ecuador."

As Alexandra Kennedy Troya explains, even if Church's visit did provide a crucial spark, the fire was already well laid.[118] Ecuadorian artists, including the Salases, hosted multiple traveler-scientists starting in the eighteenth century, and they would continue collaborations into the twentieth. A steady stream of visitors, including "Mutis, Humboldt, Caldas, Darwin, Charton, Church, Wold, Reiss & Stübel, among others, indisputably served as drivers in a process spreading first the ideas of the Enlightenment and later of romanticism across the breadth and width of the Americas," Kennedy explains.[119] Likewise, John Howat suggests that Friedrich Hassaurek, the US minister to Ecuador from 1861 to 1865, offered Salas even more pointed encouragement toward landscape painting in the years after Church departed.[120] Church was influential, in other words, but he was not the only one providing outside perspectives.

And, despite snide remarks to the contrary from Hassaurek and others, Salas and his compatriots were not mere copyists who took their experiences with outsiders and replicated them.[121] They had their own vision and purpose. Rafael Salas observed Church's painting practice carefully and was impressed by it. But he didn't adopt it wholesale. Though he began to observe terrain more carefully and started to paint rural landscapes, he still preferred to paint from memory rather than from sketches done on-site. And, Kennedy explains, based on the few still-extant paintings available, it appears that Salas also eschewed Church's detailed, scientific style. He worked more with light, ambience, and form, heightening a religious feel. That greater emphasis on the spiritual both aligned Salas with local politics and recognized the investments of the Ecuadorian art-buying market. This lesser investment in scientific realism may also be tied, ironically, to Salas's greater obligations to reality. We know that Church's obsessive detail and heightened realism frequently misrepresented the reality of Andean scenes, including its flora and fauna. Salas, on the other hand, could not pass precise-but-erroneous detail off as reality. As Kennedy muses, "Salas had an audience that knew its own territory and that had no tolerance for transgressive compositions that idealized that territory."[122]

---

118. Kennedy Troya, "Artistas y Científicos," 229.
119. Kennedy Troya, "La Percepción de Lo Propio," 113. "Figuras tan distintas como la de Mutis, Humboldt, Caldas, Darwin, Charton, Church, Wolf, Reiss y Stübel, entre otras, sirvieron como motores indiscutibles en un proceso que había arancado con el afianzamiento de la ideas de la ilustración y posteriormente del romanticism, a lo largo y ancho del territorio americano."
120. Howat, *Frederic Church*, 77.
121. Howat, *Frederic Church*, 77.
122. Kennedy Troya, "La Percepción de Lo Propio," 119–20. "Salas tenia una audiencia que concocía su propio territorio y que no admitiría composiciones transgresoras en el sentido de construcciones ideales."

His paintings served a local, national purpose and, therefore, romanticized the national terrain. Church, we can now understand, was able to become known for depicting the tropics in supposedly perfect scientific detail because those tropics were part of his audience's imagined America, not an actually existing place that they knew intimately. Such inventive science might not have been successful had Church been painting US scenes. Audiences might have recognized the fiction and so been less able to imbue its "science" with national romance.

The nineteenth-century Europeans and North Americans who visited, painted, and wrote about South America following Humboldt's summons produced work marked by "foreign visions" that were "imbued with their own predispositions with regard to nature and civilization, and that did not necessarily correspond to the [South] American reality."[123] As Ecuadorians— artists, politicians, and scientists—took up the ideas they had gained from interaction with those foreigners, Kennedy asserts, the images they produced "were enriched with the direct and daily knowledge of the phenomena that affected the newborn republic of Ecuador"—factors both ecological and political.[124] Outsiders may have brought unfamiliar perspectives and shared new techniques, but Ecuadorians took them up on their own terms, in their own place. They knew the land and saw it every day. They sometimes felt particular allegiances to the places they depicted. And they had their own nationalisms, hierarchies, and ideological purposes to serve. The supremacist, colonial attitudes of foreign artist-scientists who came to lay intellectual claim to Ecuadorian phenomena became, in the hands of white-mestizo Ecuadorian elites, a tool to advance their own visual culture of settler colonialism. Landscape became another means of extending white-mestizo claims over the national landscape not because the artists and scientists there were mimicking foreign visitors but because such visions were grounded in their own colonial, political purposes.[125] The stories they told were, in the process, also majoritarian stories that ran parallel to the stories cultivated by Church and his paintings. But they were not Church's stories. Here, again, the story of Church's magnitude is attenuated by what Royster and Kirsch might call "strategic contemplation."[126] "Linger[ing] deliberatively" with "not-so-obvious"

---

123. Kennedy Troya, "Artistas y Científicos," 227. "Estas pinturas y grabados corresponden a la vision de extranjeros, sobre todo europeos, imbuidos de sus propias prediscposiciones acerca de naturaleza y civilización, y que no necesariamente correspondían a la realidad americana."
124. Kennedy Troya, "La Percepción de Lo Propio," 113. "Se vieron enriquecidas con el conocimeiento directo y diario de los fenómenos que afectaban a la naciente república de Ecuador."
125. Christa J. Olson, *Constitutive Visions*.
126. Royster and Kirsch, *Feminist Rhetorical Practices*, 84.

stories adjacent to Church's decenters familiar accounts of American magnitude without romanticizing the patterns of domination that stretch across the Americas.[127] As I will explore further in chapter 4, Latin American interlocutors, including Salas and other Ecuadorian artists, consistently looked askance at American magnitude, scaling it down, throwing it off kilter, and repurposing its import.

Conclusion: The Story of the Great American Painter

In the traditional story, Church is imagined to have had a massive effect on Ecuadorian art. Church himself, however, is imagined to have returned home only with inspiration: with sketches and ideas for paintings that would extend his fame. That version of the story leaves Church thoroughly in control of his own path. He came and left the same artist—just with new experiences. And yet, Raab points out, Church's trips to South America were his "earliest and arguably most formative" travels.[128] Kelly, likewise, notes that seeing South America changed how Church viewed North American scenes—he brought a new humidity and softness to his Hudson River canvases even before starting to work on the scenes that would, ultimately, change him from a painter in the Hudson River School to the painter of the tropics.[129]

Church's South American paintings were not exclusively responsible for him—at the height of his career—being referred to as a "Great American Painter," but they certainly played a major role. *The Heart of the Andes,* in particular, gained recognition as a "great American painting" and, in the process, clinched Church's status. A November 1860 column on art in the *Cincinnati Daily Commercial,* for example, opined, "If we may judge from the numerous approving verdicts of writers whose opinion is law in the forum of art, [*Heart of the Andes*] is one of the greatest triumphs of American genius."[130] And the status of the painting conferred on Church not only greatness but a particular Americanness, a uniquely American magnitude. The author continued, "Mr. Church is, in the genuine and most entire sense of the word, an American artist—never having been abroad."[131] The multiple nation-state borders Church crossed in pursuit of his American art, presumably, mattered not at all. The Andes were American, they were "ours." They could not be "abroad."

---

127. Royster and Kirsch, *Feminist Rhetorical Practices,* 84, 85.
128. Raab, "Precisely These Objects," 579.
129. Kelly, *Frederic Edwin Church,* 77.
130. "Art Matters."
131. "Art Matters."

Repeatedly, Church's grand paintings and genius status compounded to enhance the claims of American magnitude in his pictures. In an 1879 retrospective that treated the past fifty years of American art, the first several sentences introducing Church made clear that his grandeur was entirely tied up with American grandeur. And the magnitude of both was, unmistakably and necessarily, a colonial magnitude. Church's art "represents the restless, unsatisfied genius of our people during this period, ever reaching out and beyond, and yearning, Venice-like, to draw to itself the spoils, the riches, the splendors, of the whole round globe."[132] Before Church's painting, the author gushed, "The vastness and the glory of this continent were yet unrevealed to us."[133] But "with the enthusiasm of a Raleigh or a Balboa he has explored land and sea, combining the elements of the explorer and the artist."[134] Lest we think readers might have missed the hints given here, at the beginning of the article, the author was even more explicit, writing of US landscape art that "one can hardly believe that where, but a few years before, the Indian and the buffalo and the wolf had roamed at their own wild will, artists now arose armed with an ability to discern the beauties of their native land, to direct the prosaic thoughts of the pioneer to the loveliness of the nature which surrounded him."[135] Painting, in this retrospective, is colonization by another name.

Stories, Ellen Cushman reminds us, are the "epistemological center of knowledge making."[136] Church's art, "a multimedia geography lesson," put the United States at the epicenter of American epistemology. Critics in his own time and today have done their best to ensure that audiences in the United States understand that point.[137] This chapter's stories have aimed to fracture and destabilize both how knowledge has been made about America through Church's paintings and the nature of that knowledge. They have attenuated the magnitude of Church's American vision.

At the height of his career, Church was *the* American painter and *the* painter of American scenes. His star fell quickly, however. By the last decade of the nineteenth century, critics understood his paintings as "theatrical, loud, decadent, too elaborate, or simply—merely—beautiful."[138] The paintings and their intense detail were feminized and so dismissed. They lacked masculinity;

---

132. Benjamin, "Fifty Years," 488.
133. Benjamin, "Fifty Years," 488.
134. Benjamin, "Fifty Years," 488.
135. Benjamin, "Fifty Years," 482.
136. Cushman, "Wampum, Sequoyan, and Story," 128.
137. Rosenbaum, "Frederic Edwin Church," 29 (paraphrasing Manthorne).
138. Raab, "Precisely These Objects," 585.

they lacked magnitude. Henry James, for example, compared Church's paintings to a beautiful woman whose fashion choices make her appear, momentarily, to be a prostitute even though she is not.[139] What it meant to be a great artist, a great scientist, a great man, and a great American had shifted, and Church no longer quite fit the criteria. By the time of Church's death, art and science had come to occupy entirely separate spheres. Humboldt's grand vision had given way to Darwin's particularity.[140] Church's effort to harmonize art and science was too Humboldtian for his era. Though the scientist-explorer remained an American masculine ideal, the scientist-artist became an oxymoron. The rise of photography, too, doomed Church's painterly realism to the realm of the passé. Science shifted visual technologies, and the spirit of American grandeur went along with it.

It should be no surprise, then, that the next chapter stays with science, with magnitude, and with an Americanness marked as white, masculine, and expansionist, but leaves fine art behind.

---

139. Raab, "Precisely These Objects," 585.
140. Raab, "Precisely These Objects," 580.

CHAPTER 3

Of Cities on Hills

At the height of his power, the ninth Inka, Pachakuti Inka Yupanki, led his armies down the Urubamba valley to conquer the Vitcos region. Perhaps to celebrate that campaign, Pachakuti claimed part of the valley, an area known as Piccho, as a royal estate. He had a retreat built on a ridge above the valley. During Pachakuti's reign, the Inka elite enjoyed the retreat as a place of rest and worship. Quechua commoners lived and worked nearby, tending its terraces. After Pachakuti's death, the retreat continued as part of his estate and was carefully maintained, sometimes housing his mummified body. Pachakuti and his descendants ruled a great empire, built complex networks of commerce and information, and extended their power across the Andes. Long after his death, Pachakuti's great-grandsons, Huascar and Atahualpa, fought a civil war to determine who would control Tahuantinsuyo, the Inkan empire. Atahualpa was eventually victorious and became the undisputed Inka. The retreat at Piccho continued to be tended as Pachakuti's legacy, but Atahualpa's reign was brief. Around the same time, across an ocean, other armies waged religious war for control over a place called the Iberian peninsula. After that faraway war came to a close, the remnants of the victorious army went marauding. They soon landed on shores contiguous with Tahuantinsuyo and made their way south toward the Andes. Driven by avarice and acting through deception, a rogue officer captured and murdered the Inka Atahualpa. With the resulting war, disease, and political collapse, royal estates like the one at

Piccho fell into neglect and out of dominant memory. But Quechua farmers—the ordinary people of the now-destroyed empire—continued to live there sometimes.

If you go online to learn about Machu Picchu today, you'll likely find elements of the story above. On my computer, the first three results of a Google search for "Machu Picchu" return a Wikipedia article, UNESCO's page on the Historic Sanctuary of Machu Picchu, and a National Geographic travel article titled "Discover 10 Secrets of Machu Picchu."[1] Each of those pages explains that Machu Picchu was built during what the Gregorian calendar calls the fifteenth century and abandoned following the Spanish conquest. Wikipedia and National Geographic specifically mention the Inka Pachakuti. All three acknowledge the power and engineering capacity of Tahuantinsuyo at its height (referring to it as the Inca Empire).[2] However, though the three sites acknowledge Machu Picchu as Pachakuti's retreat, they ultimately emphasize another story. That other story is also at the center of this chapter, though troubled.

For the last century, the story of Machu Picchu has told of a ruin abandoned in the sixteenth century and (re)discovered in 1911 by a Yale University professor named Hiram Bingham. The UNESCO World Heritage site description puts it thusly: "Built in the fifteenth century Machu Picchu was abandoned when the Inca Empire was conquered by the Spaniards in the sixteenth century. It was not until 1911 that the archaeological complex was made known to the outside world."[3] If your memory has not already reminded you of Winthrop's claim that the grandeur of the Andes "remained only a doubt and a dream, until Mr. Church became its interpreter to the northern world," allow

---

1. Wikipedia, "Machu Picchu"; UNESCO World Heritage Centre, "Historic Sanctuary"; Adams, "Discover," 10.

2. The title used by the nobility of Tahuantinsuyo appears in this chapter spelled both "Inca" and "Inka." The people of Tahuantinsuyo had many means of inscription and record keeping, but did not use alphabetic script, let alone the Latin alphabet. Spanish colonizers transliterated Quechua words and those Spanish spellings became part of English as well. In line with the position taken by many Indigenous leaders, scholars, and activists, when referring to the actual historical figure, the Inka, I replace the Spanish hard C (Inca) with a K (a letter not traditionally used in Spanish): Inka. When referring to colonial representations of Tahuantinsuyo and its leaders, I use the more traditional and more firmly Spanish spelling: Inca. Technically, "Inka" was a title reserved for the royal family of Tahuantinsuyo. Referring to all the people of the empire as "Incas" is a misnomer equivalent to calling British commoners "kings."

3. UNESCO World Heritage Centre, "Historic Sanctuary," Brief Synthesis para. 1.

me to do so explicitly.⁴ Machu Picchu, like the Andes, apparently had to be discovered by a very particular sort of outsider to achieve its natural state as a site of global heritage.⁵

In June 1911, Hiram Bingham—an adventurer turned professor of Latin American history—arrived in Peru with a team of scientist-explorers intent on discovering Incan ruins, climbing mountains, and generally placing themselves on the map by mapping southern Peru. Bingham and his Yale Peruvian Expedition (YPE) eventually meandered their way down the Urubamba valley to the home of a man named Melchor Arteaga. Arteaga told Bingham of impressive Incan ruins high on a nearby ridge. Bingham paid Arteaga to lead the way to the ruins that, he was told, were located at "Machu Picchu." When they reached the top and walked into the midst of jungle-covered stone structures, Bingham was astonished and transfixed by the grandiosity around him. His team soon set to work clearing the site, revealing incredibly preserved buildings and plazas. The YPE returned to Peru and to Machu Picchu in 1912 and 1914–15, this time funded not only by Yale and private gifts but also by the National Geographic Society. They uncovered Machu Picchu's buildings and conducted extensive excavations in the area. Bingham's presentation of Machu Picchu as the "lost city of the Incas" prompted enthusiastic reports in newspapers, magazines, and scientific publications in Peru and across the United States. Bingham was hailed as the city's discoverer, a title only sometimes amended to "scientific" or "archeological" discoverer.

Though Bingham's claim to discovery is not so patently ridiculous as Winthrop's claim about Church finding the Andes, it is nevertheless shot through with contradictions. Bingham relied on Melchor Arteaga to guide him to Machu Picchu. When Arteaga took Bingham up the steep trail to the ridge, they rested just below the ruins and ate some cold sweet potatoes offered to them by the Quechua farmers who lived there. When they entered the ruins, they walked amidst those farmers' crops. In the process of uncovering Machu Picchu's stone walls, the YPE came across a signature scrawled across one prominent rock. A local man named Agustín Lizarraga had visited in 1902 and left his name and the date behind as graffiti. Bingham, intent on dramatic finds that would shift scientific understanding of human history, argued (erroneously) that Machu Picchu was the mythic site Tampu Tocco: the origin place of the Incas. So far as I can tell, no one asked the Indigenous families living there about the origins or fate of their corn.⁶

---

4. Winthrop, *A Companion to The Heart of the Andes*, 4.
5. See, for example, "Young Americans."
6. In early twentieth-century Peru, Indigenous families living on a ridge inaccessible without a guide and quite far from the nearest hacienda were probably trying to make a go

At the time, Bingham's interpretations and his use of Machu Picchu were countered by Peruvian scholars. The early decades of the twentieth century were a time of growth for historical and social scientific scholarship in Peru. Criollo and mestizo-led academic organizations in Cuzco promoted attention to pre-Columbian archeology as essential to understanding their nation's history. Peruvian *indigenismo* was on the rise.[7] During and after Bingham's excavations at Machu Picchu, Peruvian scholars and students journeyed there to conduct their own research and incorporate the site into Peruvian national history.[8] Initially, Cuzqueño scholars were pleased to welcome Bingham and the YPE as peers engaged in scientific study. The relationship quickly soured, however. Eventually, leading intellectuals in Cuzco accused Bingham and his team of working illegally, stealing artifacts, and conducting excavations irresponsibly.[9]

In the years since, local and international tourists have flocked to Machu Picchu. In 2010, expenditures related to Machu Picchu accounted for some 90 percent of Peru's tourism income.[10] Trash and human waste have become an unrelenting problem along the famed Inca Trail.[11] In 2012, after nearly one hundred years of protest and demands, Yale University finally returned to Peru the pre-Columbian remains and artifacts that Hiram Bingham and the

---

of it outside the debt peonage and conscription structures of the feudalist Andean state. The sudden attention paid to their place of refuge wasn't welcome, and the sudden disturbance to their home and planting ground ultimately led to some of them being reensnared in the bonds of debt peonage and all of them being conscripted in the manual labor that allowed Machu Picchu's "scientific discovery." Heaney, *Cradle of Gold*, 133–34, 154; Hall "Collecting a 'Lost City' for Science," 314 n48.

7. For those familiar with my first book, *Constitutive Visions*, the term indigenismo will be deceptively familiar. Peruvian indigenismo was an earlier movement than Ecuadorian indigenismo, and while it shared with Ecuadorian indigenismo a deep grounding in intellectual circles and the emerging national scholarly institutions, Peruvian indigenismo had more in common with the romantic indianismo of early twentieth-century Ecuador than the Marxist-leaning social realism of Ecuadorian indigenismo.

8. Salvatore, "Local versus Imperial Knowledge," 75; Gómez, "Machu Picchu Reclamada." For examples of how indigenistas articulated Machu Picchu, see, for example, Valcárcel, *De La Vida Inkaica*; Valcárcel, *Machu Picchu*.

9. No chronicle of Bingham's activities can responsibly ignore the questionable methods and consistent efforts to circumvent Peruvian law that characterized his expeditions. A combination of excessive confidence, ambition, disregard for rules he disagreed with, and racism left their marks on Bingham's scholarship, the materials the YPE collected, and the communities he encountered in Peru. The coming pages offer some details of Bingham's actions. For further discussion, see Hall, "Collecting a 'Lost City' for Science"; Heaney, *Cradle of Gold*; Mould de Pease, "Un Día"; Salvatore, "Local versus Imperial Knowledge."

10. "Peru's Machu Picchu Reopens to Tourists," BBC News, April 2, 2010, http://news.bbc.co.uk/2/hi/americas/8598154.stm.

11. Maxwell, "Tourism."

YPE had removed from the country under dubious circumstances during the years of the expedition.

Since it reemerged into international and Peruvian national consciousness in the early twentieth century, Machu Picchu has attracted yet defied simple stories about its discovery and its magnitude. Bingham's tale of scientific discovery grew tattered as Peruvian intellectuals, politicians, and local residents questioned his actions and intentions. His argument that Machu Picchu was Tampu Tocco likewise frayed—though that took longer.[12] Peruvian arguments placing Machu Picchu at the center of national heritage battled imperialist attitudes that presumed North American discoverers held ultimate right to artifacts found on Peruvian soil. Those Peruvian nationalist arguments that centered Machu Picchu as a site of national heritage simultaneously ran aground on Peruvian elites' racist and exploitative treatment of their contemporary Quechua compatriots. Tourists today celebrate their trek to the picturesque city on a hill, but their shit, literally and figuratively, threatens the local ecosystem and the larger tourist economy.

There are, in other words, many conflicting stories and counterstories to tell about Machu Picchu even if we keep our focus specifically on matters of magnitude. Working across and among those stories, this chapter uses their divergent investments and purposes to illuminate how the "discovery" of Machu Picchu relied not only on the tropes and tools of magnitude in general but on those of American magnitude in particular. It emphasizes the use to which Machu Picchu was put in articulating early twentieth-century US hegemony and the crucial role that American magnitude played in those articulations.[13] In the process, it theorizes discovery, invention, and revelation as constitutive strategies of magnitude.

---

12. It took a few decades for scholars to begin offering evidence establishing Machu Picchu's more recent origins. Importantly, though, they did so using sources that would have been available to Bingham (indeed, Bingham cited at least one of those sources but failed to notice references to Picchu). The Peruvian scholar Luís Valcárcel suggested as early as the 1960s that Machu Picchu had been built for the Inka Pachakuti. Burger and Salazar-Burger place the date of realization as 1982, with Rowe's 1986 rediscovery of a 1568 document confirming their archeological findings. Valcárcel, *Machu Picchu*; Burger and Salazar Burger, "Machu Picchu Rediscovered"; John H. Rowe, "Machu Picchu."

13. For takes on the Incan empire, see, for example, Bauer, *Ancient Cuzco*; Patterson, *The Inca Empire*; Valcárcel, *Machu Picchu*. For more on colonial and republican Peru, see, for example, de la Cadena, *Indigenous Mestizos*; Rama, *Ciudad Letrada*; Rappaport and Cummins, *Beyond the Lettered City*; Salomon and Niño-Murcia, *The Lettered Mountain*.

Bingham's presentation of Machu Picchu to US audiences and its circulation in the United States, I argue, cannot be separated from themes of US nationalism. The American magnitude of an ancient city upon a hill was readily caught up in the nationalist and imperialist rhetorical ecologies of the United States during the period between the Spanish-American War and World War I.[14] As Macarena Gómez-Barris puts it, "Bingham's accidental but wrongful discovery of the fabled lost city inaugurated a shift from the foundational importance of the Spanish Conquest to the rise of the United States Empire, culturally supported through the archaeological and tourist gaze."[15] Hiram Bingham's story of his "scientific discovery" brought the "Lost City of the Incas" into an American purview. Through it, US audiences could not only appreciate the ingenuity of heroic [US] Americans abroad but also encounter Incan civilization as fundamentally and generatively related to their own. Both were exceptional. Both accomplished grand works. Both transformed the world around them. In Bingham's writing and photography, the act of discovering Machu Picchu, the process of making it known, and the place itself were all drafted into the service of American magnitude.

In this chapter, I tell stories about the YPE that focus on its accounts of itself, using those accounts to track both the processes of discovery, revelation, and American magnitude and their consequence. To illuminate how magnitude and revelation together authorized doctrines of American discovery well into the twentieth century, I look at two aspects of the YPE's work: (1) the structure of the expeditions themselves and (2) public accounts of the expeditions that circulated in the United States. In the first part, lingering with accumulation, I review procedural documents that guided YPE staff in their evidence collection. The second part goes public and emphasizes story, following along as Bingham promulgated the American magnitude of Machu Picchu by telling tales about it. In both process and product, accumulation and story, we see the YPE and its audiences laying claim to Machu Picchu. Seeing evidence and following stories, viewers in the United States saw the Incan city on a hill, no longer hidden but before the eyes of the world, reflecting their own particular magnitude.

---

14. For scholarship on related themes of Progressive-era imperialism in visual culture, science, and exploration, see, for example, Bayers, *Imperial Ascent*; Espinosa, *Epidemic Invasions*; Kaplan, *The Anarchy of Empire*; Bonnie Miller, *From Liberation to Conquest*; Murphy, *Hemispheric Imaginings*. Within rhetorical studies specifically, see, for example, Christa J. Olson, "But in Regard"; Rendahl, "The Rhetoric of Imperialism."

15. Gómez-Barris, "Andean Gateways," 343.

Discovery, Invention, and Revelation

It is easy to see that Bingham's presentation of a city on a hill, built of massive stone blocks, raised by the mythic Inca, hidden for centuries by jungles, and dramatically rediscovered by the YPE relied on themes of *megethos*. "This is important!" seems fairly easy to shout.[16] And yet, what makes Machu Picchu's magnitude particularly interesting is the immense difficulty of firmly determining the referent for the "This" in "*This* is important!" Machu Picchu itself, of course, but which version of it and under what conditions? How did a minor royal retreat become so thoroughly a symbol of American grandeur for its early twentieth-century audience that it continues to reflect that American magnitude even today?

Hall argues that Machu Picchu began its public life as "an effect from a specific way of seeing."[17] This section theorizes the rhetorical processes behind that "specific way of seeing," moving from discovery and invention to revelation and magnitude.[18] Discovering, inventing, and revealing Machu Picchu, Bingham made visible its magnitude and made clear that its magnitude came from and had consequence for America.

Though it is factually and semantically problematic, there is something appropriate about describing Hiram Bingham's encounter with Machu Picchu as a "discovery." Given the American claims Bingham made about the citadel, he had much in common with the European explorers four centuries earlier who had arrived in a thoroughly populated place and proclaimed themselves its discoverers.[19] Indeed, Bingham made the comparison himself, writing,

> I suppose that in the same sense of the word as it is used in the expression "Columbus discovered America" it is fair to say that I discovered Machu Picchu. The Norsemen and the French fishermen undoubtedly visited North America long before Columbus crossed the Atlantic. On the other hand it

---

16. Farrell, "The Weight of Rhetoric," 484.
17. Hall, "Collecting a 'Lost City' for Science," 294.
18. For more on invention and discovery, see, for example, Richard McKeon, "Creativity and the Commonplace," Carolyn Miller, "The Aristotelian Topos"; Christa J. Olson, *Constitutive Visions*, 10–12.
19. It is worth noting that Columbus's "discovery" was even more sinister than this phrasing suggests. "In 1492," Davis and Todd note, invoking work by Lewis and Maslin, "there were between 54 and 61 million peoples in the Americas and by 1650 there were 6 million." In other words, "discovery" didn't come to a place where no one had ever been before. It *made* a place that had been filled with rich, diverse, vibrant life into a sparsely populated place. Davis and Todd, "On the Importance of a Date," 766.

was Columbus who made America known to the civilized world. In the same sense of the word I "discovered" Machu Picchu—in that before my visit and report on it, it was not known to the geographical and historical societies in Peru, nor to the Peruvian government. It had been visited by a few Indians and half-castes and possibly by one European.[20]

It is telling that, for Bingham, neither the peoples living in North America when the "Norsemen and French fishermen" visited nor the families of Torvis Richarte, Anacleto Alvarez, and Tomas Fuentes who lived and farmed the land at Machu Picchu even merit consideration in his account of discovery. In Bingham's frame, one has to come from the outside, intending to find, in order to discover something. And, even then, true discovery requires revelation: The thing discovered must be made known. In this sense, Bingham offered himself as the quintessential and the ideal discoverer.

Like his predecessors, who utterly remade the place they stumbled across, what Bingham discovered was not the Inkan citadel built by Pachakuti but a ruin. Bingham would build that ruin's structures into a grand, lost city through photographs and words, diagrams and maps.[21] Bingham's "discovery," like the "discovery" of "America," in other words, was an invention. Like the "invention of America" that Edmundo O'Gorman describes as not "the result of a purely physical discovery" but "as the result of an inspired invention of Western thought," the "discovery" of Machu Picchu brought Machu Picchu into being.[22] In O'Gorman's sense, discovery-as-invention is a matter of rhetoric. Both the "New World" and Machu Picchu are places made through discourse and practice, not preexisting places waiting to be found. Both boasted vibrant human life long prior to "discovery," but they were put to new, wholly transformative (and wholly colonial) use thanks to the rhetorical explosion that accompanied the arrival of Euro-US outsiders. In this sense, by claiming to "discover," Bingham established himself as one of Machu Picchu's earliest and most influential inventors.

Invention, rhetorically speaking, leads to and requires production. It implies public dissemination of the thing invented. As a process of invention, discovery likewise requires production. A discovery unannounced is no discovery at all. And, for Bingham's "scientific" milieu, assertions of discovery required corroboration through evidence. The objects of discovery must be not only announced but *revealed*: illustrated and instantiated. They had

---

20. Qtd. in Heaney, *Cradle of Gold*, 93; qtd. in Alfred Bingham, *Explorer of Machu Picchu*, 26.
21. Hall, *Framing a Lost City.*
22. Edmundo O'Gorman, *The Invention of America*, 4.

to be brought before the eyes of an audience qualified to assess them. Thus, the reasoning with regard to Machu Picchu's discovery went like this: Many people had seen Machu Picchu before Bingham arrived. None of them, however, had revealed it. Therefore, they had not discovered it. Repeatedly in his public accounts of the YPE, Bingham introduced the ruins by marking them as "undescribed."[23] As Heaney notes, when Bingham arrived at Machu Picchu, "no one had yet described Machu Picchu, photographed the ruins, or tried to understand them . . . and that, to Bingham, was discovery."[24] Because previous visitors had not presented the ruins to wider publics, showing them in words, pictures, and artifacts, Machu Picchu had not yet been discovered. Its magnitude was untapped.

And so, when Bingham set out to "discover" what would become Machu Picchu, he set out with tools of invention in hand, with expectations for accumulation, and with plans to disseminate already in place. He and his staff would take careful notes, keep detailed diaries, and wield their cameras with care.[25] They sought permission to excavate, and they prioritized artifact collection even when permission was withheld or limited. And Bingham crafted relationships with US newspapers, magazines, and scholarly venues to ensure that the work of the YPE would reach the eyes of those whose attention would, ultimately, corroborate the magnitude of his discovery.

This interplay of discovery, invention, and revelation is, ultimately, inseparable from matters of magnitude. When Farrell notes that magnitude is "rhetorically invented and construed" and reminds us that "our criteria for what ranks as important and unimportant are themselves rhetorical constructions," he emphasizes that what "matters" is not given.[26] Discovery makes a claim to what is important, to what matters, and it establishes that import through revelation. Machu Picchu, discovered, had to be shared with specialist and popular audiences who would corroborate its importance (its magnitude) through the magnitude of the evidence about it. Every act of discovery, in other words, is an assertion of magnitude. In the specific case of Machu Picchu, that assertion brought an amazingly preserved, jaw-dropping Incan ruin to public attention and made it matter not just to Peruvians but to the world: a great American site.

Photography was crucial to Bingham's "discovery" of Machu Picchu and his assertion of its magnitude. Photographs etched Machu Picchu's white

---

23. See, for example, Bingham, "The Discovery of Machu Picchu," 709.
24. Heaney, *Cradle of Gold*, 93.
25. Bingham, "Plan for 1912," 2; Bingham, "Peruvian Expeditions. Summary of the Work of 1915."
26. Farrell, "The Weight of Rhetoric," 469.

stone and dark lines onto glass and projected it onto paper, allowing the ruins to travel. Photographs framed the city, illuminated the work of its discoverers, and shed light on the civilization that built it. Photographs and the words that accompanied them showed Machu Picchu to a very particular viewing public, one positioned to recognize the city for what (Bingham thought) it was: a great city testifying to a great civilization.[27] Tracking magnitude across those photographs and the textual descriptions that accompanied them, we can see how Bingham discovered, documented, and made public Machu Picchu. We can, simultaneously, observe Machu Picchu acquiring American magnitude.

Like the stories told in the previous two chapters, the story of the YPE is, from beginning to end, a story of entitled usurpation, masculine presumption, and colonial theft. The particulars of place and material and the changes in political and cultural environment over time should not obscure the resonances among these cases. From their willingness to exploit Indigenous laborers to their disregard for Peruvian law, the expedition's members—especially Bingham—made clear that they understood their purposes to supersede those of the people around them.[28] As Amy Cox Hall describes it, the YPE was thoroughly invested in "the notion that science had a sovereign claim on those objects that might contribute to the accumulation of its knowledge."[29] And, science, in this framework, was always the province of the northern, the masculine, and the white. Scientific sovereignty and imperialism went hand in hand.[30]

Though Bingham consistently relied on his era's notions of scientific progress to authorize his work, it is fair to say that his more central and pressing concern was the pursuit of magnitude. Even the dictates of science would ultimately be bent to his more urgent projects of revelation and acquisition: accumulating major finds, material artifacts, and—most of all—recognition. Bingham's confidence in the righteousness of his pursuits and his investment in accumulation traffic in claims of American magnitude. The rapacious mood of late nineteenth-century aggressive expansionism may have faded by this point, but the certainty that US Americans had a particular mission in and to

---

27. Gómez, "Machu Picchu Reclamada," 498.
28. For more on this point, see, for example, Gómez, "Machu Picchu Reclamada," 498–502; Mould de Pease, "Un Día," 259; Salvatore, "Local versus Imperial Knowledge."
29. Hall, "Collecting a 'Lost City' for Science," 294.
30. Carey, "Mountaineers and Engineers"; Hall, "Collecting a 'Lost City' for Science."

the rest of America was only strengthening.[31] US Americans had consequence. That consequence—Bingham and others presumed—authorized their actions.

The Yale Peruvian Expedition

Hiram Bingham was dashing, persuasive, overconfident, and ambitious. He had excellent intuition for opportunities, was an effective organizer, and had significant skill at generating public attention.[32] His self-assurance also made him a sloppy scientist. He had no training in archeology and chose not to hire an archeologist for any of the three expeditions despite planning extensive archeological excavation.[33] Bingham left Peru in annoyance and disgrace in 1915, having thoroughly tried the patience of his hosts. He and the YPE exported thousands of artifacts from the country under dubious circumstances, sometimes illegally, and Peruvians knew it. Even so, in the 1910s and in the century since, Hiram Bingham captured the spotlight as the single most recognizable name in the history of Machu Picchu. The Machu Picchu celebrated as a world heritage site is more Bingham's city than Pachakuti's retreat. More than one hundred years after its "discovery," Machu Picchu's magnitude still appears on Bingham's terms.

In the summer of 1911, Bingham took a staff of six people to Peru. He left the United States on June 8; his team joined him on July 2. Bingham's plan was to conduct investigations in southern Peru: exploring the Urubamba valley, visiting the ruins of Choqquequirau and Lake Parinacochas, and ascending Mount Coropuna. The expedition started work near Cuzco, gathering supplies and information. Before long, Bingham and a smaller group went in search of significant new ruins further down the valley. He wanted to find the capital that the last Inka, Manco Capac, built as a final refuge against the Spanish. It was early in that excursion, on July 24, 1911, that Arteaga led Bingham to the ruins that became known as Machu Picchu.[34] Three families of Quechua farmers lived on the ridge, having moved there to escape the exploitative debt peonage system of the more populated valley.

---

31. Hilfrich, *Debating American Exceptionalism*; Kaplan, *The Anarchy of Empire*; Murphy, *Shadowing the White Man's Burden*.
32. See, for example, Heaney, *Cradle of Gold*, 73.
33. Burger and Salazar Burger, "Machu Picchu Rediscovered."
34. The section of Bingham's official journal that recounts his first visit to Machu Picchu is missing from the Bingham collection in the archives at Yale University's Sterling Memorial Library.

After spending a few days at Machu Picchu, Bingham, Harry Foote (the expedition's naturalist), a Peruvian solider who had been detailed to support the expedition, and a team of muleteers continued on their way in search of other notable ruins. After much hard travel, Bingham and his team were brought to two sites that we now know were the final residences of the Inka after the Spanish conquest. Bingham quickly dismissed his most notable find, Espiritu Pampu—the refuge where Manco Capac made his last stand and Tupac Amaru was captured—because it lacked the grandeur he associated with great finds.[35] The other site, Vitcos, impressed Bingham more, but it was difficult to reach and, ultimately, seemed less grand to him than the ruins at Machu Picchu. Returning from those jungle locations, Bingham spent the last weeks of the 1911 expedition in archives, trying to find mentions of Machu Picchu in earlier accounts. By the time Bingham returned to New York City on December 21, 1911, Machu Picchu had become the expedition's major find. Bingham billed it to the crowds of reporters on the dock as Tampu Tocco, the origin site of the Incas.

Home, Bingham immediately began planning for another expedition. This one would focus on excavation, bringing Machu Picchu to light for the glory of Yale, the United States, and Hiram Bingham. Yale offered more support for this second expedition, and Bingham secured sponsorship from the National Geographic Society. Bingham and his supporters were filled with eager, ambitious plans.[36] First, though, they had to confront a new Peruvian decree banning the export of antiquities. Expeditions could take photographs, but they had to leave objects in Peru. Bingham began efforts to secure an exemption. If he couldn't promise artifacts, his sponsorships and his claim to discovery would evaporate. Those efforts, which began before departure and lasted for much of the 1912 expedition's time in Peru, were never fully successful.[37] Bingham eventually came to a partial agreement with the Peruvian government that the expedition would leave all singular objects and one of any duplicate objects in Peru. He and his colleagues were unhappy with the requirement, though, and actively defied it throughout their time at Machu Picchu.

Ten men made up the staff of the 1912 expedition, officially named the Yale-National Geographic Society Peruvian Expedition of 1912: a geologist, an osteologist, a surgeon, three topographers, three assistants, and Bingham as director. They left New York in June 1912 and returned to the United States in late December 1912. While Bingham himself spent much of his time exploring

---

35. Heaney, *Cradle of Gold*, 114.
36. Bingham, "The Peruvian Expedition of 1912."
37. The details of the "Yale Concession" and the shifting permissions given to the YPE are beyond the scope of this project, but well covered in Heaney.

other locales, his team worked to clear Machu Picchu's buildings, map them, and conduct "archeological" excavations there. Their final report indicated that "more than one hundred burial caves were opened and a large amount of anthropological material was collected."[38] It also names the large number of photographs taken as evidence of the expedition's accomplishments.

Intent on discovery and unconcerned with Peruvian sovereignty, Ellwood Erdis, the expedition's "engineer," arranged to have only the least interesting finds reviewed by the monitor that the Peruvian government had appointed to ensure that the YPE complied with its agreement. The expedition found only a handful of unique bronze, silver, and gold artifacts and relatively few complete pottery items. Erdis ensured that none of those particularly prized objects came to the attention of the monitor, however, and Bingham successfully secured their removal from the country. Still, there were rumors and complaints about their behavior. Bingham left Peru on bad terms, feeling insulted and wronged rather than contrite. He crafted plans for the 1914–15 expedition in order to reestablish his good name with Peruvian scholars, but the venture was ultimately fraught.

Bingham's initial plan for the 1914–15 expedition was extensive. Its object was to "make a geographical reconnaissance of a portion of southern Peru, including the Cordillera Vilcabamba and some portions of the Apurimac and Urubamba water-sheds."[39] A six-person vanguard of the expedition left New York in April 1914 and began work. Bingham followed a year later. Like the previous expeditions, this one had a broad mandate—treating climate, geography, archaeology, biology, and anthropology.[40] Matters of human culture remained at the forefront.[41]

Once in Peru, Bingham spent a good deal of his time dealing with objections and complaints from local authorities and prominent scholars. This expedition was intended to be the longest yet, running from April 1914 through December 1915. It was cut short, however, when the YPE was found to be excavating without permission. After a hearing, Bingham secured permission to excavate again, but the Peruvian government required that its monitors be present. When the government failed to pay those monitors, it was impossible for the YPE to work, and Bingham finally left in frustration.

---

38. Bingham, Hiram, "The Peruvian Expedition of 1912," Report. Torvis Richarte, Anacleto Alvarez, Tomas Fuentes, and other Indigenous conscripts had done most of the finding and opening, of course.

39. Bingham, "Plan for the Peruvian Expedition of 1914–15," 1.

40. Bingham, "The first point of attack for the Expedtion . . ."; Bingham, "Plan for the Peruvian Expedition of 1914–15."

41. Bingham, "Plan for the Peruvian Expedition of 1914–15," 2.

The last YPE cleared customs—carrying boxes of illicit materials—on August 19, 1915. Bingham did not return to Peru for another thirty years. By that time, though, Bingham's "discovery" was well established in the United States. Today, a plaque at Machu Picchu honors Bingham's role in revealing the site, and his date of arrival remains one of the most important dates in the site's story.

The Groundwork of Revelation

Presumptions of American magnitude pervade the story of Machu Picchu's "discovery." They are palpable not only in the reports written after the fact but also in the YPE's research practices and processes. Bingham went looking for greatness, and he primed his methods to ensure he found it. For all the attention to grandeur and awe that would eventually characterize his public accounts of Machu Picchu, the American magnitude of his work began with scrupulous attention to detail. Bingham seemed to understand the relationship between accumulation and magnitude—proliferating materials and piling them up so that they could account for the importance of his work. "Scrupulous" attention to detail is, perhaps, a misnomer, though. The contexts in which Bingham demanded detail from his staff and those in which he did not tell us a great deal about what he valued in the work of discovery. Bingham had clear purposes in mind, and his instructions for expedition staff ensured that they would collect and distribute the magnitude of Machu Picchu in line with that purpose.

Amy Cox Hall notes that the YPE's collecting practices were questionable, even for their moment. They were, she suggests, "better characterized as a late antiquarianism-inspired collecting spree—or, less generously, strategic 'grave robbing.'"[42] The collection itself—its size, variety, and uniqueness—mattered far more to the YPE than did the process of collecting. Yet Bingham sought and needed the imprimatur of scientific validity. That tension pervades the planning and practice of the YPE. For example, Bingham's scientific colleagues encouraged him to be more exacting in his methods and recommended that he bring along an archeologist to aid in excavations. But Bingham couldn't find an archeologist he could afford for any of the expeditions.[43] So, he hired men with adjacent experience. In 1912, an osteologist (Dr. George F. Eaton) and an engineer (Ellwood C. Erdis) led the archeological efforts of the expe-

---

42. Hall, "Collecting a 'Lost City' for Science," 293–94.
43. Hall, "Collecting a 'Lost City' for Science," 301.

dition. To correct for those shortcomings in experience, Bingham sought to ensure scientific credibility by providing detailed written guidance. He prepared a loose-leaf binder of instructional "Circulars" for each expedition staff member. Those circulars included extensive guidance on both archeological and photographic practice. Given that they were often working in unfamiliar territory, separated from one another for weeks at a time, and tasked with complicated, interconnected projects, YPE staff would have needed specific guidelines for their work no matter their depth of expertise. The fact that the expedition members were often doing "scientific" work for which they were not trained made such instruction all the more essential. More telling for our purposes, however, are the choices that Bingham made about what tasks to emphasize and which to skim. Analyzing them reveals not only how Bingham understood the work of scientific revelation but also his intention to invent and reveal the remains of a great, "lost" civilization.

The circulars provided guidance on proper host gifts and food rations, they outlined techniques for packing boxes and taking photographs, and they listed required reading. Some—like the instructions for topographers—assumed a level of expert knowledge. Others—like most of the photography instruction—began from the basics. On almost every page, Bingham urged precision, care, and patience. He was explicit about attending to accumulation, demanding a high level of detail and orchestrating the minutia of the expeditions' functioning. His "General Instructions" for the 1912 expedition, for example, carefully described how staff should respond if they found "ethnological material" of potential interest:

> When finds are made, the Archaeological Engineer should be notified through proper channels, at the first opportunity, and such information furnished him, by means of notes, sketches, diagams [sic], and maps, as will enable him to decide whether it is desirable that he should visit the place of interest himself. This information should, if possible, be supplemented by accurate directions for reaching and identifying the localities described, so that the Archeological Engineer can make his way there without a guide.[44]

The remainder of the eleven-page document explains how to find artifacts—especially burial sites—and how to approach excavating them. Photographic processes for representing burial sites receive a page of their own.[45] While such instructions were not necessarily up to date with scientific norms or

---

44. Bingham, "General Instructions," 1–2.
45. Bingham, "General Instructions," 5.

practices, they carried the air of scientific precision. They emphasized to staff how even the smallest task built toward the culmination of the YPE mission. And the work that mattered most, consistently, was the accumulation of evidence—both objects and photographs. Proliferation was the key to scientific accomplishment and to cementing public recognition of it.

Two specific examples from YPE practice help convey the line connecting research practices, YPE ideological purposes, and the work of revealing American magnitude. The first focuses on the circulars' guidance on collecting human remains and other artifacts from burial sites. The second looks specifically at Bingham's explanations of photographic practice. Together, they illustrate Bingham's presumption that attaining grandeur required particular kinds of everyday labor that were oriented toward the accumulation of proper, powerful evidence.

Piling Up Evidence

Bringing home artifacts was an absolute necessity for the YPE. They needed evidence to demonstrate the nature and magnitude of their labor. Throughout the YPE archive, there is a sense of urgency about objects—how to find them, how to get "better" ones, how to find more of them, and how to get them home. That urgency also translated into the research process. Though Bingham urged care, he also put clear emphasis on quick collection and proliferation. That meant that care frequently went by the wayside.

The first step in collection, of course, was finding things to collect. Bingham's "General Instructions" told staff the sorts of "places where excavation is most likely to yield valuable material" ("the earth floors of ancient ruins," "the accumulations of miscellaneous rubbish . . . found close to ancient human habitations," and "in graves") but were nearly silent on how to actually find those places.[46] In Bingham's estimation, burial sites were particularly rich finds—both for osteological material and for other artifacts—but they were also particularly difficult to find. Bingham could tell his staff what to look for, and the "General Instructions" offered a great deal of information about Incan burial practices, but the instructions were notably silent on how to actually find the "natural and artificial caves" that were the most common ancient burial sites in the region of Machu Picchu. Those caves were now buried in the jungle, and expedition staff had little luck finding them.

---

46. Bingham, "General Instructions," 3.

Into the silence of the instructions and failures of the gringo staff stepped the local Quechua men whom the YPE hired to aid them in the grunt labor of the expedition. Alvarez, Richarte, and Fuentes, though hesitant to help at first, eventually became the expedition's greatest scientific resource. They knew how to identify likely sites and found nearly every Machu Picchu burial site that the expedition reports listed among its results. Those three, and a group of Quechua peasants conscripted from the valley, also did the heavier labor of excavation. If finding sites and artifacts was the crucial opening step in scientific discovery, it is notable that it was repeatedly accomplished by Indigenous laborers. Though in reports and publications they were deemed the objects of science, not its agents, Alvarez, Richarte, Fuentes, and their Quechua compatriots were, in fact, essential to the YPE's scientific work—such as it was. Bingham's lack of a critical skill meant that the YPE relied on Indigenous knowledge and expertise but occluded it.

This same pattern of detailed explanation and telling omission continued into Bingham's instructions for excavation itself. They included multiple admonitions toward proper archeological practice, but little guidance on how to enact it. The "General Instructions" circular, for example, emphasized that excavators ought to note the depth at which artifacts were buried. It explained that depth and position "may be required for determining the age of the specimens and the relative culture periods to which they belong." "The true value of all archaeological and ethnological material," Bingham further explained, "depends largely on the possibility of determining its age of 'culture'; and to properly observe and record the requisite evidence, by notes and diagrams, is one of the most important and most difficult duties of an archaeologist."[47] Bingham did not, however, provide detailed instructions on how team members ought to identify depth and position. The instructions simply laid out a general process and the information that ought to be included in notes and diagrams.[48] They asserted, extensively, that objects' depth, position, and relation to one another was important information. They left the specifics of how to identify that information up to individual staff members who, again, had little professional training or experience in such matters. Documentation of this information was important in theory—it needed to appear to be valued—but in practice it fell to the wayside.

---

47. Bingham, "General Instructions," 6.

48. It is worth noting that the handwritten draft "Instructions for Topographers" from the 1915 expedition includes a great deal more technical information and detail on how to proceed. It is also written in a hand other than Bingham's, suggesting that one of the topographers may have prepared it. "Instructions for Topographers, 1915."

The practice of relying on conscripted Indigenous laborers for the most physically tedious labor of excavation is further evidence of this point. What might have been specialized work—carefully revealing and accounting for details of object placement—the YPE left to workers they considered backward and unskilled. YPE staff supervised much of the archeological work, but they weren't always present. To the extent that materials were uncovered safely and located accurately, Quechua peasants—much maligned by the YPE staff at the time—deserve more credit than their overseers.[49] Even so, it is clear from the choice to leave this work to conscripted labor and its relatively light treatment in circulars that the expedition's emphasis was more on the accumulation of large numbers of artifacts in a short period of time than on documenting the details of the recovery process.

This choice in emphasis is corroborated by Bingham's other instructions for handling artifacts. Where excavation processes were given relatively slight attention, instructions for recording and packing the objects were extensive and orchestrated to the finest detail. In the circulars, Bingham's guidelines for labeling specimens take a page and a half, handwritten; those for packaging take another page. Excavation—the *how* of collecting—takes just a paragraph before Bingham turns, again, to outlining what to collect and how to describe it.[50] His team obviously received the message that the collection itself was of prime importance. Mass collection was emphasized, and gathering artifacts in quantity took up the bulk of the expedition's daily labor. The sheer number of items found figures prominently in Bingham's final reports.[51] Artifacts, in this sense, would serve as evidence of the magnitude of the YPE's achievements as much as (or more than) they would be evidence of particular scientific findings.

---

49. Watson and Huntington note that such interactions have long histories, both colonial and precolonial: "Cultures have been in contact . . . for thousands of years—some of these exchanges producing the very 'Western Science' supposed to be uniquely 'Western.'" Watson and Huntington, "They're *Here*—I Can *Feel* Them," 275.

50. Bingham, "General Instructions," 7. The 1914–15 instructions on excavating are a revision of a similar circular from the 1912 expedition, this one focused specifically on collecting archeological and osteological material. The earlier text provides slightly more detail on collecting process and slightly less on identifying, labeling, and packing, but the overall balance is similar to that of 1914–15. Bingham, "Official Circulars of the Peruvian Expedition of 1912. No. 13."

51. See, for example, Bingham, "Peruvian Expedition of 1912," Report; Bingham, "Plan for 1912."

Accumulating Images

If burial sites, human remains, and pieces of pottery—in aggregate—pointed to the significance of the YPE's accomplishments, photography revealed its magnitude. That meant that photographic practice was a crucial part of the everyday work of the expeditions. As the next section emphasizes, the YPE's pictures generated much excitement in the United States.[52] Such visual success didn't happen by accident. Bingham's circulars offered detailed and extensive guidance on photography: how to do it, what to capture, and how to document practice. In many ways, careful photography seems to have stood in for the rigors of archeology.[53] Where the instructions for finding, excavating, and documenting artifacts are rife with omissions, the instructions for photography leave nothing to the imagination, and nearly every member of the YPE staff was accountable for their photographic practice.[54] As Bingham explained in his "Plan for 1912," "the photograph collection" would be "one of the most important results of the expedition's work."[55]

Instructions for photography appear in multiple circulars, and not just the ones explicitly dedicated to instructing expedition staff in photographic practice. For example, in the "Daily Journal" that each staff member was instructed to keep, attention to photographic detail took prime place. After a brief paragraph outlining important topics to include, the circular on the daily journal concluded with a longer paragraph about photography:

> A minute and careful record of all photographs taken is to be kept in the photographic record-book supplied to each member. In all cases it is expected that the date, time of day, and direction of the camera will be stated, and it is particularly important that until the weather and light conditions are thoroughly understood a careful record should be kept of light conditions, length of exposure, and size of diaphragm, etc., places for all of which will be found in the record-book. It is very important that the numbers in the book and on the negatives correspond exactly, and that extreme pains should be taken to record the exact time of day and date.[56]

---

52. See, for example, the gushing review of a 1916 exhibit of the YPE's collected photographs published in the Washington, DC, *Evening Star*. "Evening Star Washington, DC."
53. See, for example, Bingham, "Circulars of the Peruvian Expedition of 1912. No. 1. Suggestions for the Work of Assistants"; Bingham, "Official Circulars of the Peruvian Expedition of 1912. No. 9," 9; Bingham, "No. 19. Directions for Using Color Chart."
54. See, for example, Bingham, "Plan for 1912," 4; Bingham, "The first point of attack . . . ," 1.
55. Bingham, "Plan for 1912," 2.
56. Bingham, "Peruvian Expedition of 1914–15. Official Circular #10. The Daily Journal."

The daily journal's purpose, at least in part, was to index photographic practice and put photographs in context. Photographs weren't merely a means to document artifacts that had been collected or collect those findings that could not reasonably be carried home (e.g., stone buildings, Indigenous bodies, panoramic landscapes); they stood in for scientific practice. The YPE's accomplishments, frequently, played out through photography and in photographs. Careful photographic practice showed scientific care. Extensive photograph collections showed the scope of the expedition's achievement.

And, in that light, the kind of photographs taken also mattered. They enacted the YPE's discoveries and, therefore, what they showed mattered immensely for communicating the magnitude of the expedition's work. Bingham paid attention to staff members' photographic skill and delegated photographic responsibilities accordingly.[57] Nearly as often as he reminded staff members to be careful photographers, Bingham weighed in on aesthetics and style. While Bingham warned that "it is not expected that films will be used merely for taking pretty views that have no bearing on the work at hand" and bluntly asserted that "snapshots are not desired," the YPE photography collection includes a lot of pretty views.[58] Apparently those pretty views did have bearing on the work at hand. Bingham's warning, in other words, was not intended to distinguish beauty from science but to clearly tie photography to the central work of the expedition. Photographs were meant to be purposeful and effective. Potential impact—scientific or popular—determined whether something was worth photographing. And, sometimes, collecting a beautiful scene was crucial to establishing magnitude. Panoramic scenes showing the awe-inspiring scope of Machu Picchu were relevant for the scientific work of the YPE because they documented something important: the sheer scope of the YPE's discovery. A revised version of the instructions above acknowledged just that need: "It is not expected that films will be used for landscapes, or for objects properly connected with other departments, except as requested by the Dierector [sic], or in cases where it is known to the member that it is probable that he is the only member of the Expedition who will have an opportunity to get the picture in question."[59] Rare, inspiring landscapes were worth capturing because Bingham needed to be able to represent the full scope of the expedition's accomplishments: grand scenes, grand work. Ultimately, Bingham

---

57. Bingham, "Assignment of Photographic Negatives and Numbers," 1; Bingham, "Peruvian Expedition of 1914–15. Official Circular #20, Revised."

58. Bingham, "Assignment of Photographic Negatives and Numbers," 2; Bingham, Hiram, "Peruvian Expedition of 1914–15. Official Circular #20, Revised," 2.

59. Bingham, Hiram, "Peruvian Expedition of 1914–15. Official Circular #20, Revised," 2.

wanted viewers in the United States who looked at these photographs to see not only the greatness of Machu Picchu but also the importance of the YPE's discovery of it.

Gathering artifacts and taking pictures was scientific work. Accumulating evidence in objects and images was, for Bingham, the object of discovery. But actually discovering Machu Picchu—in the full sense of the word—required making that scientific accumulation public. In order to establish the magnitude of the YPE's work, they needed to reveal it to audiences that mattered. At this point, therefore, we shift from magnitude as accumulation to magnitude as story.

Making Machu Picchu Matter[60]

As Bingham repeatedly reminded his audiences, the results of the Yale Peruvian Expedition included as many as twelve thousand photographic negatives, thousands of shards of pottery, and hundreds of skeletons and individual bones. They also included accounts of those materials and the processes involved in uncovering them. Together, materials, photographs, and accounts became the story of Machu Picchu and made it into the "lost city of the Incas."

Bingham claimed that "the ruins of Machu Picchu [were] the most important that have been discovered in South America during the past three centuries."[61] That assertion of *megethos* continues to resonate today as, for example, the UNESCO web page for the "Historic Sanctuary of Machu Picchu" asserts, "It was probably the most amazing urban creation of the Inca Empire at its height."[62] But in 1911 and 1912, that magnitude was but a "doubt and a dream."[63] Bingham brought it into being by making Machu Picchu widely known and widely seen. By the time scholars realized that the origin story for Machu Picchu might not be so grand as Bingham thought, the site had been invented as a "lost city" and as the most important ruins in South America.

---

60. A nod to both Farrell, "Sizing Things Up" and Finnegan, *Making Photography Matter*.
61. Bingham, "The Peruvian Expedition of 1912," Report.
62. UNESCO World Heritage Centre, "Historic Sanctuary," para. 1. The elision of Cuzco here is telling: substituting postcolonial preservation for pre-Columbian importance.
63. Winthrop, *A Companion to The Heart of the Andes*, 4.

Accounts of Machu Picchu's discovery appeared in scholarly journals, in maps of previously uncharted corners of Peru, in reports for funding agencies and employers, and in stories published in newspapers and popular magazines.[64] Though YPE publications in scientific venues were extensive, Bingham's popular publications took pride of place. He maintained a constant awareness of the public possibilities accompanying his adventures. Despite his frequent protestations that the expeditions were scientific in nature—not the stuff of treasure hunts and adventure novels—he carefully sought out media attention and wrote numerous popular articles and books. In the end, Machu Picchu was invented through its revelation in objects, images, and words that circulated to popular viewing publics in the United States.[65]

This section looks closely at Machu Picchu's public revelation as the work of "strenuous Yankees."[66] It traces the invention of American magnitude that pervaded accounts of Machu Picchu's "discovery." My account of that invention begins with the first announcements of Machu Picchu's discovery in US newspapers, showing how they positioned Bingham and the expedition in relation to other people, cultures, and civilizations. It then turns to the two most extensive illustrated accounts of the discovery that appeared during spring and early summer 1913, highlighting how the revelation of Machu Picchu happened across word and image. The section ultimately demonstrates how seeing Machu Picchu, discovered, revealed both the ruins and the YPE as exemplars of a grand civilization.

Setting Scenes and Establishing Claims

Reports of Machu Picchu's discovery appeared in newspapers across the United States. These accounts storied the site as the "lost city of the Incas." They also, crucially, cleared the scene to allow Bingham and company to be Machu Picchu's first and rightful narrators.

Crowds of reporters awaited Bingham on each return to the United States.[67] Bingham had primed that attention even before departing, and he

---

64. For a partial list of YPE publications prior to 1914 see, for example, Bingham, "Table of Contents." For newspaper reports celebrating the materials accumulated and the magnitude of the findings, see, for example, "Marvelous Lost City Found by Yale Men"; "Finds Bones of Ancient Man."

65. Hall, *Framing a Lost City*.

66. "Lost City in the Clouds," SM 1.

67. Heaney, *Cradle of Gold*, 73, 126.

sent cables home announcing important finds, ensuring a warm reception.[68] Before the 1911 expedition left for Peru, the *Los Angeles Times* ran columns celebrating the expedition's plans for discovery. In "Seek Lost Incan Cities," the *Times* explained that Bingham had visited Incan ruins before and "hope[d] to find more cities."[69] A month later, while the expedition was in progress, a somewhat longer *Times* article again emphasized the search for "lost cities."[70] Even before Bingham found ruins, audiences back home were prepared to encounter lost places. When the YPE arrived home, then, reporters were waiting for stories framed in terms of the lost and the found.

The rhetorical work of making ruins into "lost cities," as Hall explains, was central to the YPE's visual strategy.[71] Before and after the first expedition, Bingham carefully framed what it would mean for the YPE to reveal "lost cities." Though excavation would eventually become important, in his initial explanations he emphasized making the places themselves visible. "Getting at these places," he explained, "will be mostly clearing work."[72] The first step of discovery was to rescue "lost cities" from neglect (in the form of overgrowth) and, in the process, make them photographable.

This story of the YPE's mission, though apparently innocuous, set several important parameters that would shape future interactions with Machu Picchu. If a place was lost, then someone had lost it—through neglect, lack of understanding, or lack of capacity. Likewise, if the crucial first task of discovery was to uncover and reveal those lost cities, then the people who did that work had a special claim to the places discovered. Bingham primed his US audiences to recognize responsibility for loss and for discovery, and he took care to establish the levels of skill and effort that discovery required. Quotes from Bingham in those early newspaper accounts drew attention to the challenges the expedition would face in accomplishing its aims. He commented, for example, "Of course, the Incas [sic] cities on the plateau have been known, but their fortified cities they were accustomed to hang in almost inaccessible spots on mountainsides, and it has only lately been possible to get near them."[73] Peruvians and other explorers knew all about the easily accessed Incan ruins—those "on the plateau"—but reaching the true magnificence of the Incas required bolder action. And the YPE was uniquely equipped to take

---

68. See, for example, Bingham, Letter to Manager; Bingham, "Peruvian Expedition of 1915"; Bingham, "The New Peruvian Expedition."
69. "Seek Lost Inca Cities."
70. "Will Seek Lost Cities."
71. Hall, *Framing a Lost City*.
72. "Will Seek Lost Cities."
73. "Will Seek Lost Cities."

that action, never mind that Quechua farmers had been "getting near" such ruins for generations and it was a new Peruvian road that most facilitated the YPE's access. Peruvians had "lost" those cities, but rugged, virile US American scientist-explorers would (re)discover them.

Articles published when the 1911 expedition returned the following December made good on the groundwork that Bingham had laid. Three consistent themes cut across the articles, whether they filled a column or only a single block: accessing Machu Picchu had required great effort and ingenuity, members of the YPE were the only white men to set foot there since the Conquest, and the city stood as evidence that pre-Columbian cultures had built great civilizations. These articles framed the actions of the YPE parallel to those of Machu Picchu's original creators, raising the scale and quality of both groups' labors over those of the present local population.

Across the United States, major newspapers and small-town weeklies celebrated the YPE's effort in the familiar terms of rugged individualism. Bingham's framing of the ruins as inaccessible was repeated and used to emphasize the ruined citadel's grandiosity and the caliber of the expedition's accomplishments.[74] It took effort and skill to make it to Machu Picchu, reports emphasized, and the members of the YPE had both in abundance. One frequently reprinted article explained, for example, that in order to access Machu Picchu, "it was necessary for them to travel though rough country and climb to dizzy heights in a tropical climate."[75] Other articles reveled in the dangers the expedition faced and overcame, heightening the scope of their accomplishments by advancing their degree of difficulty.[76] In these articles, the connection between the YPE and the Incas was implicit, but it is still notable: The Inca had built and inhabited cities "in almost inaccessible spots on mountainsides," and the men of the YPE, in parallel, had accomplished the journey there without significant cost: "All returned strong and well."[77]

That implicit comparison between Incan and US capacity was underscored every time a newspaper asserted that the YPE's [US] American scientist-explorers were the first people to access the ruins since the Conquest. Those claims to primacy and exclusivity both established who had "lost" Machu Picchu and signaled the expedition's superiority over them. One representative article referred to Machu Picchu and other newfound Incan sites as "places

---

74. See, for example, "Older Than the Incas"; "Discover Lost City of the Andes"; Untitled article, *Duluth News-Tribune*.

75. "Marvelous Lost City Found by Yale Men"; "Ancient Incas Ruined City."

76. See, for example, "Bingham Back with Pre-Incas' Skulls."

77. "Will Seek Lost Cities"; "Marvelous Lost City Found by Yale Men"; "Ancient Incas Ruined City."

heretofore unseen and even unknown," strangely erasing not only Indigenous residents but also the Inka himself.[78] The irony of such claims, given that those same articles sometimes acknowledged that the ruins were occupied when Bingham arrived, appears to have been lost on everyone involved in writing them.[79]

When the Indigenous people so crucial to the YPE's successes did appear in articles, they showed up only so that they could embody local failure to recognize and reveal Machu Picchu's grandeur. The *New York Times* quotes Bingham saying, "We discovered it [Machu Picchu] by following some Peruvian Indians up a narrow goat path. When we got to the top of the hill we found that the Indians had planted corn among the ruins of the ancient Inca temple."[80] Likewise, the *New York Tribune* lays the city's ruin at least partially at local feet: "On the top of the plateau they found an ancient city all in ruins, with a new one springing up. . . . Some of these walls and ruins had been removed by the inhabitants of the place to allow them to raise corn."[81] It is hard to miss the disdain driving these references to people who would plant corn in such magnificent places. The "Indians" could not be the city's discoverers because they could not recognize it for what its Yankee inventors believed it to be. It did not occur to Bingham or his audiences in the United States that the site's residents might have their own stories of the place. Instead, the presumed failure of Indigenous residents' vision cleared them from the scene even though they were the ones who had made the YPE's discovery possible.

Spaniards who might have visited Machu Picchu during the Conquest received more attention than "Indians" did, but they were also, eventually, pushed out of the "discovery" frame. The lingering power of the Black Legend meant that it was easy for US audiences to dismiss Spanish conquistadors as cruel, greedy, and rapacious. They were certainly not scientists, and only nominally explorers. A *New York Times* headline celebrating the 1911 expedition's return announced, "Its Members First White Men in 400 Years to Enter Pre-Inca, City of Macchu Pichu [sic]." The article, like many others, repeated an erroneous suggestion that Pizarro had visited Machu Picchu at the time of the Conquest.[82] Other articles similarly invoked Pizarro's soldiers'

78. "Newspaper Clipping." For additional examples, see, for example, "Peru Report Is Awaited"; "Seek Lost Inca Cities."
79. "Will Seek Lost Cities."
80. "Yale Expedition Back from Peru."
81. "Sees Old Peruvian City."
82. See, for example, "Marvelous Lost City Found by Yale Men"; "Literary Notes." In his early efforts to identify Machu Picchu, Bingham thought it might be the city he had been looking for, the last refuge of Manco Capac. Pizarro and his soldiers had described that refuge as "a city of white marble," and Machu Picchu seemed to fit the bill. Newspaper reports suggesting

supposed visit to the city while drawing a distinction between their focus on conquest and the YPE's investment in discovery.[83] Spanish soldiers destroyed and plundered; the YPE revealed and preserved. The afterlife of the Black Legend quietly undergirded the YPE's claims to Machu Picchu's American status. Bingham's contemporaries, immersed in the ongoing debate over US imperialism, would recognize this crucial distinction between European and US expansion.[84] They could readily accept having Spanish conquistadors dismissed from the scene.

Peruvian elites posed the greatest threat to Bingham's claims of discovery. They, in particular, needed to be cleared from the scene in order for the YPE to claim Machu Picchu's magnitude for [the United States of] America. Perhaps not surprisingly, then, they were the only group whose relationship to the site was explicitly critiqued in newspaper reports. They consistently appeared as either neglectful or outright hostile to scientific advancement. As such, they also could not possibly be the proper inheritors of Machu Picchu's grandeur. One column, for example, quoted Bingham warning that Machu Picchu would disappear again "unless steps are taken by the Peruvian Government."[85] Context in the article suggested that such intervention was unlikely.[86] Likewise, newspapers frequently cited Bingham's political difficulties with the Peruvian government as evidence that the government's intransigence put scientific progress at risk. In some cases, Peruvian resistance to the YPE was a sign of not only incompetence but destructive negligence. Several accounts of the 1912 expedition's return contrast the Peruvian government's meddling in YPE efforts with its failure to care for its own people during a typhus and smallpox outbreak.[87] There is a clear sense in these reports that the Peruvian government was obsessing over the wrong thing and, thereby, showing just how far Peruvian leadership had fallen since the construction of Machu Picchu. They were cleared from the scene by the supposed evidence of their own failed civilization.

Discounting Spanish soldiers, Peruvian elites, and Quechua farmers, articles repeatedly confirmed for US readers that "no white man had trod their

---

that Pizarro or other Spanish soldiers had seen the city appear to have elided Bingham's initial purpose and subsequent explanation.

83. "Ancient Incas Ruined City."

84. For scholarship addressing various strategies of imperial justification during the Spanish-American War, see, for example, Kramer, *The Blood of Government*; Lowry, "The Flower of Cuba"; Louis Pérez, *Cuba in the American Imagination*.

85. "Ancient Incas of Peru."

86. "Ancient Incas of Peru."

87. See, for example, "Ancient Incas of Peru"; "Braved Perils in Peru"; "Bingham Back with Pre-Incas' Skulls"; "Peruvian Ruins."

silent streets before, and the hand of man has done nothing to disturb the solitude except in turning over the earth to raise a little corn."[88] Machu Picchu had been waiting for Bingham and the YPE. And by discovering it, they brought to light not only that specific Incan ruin but a wider American consequence. A handful of truly over-the-top columns bring this point home with particular force. The *Grand Forks Daily Herald,* extrapolating wildly from Bingham's words, expressed hope that the expedition's work might "[reveal] the vast and now mystic history of the occupation of the American hemisphere by peoples who, in civilization, will compare with those who built Babylon and Nineveh, or who erected the highest type of ancient civilization along the valley of the Nile."[89] Likewise, the Pittsburgh *Post* announced, "Professor Hiram Bingham's expedition to Peru unearthed the famous lost city of Machu Picchu. . . . These studies point to a marvelous past development and what, after all, may be the home where earth's first culture was cradled."[90] Several years later, the *New York Herald* made the link between that first civilization and Bingham's own explicit. It celebrated in one sentence "that wonderful race which had reached the height of its marvelous civilization at the time of the Spanish conquest" and the "race" of its discoverer, "Professor Hiram Bingham, an American explorer."[91] Those seeking a grand American history that would, finally, raise the New World above the Old even in the realm of history found much promise in Machu Picchu. Here, they declared, was a city on a hill that presaged that of the United States.

Americans Looking at Machu Picchu

On June 15, 1913, the front page of the *New York Times* Sunday Magazine offered Machu Picchu's city on a hill for easy viewing (figure 3.1).[92] A panoramic photograph of the recently uncovered ruins stretched across the page, bringing the Lost City of the Incas before the eyes of its [US] American audience. This was not the first time viewers in the United States were able to look at Machu Picchu. That event happened two months earlier, when the *National Geographic Magazine* and *Harper's* published Bingham's accounts of the 1912 expedition. But, as I will discuss in a few paragraphs, those earlier

---

88. "Marvelous Lost City Found by Yale Men"; "Ancient Incas Ruined City." See also "Important Pre-Inca Finds"; "Bingham Back with Pre-Incas' Skulls."
89. "Peru Report Is Awaited."
90. "Renewing Interest in Geography."
91. "Mystery and Romance," 2.
92. "Lost City in the Clouds."

FIGURE 3.1. "Lost City in the Clouds Found After Centuries," *New York Times*, June 15, 1913. Photograph by Hiram Bingham. Original caption: "Panorama of Machu Picchu, Peru, Lost Inca City, Discovered by Prof. Bingham, Who Declares It Is Rivaled Only by the Celebrated Ruins of Cuzco." Photograph: Wisconsin Historical Society.

accounts had made viewers wait for the big reveal—delaying Machu Picchu's appearance by inviting reader-viewers to join the expedition in its search. The *New York Times* offered reader-viewers the culmination of that labor: a grand city perched in the clouds and uniquely available to their eyes. If the *Times* gave easy access to Machu Picchu in all its magnitude, though, it also directed its readers to invest in the work of exploration. Most of the article's text was composed of excerpts from the April *National Geographic Magazine* article. The opening paragraphs of the *Times* story pushed readers to access the full *National Geographic* article, inviting them to view its photographs and share the feelings of the men who took them. The two hundred and fifty photographs in the *National Geographic* article, the *Times* gushed, "give such a vivid idea of Machu Picchu and its glories that one can easily understand the thrills of awe and delight which, says the fortunate explorer, were felt by himself and his companions as they sallied forth from their camp day after day to burrow into the ruins."[93] To truly appreciate Machu Picchu's magnitude, the *Times* suggested, reader-viewers ought to participate, virtually, in the expedition and feel the thrills that only American magnitude could provide.

The *National Geographic* article excerpted in the *Times* was titled, "In the Wonderland of Peru," and it filled the entire April 1913 issue of the magazine. That same month, *Harper's* published "The Discovery of Machu Picchu," a shorter, parallel account. Both were written by Hiram Bingham. Both use photographs and rich descriptions to invite broad audiences of US Ameri-

---

93. "Lost City in the Clouds."

can reader-viewers to participate in the work of the YPE. In them—as in the *Times*—the discovery of Machu Picchu is revealed as a matter of [US] American, not just scientific, accomplishment.

Bingham's contract with the National Geographic Society stipulated that he would publish the first account of his discovery in *National Geographic*. An early draft of the 1912 agreement between Yale and the National Geographic Society includes a crucial edit in this regard. Among the conditions outlined is that "Prof. Bingham agrees to give the Society the preliminary account of the results of his work for publication in the Nat. Geog. Mag."[94] In the draft, "preliminary" is crossed out and replaced with "popular." Subsequent typed versions of the agreement retain the expectation of a first *popular* accounting published in *National Geographic*.[95] The work of the expedition as presented in *National Geographic* was, in this sense, aimed first toward a popular readership or, more accurately, toward a popular viewership. Those viewers, and not just archeologists, historians, and geographers, were invited to corroborate and participate in the expedition's discovery.

National Geographic was not Bingham's only popular venue. His 1912 agreement with the National Geographic Society stipulated that the editor had first pick of photographs and right to the initial long-form publication on the discovery. However, the agreement also allowed Bingham and his staff to publish elsewhere starting "three months after date of delivery of the articles and their acceptance by the editor of the National Geographic Magazine."[96] Bingham clearly did just that. "In the Wonderland of Peru" offered the most extensive account of Machu Picchu and by far the most thoroughly illustrated. But, Bingham's article in *Harper's* echoes and extends elements of the story, offering another audience another way of engaging with the discovery of Machu Picchu. Through pictures and vivid description, the two articles, together, accomplished the basic requirement for discovery: being seen and reported by proper subjects to proper publics. Those American viewers accompanying American explorers could take part in the American claim to Machu Picchu.

Where the *Times* allowed reader-viewers immediate access to Machu Picchu, both "Wonderland" and "Discovery" invite them to start at the beginning and make their way, slowly, to the moment of revelation. In *Harper's*, the photographs begin in the wide Urubamba valley, looking toward a wall of mountains. The destination is out there but hidden, and the ascent promises to be challenging. Subsequent photographs show treacherous paths and then, finally, the ruins themselves. The first sixteen pages of "Wonderland" feature

---

94. "The Research Com of the Nat Geog Soc . . . ," 2.
95. "Memorandum of Agreement . . . of 1912," 1.
96. "Memorandum of Agreement . . . of 1912," 1–2.

twelve pages of photographs that carried reader-viewers gradually into the Andes. When, on the eighteenth page, they got their first glimpse of a still jungle-covered Machu Picchu, they were well aware of the distance the expedition covered and the altitude it gained. In both articles, revelation was the reward for patience, diligence, and labor.

Bingham repeatedly staked his claim to discovery by emphasizing the YPE's revelatory work, and he invited reader-viewers to take part in that revelation. In "Discovery," Bingham encouraged readers to walk alongside him as he slowly realized Machu Picchu's magnitude: "The character of the stone-faced *andenes* began to improve, and suddenly we found ourselves in the midst of a jungle-covered maze of small and large walls." Soon, Bingham continued, they began to see well-built buildings under the vines, and "surprise followed surprise until there came the realization that we were in the midst of as wonderful ruins as any ever found in Peru." By this point, reader-viewers may well have felt at least an echo of the thrill and surprise Bingham himself felt. It is notable, then, that Bingham quickly reminded them that they—US American actors—were the ones to find Machu Picchu, not locals: "It seemed almost incredible that this city, only five days' journey from Cuzco, should have remained so long undescribed and comparatively unknown."[97] Over four centuries, Bingham implied, Peruvians had failed to find it. The YPE, however, found it within a month of arriving in Peru. Parallel to the newspaper articles that cleared away other claimants, Bingham's articles invited reader-viewers to uncover the ruins and claim their consequence for [the United States of] America.

Likewise, in "Wonderland," photographs and text emphasized the work of revelation. Sometimes the caption (or article text) carried the burden of describing that work, but more often than not, the change was shown through photographs. Again and again, Bingham staged before and after scenes that showed how the expedition rescued Machu Picchu's extraordinary stonework from the jungle. The story that Bingham told about those photographs made reader-viewers active participants in the YPE's revelatory work.

The photographs reproduced in figures 3.2, 3.3, and 3.4 show Machu Picchu's Intihuatana hill at various points in its revelation. In "Wonderland," they appear in a chronological circle: The first picture shows the ruins uncovered; the second, on the next page, shows roughly the same scene but still obscured by jungle; and the third, ten pages later, returns to the cleared hill. The first "after" image is titled "An Architectural Triumph: Machu Picchu." The "before" photograph beside it is captioned "A picture of the same part of the city of Machu Picchu as shown in the preceding illustration, but photographed the

---

97. Bingham, "The Discovery of Machu Picchu," 714.

FIGURE 3.2. Hiram Bingham, "An Architectural Triumph: Machu Picchu," *National Geographic Magazine,* April 1913, p. 498. National Geographic Image Collection.

year before." The third photograph, an "after" image titled "Intihuatana Hill and the Terraces West of the Sacred Plaza," cross-references the earlier pair in its caption.

Visually, it is no mistake that the two post-clearing photographs of Intihuatana hill and the main plaza are shown in landscape view. In both cases, the ruined city appears vast, spreading out across the page and inviting the viewer to marvel at the sheer scope of its construction. The visual strategies that Church used in "Heart of the Andes" to establish magnitude appear in these photographs as well—though they were printed in the pages of a magazine, not displayed alone in a room. Bingham's photographs could be held in the hands, but in them, too, the viewer stood with the image-maker on a slice of solid foreground and gazed into vastness. Unlike Church's scenes, however, the vastness that viewers confronted in Bingham's photographs of Machu Picchu was at least partially human-made: white stone terraces, stairways, and buildings set firmly yet precariously on that "inaccessible" ridge. In "Intihuatana Hill," the snow-capped peaks visible in the background emphasize the epic scale on which viewers should view the photograph and, in the process, measure the significance of Machu Picchu. The other "after" photograph, "An Architectural Triumph," achieves similar effect by setting the city against the rocky escarpments of a closely neighboring mountain, emphasizing the skill required to reach the ridge, let alone achieve the architectural triumph in the title. The magnitude of nature and of human accomplishment reinforced one another in the photographs. Though they reached public view in 1913, well

FIGURE 3.3. H. L. Tucker, "A Picture of the Same Part of the City of Machu Picchu as Shown in the Preceding Illustration, But Photographed the Year Before," *National Geographic Magazine,* April 1913, p. 499. National Geographic Image Collection.

FIGURE 3.4. Hiram Bingham, "Intihuatana Hill and the Terraces West of the Sacred Plaza," *National Geographic Magazine,* April 1913, p. 508. National Geographic Image Collection.

after the romantic era that gave us Church's mountain landscapes, such photographs appeal to earlier narratives about the power and mystery of the snowy Andes. They set the Incas' architectural skill in that same scale and gently imply that the YPE shared in it too. The photographs, in that sense, prime viewers to recognize magnitude: a great city in the majestic Andes, built (and recovered) by a great civilization.

The extent of that greatness and its implicit connection to the power of US civilization may have come even more clear to viewers as they looked from the "after" photographs to the "before" photograph. In portrait view and closely cropped, the before-clearing photograph emphasizes height and claustrophobic overgrowth. There is little distinction between the hill that is the subject of the photograph and the forest-crusted hills in the background, and the middle left of the photograph is nearly lacking in contrast. In the mid-ground of the photograph, viewers can just distinguish a few ruins, but the overall effect is fuzzy and wild. The "lost city of the Incas" is "a doubt and a dream" in this photograph. It is difficult even to orient oneself to the connection between the side-by-side "before" and "after" photographs, and hard to identify the marvel that would be. The substantial difference in framing between the photographs emphasizes the temporal and laborious distance between them. The YPE's revelation of Machu Picchu was, in other words, itself an extensive and consequential accomplishment.

And viewers were encouraged to do that work themselves. In the caption for "Architectural Triumph," Bingham made that invitation explicit, writing, "Contrast this picture, which was taken in 1912, after months of strenuous work in cleaning the city, with the picture on the following page, which was taken in 1911."[98] Similarly, the caption for "Intihuatana Hill" reads, "By comparing this with the view on page 499, the effects of the clearing in 1912 are brought out very clearly."[99] Moving their eyes back and forth between the photographs, searching out starting places, viewers took part in the slow labor of uncovering the buildings and terraces hidden in the second picture and revealed in the first. Rarely, in these contrast scenes, is the labor required to clear the ruins visible itself. That omission made the change more dramatic, and it conveniently omitted the Indigenous laborers who had done the clearing. The tangled and overgrown terrain of the "before" photograph transformed almost by the force of the readers' vision alone into the magnificent lost city of the Incas. In this sense, the reader-viewers of *National Geographic* participated enthymematically in revelation. They filled in the time and labor it took to move Machu Picchu from a jungle-covered hillside to an "architectural triumph." And just as an enthymeme, ideally, entangles listeners in

---

98. Bingham, "In the Wonderland of Peru," 498.
99. Bingham, "In the Wonderland of Peru," 508.

the argument by inviting their participation, looking between photographs and filling in the labor invited viewers to affiliate themselves with it. They accomplished a small piece of the YPE's discovery, revealing Machu Picchu to themselves.

Uncovering the city and revealing it to the world required "months of strenuous work" by the YPE.[100] The effects of that labor—namely, *clarity*—were effects inevitably amplified by the clarity of photography and the clear views those photographs made available to *National Geographic* readers. "Wonderland" taught its audiences that hard work, ingenuity, and clarity of purpose—*American* values—were essential to the revelation of Machu Picchu and its full magnitude. In the caption for the "before" photograph, Bingham explicitly extends that American success from the YPE to his audience back home. He explains that the effort of the expedition was specifically expended "so that the members of the National Geographic Society could obtain a good conception of the city."[101] That hard, protracted labor on-site and the viewer's labor looking at the photograph, Bingham suggested, allowed the members of the National Geographic Society—an explicitly US American audience—to see Machu Picchu for themselves, replicating and authenticating the YPE's discovery. In this way, reader-viewers participated in discovery by participating in revelation. In the process, they enacted and claimed American magnitude.

But American magnitude, Bingham insisted, wasn't just about panoramic triumphs. The accomplishments of a great civilization required attention to detail. Bingham, perhaps, shared Farrell's understanding that magnitude resides in both the large/extensive and the particular/refined.[102] That story of magnitude's precision was present in "Wonderland," but "Discovery" told it more explicitly and directly. "It is difficult to describe Machu Picchu," Bingham explains in "Discovery," and then he proceeds to describe it by zeroing in on particular evidence of Incan skill. Rather than treating the city overall, Bingham drew readers' attention to the lingering question of how Incan architects provided the site with water. His thick descriptions of stone-lined watercourses, irrigation ditches, a bathhouse, and fountains toured readers through the city and, in the process, revealed Incan engineering skill, agricultural acumen, and attention to basic hygiene.[103] Where "Wonderland" asked viewers to feel awe at sheer scope, in other words, "Discovery" emphasized the refinements of an advanced megalithic civilization. The article's photographs likewise focused closely on building techniques, corroborating the

---

100. Bingham, "In the Wonderland of Peru," 498.
101. Bingham, "In the Wonderland of Peru," 499.
102. Farrell, "The Weight of Rhetoric," 471.
103. Bingham, "The Discovery of Machu Picchu," 715–16.

detailed specificity of Bingham's words. Reader-viewers could see the rectangular blocks, carefully cut, and (thanks to Bingham's guidance) could make out notable features of Incan design.[104] Bingham gave precise measurements, marking out large buildings and massive blocks and directing viewers to the photographs, which, he asserted, would confirm that the blocks were "considerably higher than a man."[105] Repeatedly, in other words, "Discovery" included reader-viewers in the details of scientific discovery, pacing out the major accomplishments of the Incas and the YPE step by step. The great civilization the YPE revealed wasn't just for show; it was built with care and insight. Guiding reader-viewers through those details, Bingham revealed his own team's grasp of them.

Just as we might recognize resonances between the visual experiences Bingham staged and the ways Winthrop described Church bringing the Andes into being through sight, we ought to also recognize a contemporary resonance that Bingham's reader-viewers likely felt. As Bingham revealed the scope and detail of Machu Picchu's construction as the accomplishment of a great civilization, his readers would have been aware of their own great civilization's grand feat of engineering taking place farther north. The Panama Canal Zone had passed into US control in 1904 and the canal was nearing completion in the spring of 1913. It would open a year later. Bingham's US audience knew its own accomplishments and the importance of both grand vision and great skill. It would not be much of a leap to see their nation's grand American engineering project reflected in Machu Picchu's stone. Bingham doesn't appear to have made the comparison, but it is hard to imagine that US viewers would have missed it. And as they considered it, they could imagine their own nation continuing the magnitude of a previous great American civilization.

This sense of affiliation with Machu Picchu's greatness did not require that US viewers become one with Peruvians or even with the Incas. They would not have been amenable to such suggestions anyway. Instead, it encouraged viewers to inhabit the magnitude of their own grand, present-day, American empire by seeing it reflected in pictures of a previous American empire. Those following Bingham's tale of discovery in "Wonderland" and "Discovery" encountered a singular city built by a great civilization. That celebration of Incan magnitude quickly came to serve as a warrant for the skill of the YPE

---

104. See, for example, his description of a "semi-circular bastion." Bingham, "The Discovery of Machu Picchu," 716.

105. Bingham, "The Discovery of Machu Picchu," 716. Strangely, the particular photograph he invokes does not actually appear in the article, though one a few pages later does show a man standing beside the massive stones of the "Temple of the Three Windows," which, stacked on top of each other, rise a third taller than him.

and the importance of its discovery. In revealing Machu Picchu's magnitude, the YPE also revealed the magnitude of its home country.

At a moment when US influence in Latin America was growing—thanks, especially, to the canal project—such claims to connection and preeminence are both unsurprising and noteworthy. Theodore Roosevelt's "Corollary to the Monroe Doctrine," articulated in 1904, asserted US authority over the hemisphere. The "civilized" United States, in its greatness and paternal hegemony, would ensure that the Americas were efficient, decent, ordered, and responsible.[106] Bingham deplored the Monroe Doctrine and Roosevelt's "Corollary." In his June 1913 pamphlet, *The Monroe Doctrine: An Obsolete Shibboleth*, Bingham dismissed the notion that there was "natural sympathy" between North and South America and recognized the insult implied in the United States' assertions of hemispheric sovereignty.[107] The original doctrine was obsolete, he declared, and the new one was patently offensive. Both ought to be abandoned. And yet, the YPE's research practice and Bingham's presentation of it to US audiences belie his own words. The "discovery" of Machu Picchu, revealed in photographs and words, radiated American magnitude as a matter of science, culture, and vision. *An Obsolete Shibboleth,* with its more limited audience and attempted political intervention, was no match for the story Bingham told in actions and pictures.

What Wasn't to Be Seen—On Opacity

I have argued thus far that revealing discovery was the YPE's primary task—enacted through research practice, touted in newspapers, and visualized in magazines. All that work of revelation, however, was premised on strategic opacity. Bingham's sense of accountability to scientific and popular publics in the United States was accompanied by a refusal to be held accountable by or to his Peruvian counterparts, let alone the Quechua farmers and mestizo muleteers whose labor quite literally made revelation possible. This habit of colonial exploitation is, on the one hand, utterly familiar. As myriad scholars have reminded us, "exploration" was and is built upon a premise of superiority and the right to claim and take.[108] It presumes that scientific outsiders entering what (they deem) unclaimed or undescribed space bring knowledge with them from the outside and take that same knowledge home with them when

---

106. Roosevelt, "Corollary to the Monroe Doctrine," para. 5.
107. Bingham, *The Monroe Doctrine*, 19, 24.
108. See, for example, Hall, "Collecting a 'Lost City' for Science"; Poole, *Vision, Race, and Modernity*; Pratt, *Imperial Eyes*; Quijano, "Coloniality of Power"; Wynter, "Unsettling."

they leave. They may carry away evidence gathered on-site, but they do not gain new ideas through interaction. At best, the presumption goes, explorers may teach the "natives" some useful skills (see, e.g., Church "teaching" Salas landscape painting).

That presumption is simply wrong. As Watson and Huntington make clear, knowledge is always assembled through interaction and copresence.[109] And, as Carey establishes, even if colonial scientists from the Euro-American North invented the objects of their "discoveries," the knowledge they claimed to own and produce frequently originated in the "South" and was developed and circulated through complex networks of exchange that belie presumptions of periphery and metropole.[110] Church returned from the Andes with his vision and painterly practice changed. Bingham, too, learned from his interlocutors—even if he frequently resisted the lessons. The news that Bingham's practice was profoundly white supremacist and neocolonial and that it relied on, but failed to credit, physical and intellectual work done by Peruvian farmers, muleteers, and scholars should surprise no one. But focusing only on Bingham's racist, colonial presumption centers the story he told and obscures the stories he elided.

Therefore, in closing, I linger with another story. Writing about early twentieth-century representations of Machu Picchu, Gómez notes, "The archeological, historical, literary, and photographic work [produced about Machu Picchu] has attempted to reconstruct and redefine the invisibilities, the hidden [things], and the absences in its fragmented structures."[111] The invisible, the hidden, and the absent are constitutive of any ruin-made-into-place, including Machu Picchu. Discovering (inventing) one story and revealing it as *the* story requires obscuring the multitudes of other stories that are always there.[112] Common definitions of discovery presume that it brings to light places and things that hadn't ever been seen before. As the beginning sections of this chapter established, however, discovery and revelation are generative, not managerial. They do not merely show what already existed but was unknown. Instead, they make the things that they bring to light. As I close this chapter, Gómez's words and the stories of Machu Picchu require us to add another layer: Revelation, by necessity, hides. Discovery is always accompanied by opacity. For something to be claimed as a discovery, other possible

---

109. Watson and Huntington, "They're *Here*—I Can *Feel* Them," 259.
110. Carey, "Mountaineers and Engineers," 111.
111. Gómez, "Machu Picchu Reclamada," 497. "El trabajo arqueológico, histórico, literario y fotográfico [acerca de Machu Picchu] ha intentado reconstruir y redefinir la invisibilidad, lo oculto, y lo ausente en sus estructuras fragmentadas."
112. Querejazu, "Encountering the Pluriverse."

understandings of that thing must be covered over, obscured. A painstakingly framed shot cuts out undesirable elements. A correctly focused lens renders stonework sharp and consigns the populated foreground to fuzzy oblivion. A carefully packed crate reveals pottery shards and age-pitted bones while smuggling bronze pins and undamaged vessels out of sight. A populated, story-rich place becomes an undescribed space waiting to be discovered.

Bingham originally set out to find the last refuge of the Inka Manco Capac. He was looking for a specific lost place and a specific story about the Incas—one in which the heroic but doomed last Inca fled into the jungle, built a stronghold, and made one last stand against the Spanish. At first, Bingham thought that Machu Picchu might be that refuge, but he was quickly dissuaded. Instead, still looking for that specific story of Incan romance and grandeur, Bingham determined that he had found the origin site of the Incas. Machu Picchu, to Bingham, wasn't the end, it was the beginning. When the site he found didn't fit the story he wanted to tell, he kept the story and found the place a new position in it. Incan magnitude remained great, pure, and—most importantly—past.

Machu Picchu was relatively amenable to that story. It lent itself to discovery and revelation on Bingham's terms because it also lent itself readily to strategic opacity. Its previous European visitors—if they existed—had left scant traces to constrain his choices. Its previous criollo and mestizo Peruvian visitors, likewise, had offered little by way of interpretations. And, of course, racism and ethnocentrism made it easy for Bingham to frame Machu Picchu's present inhabitants out of the picture. They were Indigenous farmers. Though they had planted on the terraces, borrowed stones for their own constructions, and sometimes lived in Machu Picchu's buildings, they had mostly lived parallel to the clearly pre-Columbian site. The site itself—at least the aspects of it that mattered to the YPE—was free of any post-Columbian taint. Bingham, therefore, could easily lift up a purified picture of Machu Picchu as the preeminent Incan site. And he could easily leave out or dismiss the other stories that were also there.

Once one story has gained prominence, it can be difficult to recognize the presence of stories that might have been otherwise. The revelation of Machu Picchu is like that—the other stories are hidden deep. But we can begin to uncover some of those stories by looking away from Machu Picchu and turning instead to the two places Bingham chose not to reveal. After "discovering" Machu Picchu, Bingham did also eventually find his way to Manco Capac's last places of refuge. However, those sites, Vitcos and Espiritu Pampa, didn't fit Bingham's discovery needs. Those were syncretic spaces. Manco Capac and his followers had integrated Spanish architectural features, like tiled roofs, into their craft—making use of the tools available to them. This shouldn't surprise us. They were part of a living culture that adapted and changed over time, even in the midst of the cataclysm that was the Conquest. Bingham's story, however, couldn't accommodate the idea that the Inka and his people were part of a living, progressing human culture. His story also couldn't accommodate the reality that, while Tahuantinsuyo had been destroyed and the royal line had faded, Indigenous cultures lived on, changing and growing over time. Indigenous communities had continued to live at Espiritu Pampa, using the buildings and defending the place from interlopers. "Espiritu Pampa," as Heaney concludes, represented "Inca history as it was and continued to be: damaged but alive, besieged but remembered, still a refuge for resistance."[113] Espiritu Pampa—as an ongoing refuge for resistance—was so opaque to Bingham that he could not even imagine discovering it. Its revelation would not allow a claim to American magnitude because Espiritu Pampa's magnitude looked nothing like the sort of magnitude claimed by the United States and because it was so thoroughly connected to a living Indigenous community, the Asháninka. Bingham's story, by necessity, required covering over that story.

In a way, Espiritu Pampa's distance from Bingham's white-supremacist vision (and from that of his Peruvian counterparts) gave the Asháninka space to pursue their own purposes. Focusing the story on Machu Picchu, however, denied the Richarte, Alvarez, and Fuentes families that same opportunity. Unfortunately for the residents of Machu Picchu, Bingham oriented the YPE toward the invention and revelation of Machu Picchu because it fit "the Incas' history as he wanted it to be: beautiful, soaring, imperial, pure."[114] That story, and the actions it demanded, uprooted Alvarez's, Richarte's, and Fuentes's corn and inked out their home.[115] Hall points out that YPE publications systematically obscured the labor of Indigenous and mestizo peasants, hiding it from sight so that the expedition's accomplishments could accrue to Bingham and his staff. Over time, as Bingham's publications revealed Machu Picchu for US audiences, not only Indigenous labor, but also their farms, their homes, and their family stories "effectively disappeared."[116] In their stead, Machu Picchu came to light for US viewers "as a persistent antiquity, always there; not made but found."[117] Revelation was founded on erasure.

So, Bingham's revelation of Machu Picchu depended on obliterating the stories of Peruvian Indigenous communities that had survived and continued

---

113. Heaney, *Cradle of Gold*, 115.
114. Heaney, *Cradle of Gold*, 115.
115. Hall, "Collecting a 'Lost City' for Science," 309.
116. Hall, "Collecting a 'Lost City' for Science," 309.
117. Hall, "Collecting a 'Lost City' for Science," 309.

to do so.[118] And yet those communities remained live. Torvis Richarte, Anacleto Alvarez, and Tomas Fuentes and their families had not lost track of the stonework surrounding them. They had little investment in the version of the Incan story that Bingham told, but they were still part of that story and many others. Even as Bingham did his best to push them out of the frame, they and their peers remained. Their survivance, rhetorical and otherwise, took many forms, as it had for five hundred years.[119] For the three families living at Machu Picchu, it included their having found a home away from the populated valley in order to avoid being caught up in debt peonage. After Bingham arrived, it included their choice to work with the YPE and accumulate some local authority. It also included appearing at the edges of photographs that were trying hard to reveal something other than their presence. Even as those photographs sought to contrast contemporary Peruvians with the grandeur of the pre-Columbian site, the presence of Indigenous bodies in the frame also put the lie to "discovery"—reminding audiences then and today that the place held stories beyond the one offered by Bingham.[120] The Richarte, Alvarez, and Fuentes families didn't need Machu Picchu to be a sacred space in order to live their own Quechua stories. Indigenous communities today may make strategic use of Peru's investment in the Machu Picchu story and the Incan empire it reveals, but the site does not figure much in their stories of the world around them.[121] Bingham and present-day US Americans may make much of a trek to Machu Picchu just as they make much of American magnitude, but that is just one story among many.

In the story of American magnitude, opacity and revelation always coexist. The stories, places, and lives occluded by one revelation nevertheless find inventive means of their own. Those returned gazes—skeptical and resolute—take center stage in the next chapter.

---

118. See, for example, de la Cadena, *Earth Beings*; Salomon and Niño-Murcia, *The Lettered Mountain*.

119. Powell, "Rhetorics of Survivance"; Vizenor, *Manifest Manners*.

120. For more on this sort of resistance directed toward the possibility of witnessing, see Olson and Casas, "Felipe Guaman Poma de Ayala's *Primer Nueva Corónica y Buen Gobierno*."

121. de la Cadena, *Earth Beings*.

CHAPTER 4

Animating Interests

"The pictures for teaching reading and writing to the Mexicans that were made in the United States should not be shown—they are offensive to our nation."

—María Elena Sodi de Pallares, "Genialidad de Walt Disney Desvirtuada por Extraños"

During World War II, the US Office of the Coordinator of Inter-American Affairs (OIAA) collaborated with the Walt Disney Company on what could have been a feel-good project: a series of health and literacy films designed to turn impoverished, illiterate Latin Americans into productive hemispheric citizens. In fall 1944, the OIAA and Disney took the completed films to Mexico for a test run. Following the initial showings, *El Universal,* a major Mexico City newspaper, published an extended critique of the films written by the journalist, teacher, and women's rights advocate María Elena Sodi de Pallares. Sodi de Pallares saw the films as a pedagogical travesty, and she laid the blame for the film's poor quality squarely at the feet of the OIAA. More than just excoriating the films' failures as teaching tools, Sodi de Pallares presented them as signs of bad faith and, ultimately, an offence to the Mexican people. In the process, Sodi de Pallares used the films as evidence that the United States was thoroughly lacking in culture and suffered from a parochialism grounded in excessive self-regard.[1] Her editorial, in other words, aimed to deflate the United States' claim to American magnitude.

The original idea, Sodi de Pallares explained, had been a good one. The OIAA could have served a true coordinating role, uniting the "technical and

---

1. Sodi de Pallares, "Genialidad de Walt Disney." All translations are mine unless otherwise noted.

artistic potential" of the US motion picture industry with "our [Mexican] spiritual and intellectual resources."[2] The project could have signaled a generous investment by "a great country and friend of ours."[3] But things went sour quickly. Instead of a collaboration, the three Mexican teachers who had been sent to aid Disney found their advice ignored and their comments disregarded. And the OIAA was to blame, Sodi de Pallares explained: "Walt Disney had not been authorized to receive suggestions from our three envoys." Instead, "the artist [Disney] had to subject himself to the program of the Office of the Coordinator which imposed its own criteria."[4]

Critiquing the pedagogy of the films, Sodi de Pallares continued, "These persons [the experts chosen by the OIAA] did not accept any of the pedagogical methods currently in use in Mexico," and "they were not the least bit culturally competent enough to understand" the most basic facts about the Spanish language.[5] In other words, the "experts" appointed by the OIAA, at least so far as Sodi de Pallares saw it, started and ended with the presumption that US knowledge and educational theory trumped that of Mexico, even with regard to Mexican topics and the Spanish language.

The final straw came when the OIAA planned to end the films with "these or similar words": "This is what Uncle Sam has done for Latin America." Sodi de Pallares protested, "Even Mr. Disney, respectful of the dignity of the Mexican people, opposed this idea, but the aforementioned Office explained that only with a closing of this nature would the American Government be willing to cover the cost of the films."[6] This was insult added to injury. Not only was Mexican expertise dismissed and ignored, not only would the pedagogical approach impair rather than aid students' learning, but this bad gift was to be presented as an act of charity. In this sense, the Disney-OIAA health and literacy films were everything problematic about American magnitude as wielded by the United States in its long relationship with the "other American republics." The United States was conceited, overbearing, insensitive, and even destructive. Excessive self-regard impeded its vision, and its presumption of particular importance made it a terrible neighbor.

There is deep irony in the OIAA's apparent failure to meaningfully incorporate Latin American expertise into their work. After all, the office was estab-

---

2. Sodi de Pallares, "Genialidad de Walt Disney."
3. Sodi de Pallares, "Genialidad de Walt Disney."
4. Sodi de Pallares, "Genialidad de Walt Disney."
5. Sodi de Pallares, "Genialidad de Walt Disney."
6. Sodi de Pallares, "Genialidad de Walt Disney." Ultimately, the films opened with the seal of the United States and a title page giving credit to Disney and the OIAA, not the overt propagandizing that Sodi de Pallares described.

lished to promote hemispheric solidarity and attend to Latin American public opinion. They should have known better. There is deeper irony—though little surprise—in the fact that the joint literacy project's creators were, apparently, impervious to the critique. At the end of the project, though they touted the potential of motion pictures as a teaching tool, educational testers proclaimed the films less effective than a teacher alone. They also determined that the project was unsustainable because of Latin American shortcomings: Governments in the "other American republics" lacked the resources to provide projectors, screens, and electricity in the venues where they would use the films. The final reports made no mention of more fundamental criticisms, however. There was no hint that the language-teaching method might have been inappropriate for Spanish-language contexts, let alone contexts where the target audience—largely Indigenous people—were themselves non-native speakers of Spanish. The project had fatal flaws, the final report accepted, but perhaps the most fundamental of those flaws went unmentioned.

OIAA staff were aware of pedagogical critiques like the one leveled by Sodi de Pallares. A clipping of her article, a full translation, and a note calling a supervisor's attention to it sit in the agency's files at the US National Archives. Roy Disney received a copy and translation of another article making similar critiques, and the copies he forwarded to the OIAA also appear in the literacy program's files.[7] And while there is evidence that such critiques concerned agency staff, there is little sign that it troubled them enough to prompt a course change.

To be fair, such critical articles were vastly outnumbered by celebratory ones that pictured the magic of motion-picture literacy as transformative. In multiple letters, newspaper columns, and official reports, the OIAA-Disney literacy films sparkled with the light of progress and hemispheric cooperation. Critiques of US arrogance and OIAA presumption appear sprinkled throughout the OIAA archives, but they never seem to have achieved sufficient scale to tip the balance of OIAA activity. For the OIAA, critique was a problem to be managed or an impediment to negotiate, but never a fundamental check on the organization's American mission.

I open with Sodi de Pallares's editorial, however, because it serves as a bracing reminder of a fact that is at the heart of this last chapter: The pre-

---

7. "Translation of an Item." This article, by Carlos Denegri, makes the same pedagogical critique as Sodi de Pallares's, but blames the three Mexican teachers for failing to protect Mexican national integrity, commenting, "It is not the Americans fault not knowing the language. They already do plenty by trying to teach it to us." It is possible that Sodi de Pallares's column was, in part, intended to defend the three teachers, Eulalia Guzmán, Guadalupe Cejudo, and Estella Soní, from Denegri's attacks.

sumed magnitude of the United States has never gone uncontested, and it cannot stand on its own. Despite the consistent tendency of US image-makers to ignore, suppress, minimize, or curate Latin American perspectives on the United States, Latin Americans—elites and subalterns, allies and antagonists—have consistently responded to US looking with visions of their own. In politics, art, culture, and beyond, time and again, Latin Americans assert their own import and diminish the overbearing grandeur of the United States. Theirs is a consistent and persistent response to imperial presumption.[8] Sodi de Pallares's voice is not isolated—even if it might appear so in the records of the National Archives.

That persistent refusal to accept the US version of American magnitude at face value matters to my argument in this book not only because it demonstrates that US hemispheric hegemony has never been absolute but also because it reveals a tension that is endemic to American magnitude. The previous chapter established that magnitude must be revealed in order to have consequence. This chapter takes that further: Magnitude must be recognized by others. Claiming particular magnitude requires the existence of audiences who do not share in it—at least not fully—but who accept and accede to it. The underlying pattern in the OIAA's work—and its constant problem—was the pursuit of Latin American acquiescence to US American magnitude and to the United States' claim to be particularly American among Americans. Though OIAA staff and materials asserted that magnitude and sought to extend it, Latin American acquiescence to it also always eluded them.

In each of the previous chapters, US image-makers, audiences, and their mediators have presumed unidirectional vision and a centripetal definition of magnitude. They have looked at Latin America and used Latin American scenes to picture their own American consequence, but they have only occasionally imagined a counterpart looking back. They have certainly never imagined those counterparts asserting their own magnitude. Of course, the pictures themselves and their processes of creation call that assumption of privileged looking into question. Even as US image-makers have presumed a particular "right to look," their subjects have destabilized those assertions of grandeur and unmarked Americanness.[9] Quechua laborers and Peruvian soldiers stared back at Bingham's camera, observing and assessing. Quechua residents in the Urubamba valley and the Amazon basin watched Bingham's progress and gauged their moments of interaction carefully. Cuzqueño elites

---

8. For more on the need to center such critiques of imperialism, rather than presume an all-encompassing United States, see, for example, Levander and Levine, "Introduction"; Murphy, *Shadowing the White Man's Burden*.

9. Mirzoeff, *The Right to Look*.

visited Machu Picchu on their own terms, wove public stories that painted Bingham in unfavorable light, and took him to court to contest his vision of civilization. Likewise, the Kichwa pilgrims on the trailside in Church's *Heart of the Andes* may not themselves look out beyond the frame, but if viewers imagined themselves into the scene and walked along the path—as Church invited them to do—they could hardly presume to avoid curious eyes and whispered comments as they passed. And Church's diaries and letters make clear that Colombians and Ecuadorians were consistently alert to his actions and regularly facilitated or curtailed his opportunities for art-making. Kichwa guides looked at local conditions and determined what progress Church could make. Church's criollo interlocutors, in turn, took up their own brushes and offered their own visions of national landscape and their own theories of painting's power. And, of course, the Mexican soldiers and civilians pictured in letters and prints from the US-Mexican War not only looked back, they shot back. And they produced their own prints, photographs, letters, and spectacles that circulated within Mexico and beyond. To the extent that those looking from the perspective of the United States imagined themselves to look undisturbed, standing at the unquestioned center of America, they were imagining things.

But, of course, the image-makers themselves and at least some of their US audiences were aware that Latin Americans looked at the United States and weren't always pleased with what they saw. They knew that Latin Americans had their own sense of importance and consequence. Omitting that fact was a constitutive choice and racist habit as well as an act of oblivious imagining. US wartime audiences in 1846 could not conceive of Mexicans expanding their own territory farther north, but they knew that Mexicans objected to the invasion of their territory. Bingham spent significant time writing and speaking about how Latin Americans responded to the indignities of the Monroe Doctrine even as he failed to apply those insights to his own behavior.[10] Church's public, perhaps, managed to persuade itself that there was no one to look back at them, if Winthrop's framing is to be believed. However, Cyrus Field—Church's companion on his 1853 trip—was actively looking for business opportunities in South America. And markets require interlocutors.

While the soldiers, travelers, artists, and scientists of the previous chapters all—at least sometimes—positioned themselves as purveyors of new forms of sight and American benevolence (establishing newspapers and printing presses in conquered Mexican cities, teaching new painting techniques to criollo artists in Ecuador, and sponsoring scientific knowledge in Peru), those traveling image-makers would also have been aware of resistance, even

---

10. See, for example, Bingham, *The Monroe Doctrine*.

if they dismissed it as unjustified or uncouth. For as long as the United States has existed and certainly since the Monroe Doctrine, Latin Americans have looked critically at the colossus of the North.[11] Simón Bolívar and other leaders of the South American independence movements sometimes looked to the United States for inspiration, but they did so with a healthy dose of skepticism.[12] For one thing, the Monroe Doctrine had made quite clear that the United States would not declare itself an ally until after South American republics actually achieved independence.[13] The US-Mexican War put to rest any remaining beliefs about benevolent familial relations among the nations of the Americas. With the arrival of the twentieth century, Latin Americans frequently acknowledged the economic and military might of the United States, but they just as consistently called its culture, decency, and—most of all—its intentions into question. The rise of "big stick" diplomacy following the Spanish-American War and Theodore Roosevelt's presidency led Latin Americans across the continent and across socioeconomic strata to decry US imperialism, and they formed alliances to resist it. Latin Americans have, without question, actively and productively looked at the United States without being particularly enamored of what they saw. The accumulating consequence of US actions in Latin America may have made US hegemony in the region a palpable fact, but that didn't mean that Latin Americans appreciated it nor that they acquiesced to it as an inevitable outcome of the United States' particular American magnitude. Anyone in the United States who was paying the least bit of attention would have known that.

With the outbreak of World War II, however, critical glances from Latin America took on new significance for the United States. Suddenly, a Latin America at odds with the United States—even on cultural grounds—posed a threat to US security. Those Latin American nations might well become breeding grounds for "fifth column" activities, policy makers fretted. Likewise, the economic and military weakness that US leaders saw in their Latin American counterparts potentially put the United States at military risk. As Franklin Delano Roosevelt made clear in his "Arsenal of Democracy" address, an Axis base in South America was a specter not to be considered. Suddenly, it mattered a great deal that Latin Americans not only look *at* the United States but that they look *to* it. The security of the United States, the Roosevelt administration suggested, might well depend on the "other American republics" acquiescing to the United States' place at the center of America and fol-

---

11. For more on this, see, for example, Saldívar, *Trans-Americanity*; Stern, "The Decentered Center."
12. Pividal, *Bolívar*; Ramírez Novoa, *Monroismo y Bolivarismo*.
13. Christa J. Olson, "But in Regard."

lowing its lead. For, arguably, the first time in US history, US leaders saw good and nearly (but not fully) equitable relations with Latin America as very much in US interests. Such relations were not just good for business or the moral obligation of good neighbors, but critical to the safety and security of the United States.¹⁴ As world war loomed, the US government needed people in the United States to see Latin Americans as their neighbors and wanted Latin Americans across countries and social spectra to look to the United States as not only a good neighbor but an ideal one—a nation to follow, admire, and emulate.¹⁵

Enter the Office of the Coordinator of Inter-American Affairs. This wartime agency was formed as part of the State Department by executive order in July 1941. It was led by Nelson D. Rockefeller throughout its existence.¹⁶ The OIAA was charged with the task of "formulating and executing a program which, by effective use of Governmental and private facilities in such fields as the arts and sciences and education, will strengthen the bonds between the nations of the Western Hemisphere."¹⁷ That mission, as Monica A. Rankin emphasizes, always presumed that hemispheric unity would be led by the United States.¹⁸ The OIAA was, in other words, primarily concerned with the rhetorical coordination of Latin American acceptance of US primacy. That

---

14. See, for example, "Report on Conference," 2.

15. See, for example, "Report on Conference," 3. In a chapter written after World War II, looking retrospectively at US-Latin American relations, Rockefeller bemoaned the failure of US leaders in Latin America, especially businesspeople, to concern themselves with the people around them. Giving examples of investment in local conditions, Rockefeller repeatedly suggested that such investments would result in better relationships more broadly. He also warned that people across the Americas looked to the United States and resented anything that stood in the way of their efforts to emulate US lifeways. See, for example, Rockefeller, "Chapter II," 30, ch. 2 outline 2, ch. 2 outline 3.

16. The OIAA was preceded in its role by the Office for Coordination of Commercial and Cultural Relations Between the American Republics (OCCCRBAR), which was created by the Council of National Defense the previous summer (August 1940). The OIAA took over the OCCCRBAR's responsibilities but had greater latitude for its work and a new home—the Office for Emergency Management in the Executive Office of the President. The agency's name was changed to Office of Inter-American Affairs in 1945. The National Archives uses the acronym OIAA to refer to the entire four-year history of the office, and I follow suit, though historical documents sometimes use CIAA or OCIAA rather than OIAA. Nelson Rockefeller headed both the OCCCRBAR and the OIAA. When Rockefeller left the office at the end of the war, his deputy, Wallace K. Harrison, became director. The activities of the office were quickly curtailed following the return of peacetime norms and the OIAA was finally closed and its remaining functions returned to the State Department in spring 1946. Anthony, *Records of the Office of Inter-American Affairs*, 1, 5, 7.

17. A common variation of a contract clause for the OIAA; this one is taken from an October 16, 1941, contract with the Museum of Modern Art. "Memorandum of Agreement" 1941.

18. Rankin, *¡México, La Patria!*

investment in US preeminence, Rankin notes, is spread across every piece of propaganda the agency created, frequently undermining its effectiveness. The frameworks of American magnitude, in other words, both authorized and troubled the OIAA's work.

Cramer and Prutsch, in their comprehensive overview of the OIAA records in the National Archives, note that the OIAA's efforts were directed to audiences in the United States and in Latin America but emphasize that the agency's message changed in subtle ways depending on where one encountered their materials. For audiences in the United States, "the OIAA sought to inspire a 'sympathetic understanding' of Latin America and a positive interest in the region as an object of study, travel, or investment."[19] In the "other American republics," OIAA efforts combined propaganda, economic development, and demonstrations of military prowess with a consistent effort to "evoke a unifying spirit and identity of the Americas."[20] US viewers were to cultivate sympathy and understanding toward Latin America. Latin Americans, looking north, were invited to affiliate themselves with the United States. Though the OIAA had this dual audience, its efforts to shape US visions of Latin America cannot be extricated from the labor of framing the United States for Latin American viewers. The two audiences received divergent messages, but they worked toward the same end: The United States would accept its place at the forefront of America and the other American republics would fall into place behind it. The American republics, together, would lead the world, on the United States' terms and in a US model.

The OIAA's purpose, writ large and extending across all of its activities, was to pursue American visuality—the production of oversight and wide-ranging hemispheric vision.[21] The records of these efforts, held at the US National Archives and the Rockefeller Archives Center, are rife with visual objects and visual projects that support and sustain that visuality. In explicitly visual endeavors (e.g., art exhibits and film projects) and seemingly nonvisual ones (e.g., the fifty-nine "Coordination Committees" made up of US citizens living in urban centers across Latin America), the OIAA "[kept] a watchful eye on" Latin America while seeking to draw Latin American eyes northward.[22] This chapter features three of those explicitly visual projects: the health and literacy films already introduced, a touring exhibit of [US] American fine art, and two feature-length films coproduced by Disney and the OIAA. These projects are

---

19. Cramer and Prutsch, "Nelson A. Rockefeller's Office of Inter-American Affairs," 795.
20. Cramer and Prutsch, "Nelson A. Rockefeller's Office of Inter-American Affairs," 796.
21. Mirzoeff, *The Right to Look*.
22. Cramer and Prutsch, "Nelson A. Rockefeller's Office of Inter-American Affairs," 788, 791.

representative of the OIAA's larger operations: They are fundamentally committed to fostering hemispheric vision in which people in the United States look generously *at* Latin America and people in Latin America look expectantly *to* their undisputed leader, the great United States of America.

Presenting those three projects, I map three fronts along which the OIAA sought to train Americans to look properly at one another and to the United States: education, exchange, and entertainment. On each front, the OIAA's hemispheric vision of American magnitude is fraught with conflict and contradiction. The OIAA sought to focus hemispheric vision, yet its control consistently slipped. Latin American viewers, repeatedly and recalcitrantly, saw something other than US American greatness in the pictures the OIAA provided to them. To the extent that American magnitude required outside affirmation, its full culmination was always withheld. The OIAA's work may, indeed, have fostered opportunities for Latin Americans to look *to* the United States. However, that gaze was often a look *askance*—obliquely and from the corner of the eye. Latin Americans, gazing north, took in the grandeur they were supposed to see, and then they gave it definite side-eye.

The OIAA's Hemispheric Rhetorical Problem

Early in his presidency, Franklin Delano Roosevelt called for a new era of US-Latin American relations framed not in the now-tired terms of the Monroe Doctrine nor his cousin's imperialist "Corollary," but in terms of neighborly relations. Mary Stuckey has argued persuasively that the frame of the "good neighbor" fit not only Franklin Roosevelt's foreign policy but his presidency in general, and it had lasting effects. From the Roosevelt administration on, Stuckey argues, "the federal government, dominated by the presidency, was a significant force in American life, and the United States was a significant force in the world."[23] Roosevelt's "good neighbor" policy introduced a new American version of international relations for which Latin America was both the test study and the pattern.

For the "other American republics" of Latin America, the good neighbor policy brought both consistency and change. On the one hand, Roosevelt's claim that the United States was "first among equals in a tiered system of global administration" was not a significant change for the hemisphere.[24] The suggestion of possible equality may have been welcome, but it still came

---

23. Stuckey, *The Good Neighbor*, 21.
24. Stuckey, *The Good Neighbor*, 23.

with the expectation that Latin American nation-states would recognize US preeminence. On the other hand, Roosevelt framed that relationship in new ways that did matter. They weren't "mere rhetoric." Roosevelt's "promise that the United States would no longer intervene in the affairs of its neighbors" didn't hold true. However, US intervention under Roosevelt took forms more coercive than violent, and the administration's stated commitment to nonintervention provided a significant brake on its responses to potential threats in Latin America.[25] In addition, Roosevelt sometimes suggested that not just the United States but the entire hemisphere "represented democracy at its best, and that the New World in general, and not just the United States, was the last best hope of civilization."[26] Occasionally, Roosevelt's United States would share the stage with its neighbors without needing to remind everyone that it was exceptional.

Of course, even if the good neighbor policy was benevolently framed, it still rested on presumptions of supremacy. As Rankin notes, US messages to Latin America defined a common "Americanness" around geographic location but also emphasized democracy as a quintessentially American characteristic, the root of American magnitude. And that democracy was always US American in character.[27] Ultimately, the Roosevelt administration's invocations of a hemispheric America "modeled a definition of American after the United States."[28] Inevitably, as Stuckey reminds us, "the metaphor of the good neighbor, while not as obviously paternalistic and damaging as some other alternatives, also served to mask many commitments to unequal and even imperialistic practices."[29] Roosevelt, Stuckey explains, consistently closed his eyes to the problems that his policies caused for Latin American republics. While extoling the virtues of democracy and the model that exceptional American democracy could provide for a post-Hitler world, Roosevelt was more than willing to overlook antidemocratic elements of his own nation's past and present. Less forgiving of others, he repeatedly demanded that Latin American republics acknowledge their own shortcomings.[30] American magnitude covered many sins, but mostly for the United States.

---

25. Stuckey, *The Good Neighbor*, 173. With regard to nonintervention, see, for example, Nelson Rockefeller's counsel to the State Department regarding how to deal with Argentina's support for the Axis. Rockefeller to US Secretary of State, September 7, 1944; Rockefeller to US Under Secretary of State, October 31, 1944.

26. Stuckey, *The Good Neighbor*, 175.

27. See, for example, Rockefeller to US Secretary of State, September 7, 1944.

28. Rankin, *¡México, La Patria!*, 164–65.

29. Stuckey, *The Good Neighbor*, 22.

30. Stuckey, *The Good Neighbor*, 23.

With US involvement in World War II looming, Roosevelt's promise not to intervene in the other American republics quickly wore thin. The OIAA became the face of both continued investment in "good neighbor" orientations and a more urgent, paternalistic wartime engagement. The OIAA, as Cramer and Prutsch put it, facilitated both "softer methods of persuasion and attraction and harder strategies of coercion to achieve given foreign policy goals."[31] It was responsible for coordinating interventions in Latin America and for making them palatable to the other American republics. OIAA intervention came in many forms, including pressure to acknowledge blacklists, targeted development and education projects, and a broader effort to hold the attention of Latin Americans. The OIAA did some covert work, but the vast majority of its work was intentionally public—it aimed to foster commonly held and widely shared feelings of hemispheric solidarity.[32] In this sense, the OIAA served as a public-oriented counterpart to US diplomatic efforts. Trade agreements and formal alliances were effective "good neighbor" strategies at the national level, but, Rankin explains, "those formal agreements frequently met a cool reception at the popular level."[33] Therefore, the OIAA took on the task of disseminating hemispheric solidarity to the Latin American masses.[34] This kinder, gentler, public intervention was, certainly, preferable to armed invasion and covert destabilization of governments (equally common in US foreign policy), but kinder, gentler intervention was still intervention.

The OIAA, then, had a clear rhetorical purpose. It also had a lingering rhetorical problem. People across Latin America had reasons to resent and mistrust the United States. Even those who had respect for US power and economic might had questions about its dignity and class and, by extension, its status as the preeminent American nation. For many Latin American elites, the United States was glitz, consumption, and force while Latin America was feeling, refinement, and grace. Persuading Latin Americans to look *to* the United States, not just *at* it, required moving the needle on both the macro issues of justified resentment and the micro issues of cultural divergence.

To persuade good Latin American neighbors into acquiescing to American magnitude, the OIAA engaged a full sensory press. Vision was the ubiquitous, predominant sense, but vision was always in tune with a broader panoply of bodily elements. Looking to America meant cultivating behavior, mold-

---

31. Cramer and Prutsch, "Nelson A. Rockefeller's Office of Inter-American Affairs," 806.
32. Cramer and Prutsch, "Nelson A. Rockefeller's Office of Inter-American Affairs," 794.
33. Rankin, ¡México, La Patria!, 64.
34. Rankin, ¡México, La Patria!, 64.

ing affect, promoting encounters (both physical and virtual), and generally putting people in touch with one another. Given the distances and numbers, vision often served as a proxy for all that. Pictures of many sorts flowed back and forth across the hemisphere. The artists, filmmakers, museum designers, government officials, and event participants involved in OIAA activities consistently and self-consciously articulated their encounters with the hemisphere in terms of neighborly feeling and American spirit. They presumed and pursued acceptance of American magnitude on US terms. Projects for education, exchange, and entertainment all took on that effort.

Training Whole, Literate Bodies

Education was at the heart of the OIAA's work, both in the United States and in Latin America. Even the exchange and entertainment projects explored below were also, ultimately, education projects. They taught Americans about each other and trained them to see one other as neighbors. For that reason, when considering the OIAA's "pedagogy of sight," we must begin with pedagogy itself.[35]

The OIAA curated a wide array of educational materials for use in the United States—pamphlets, resource lists for teachers, lecture circuits, and more. Those US-focused materials frequently equated exchange and education. They were designed to teach audiences in the United States, both children and adults, about their "neighbors" in the "other American republics." A project authorization supporting a series of "three descriptive films" about Latin America for distribution in the United States, for example, aimed "to provide the American public with a wider and more comprehensive view of the manner in which people of the other Americas live and their economic and social problems."[36] For the imagined US audience (white, middle class, educated), in other words, "economic and social problems" belonged to other Americans. To ensure hemispheric solidarity, Americans in the United States must develop benevolent understanding for their neighbors' struggles. US audiences did not need to learn skills, they needed to learn to be good neighbors to other Americans.

Those neighbors, however, apparently had a lot to learn. Promoting hemispheric solidarity frequently meant improving Latin American capacity. If the United States was to be first among equals, OIAA activities presumed, the

---

35. Jack, "A Pedagogy of Sight."
36. "Project Authorization. Identification No. MP-1302."

other American republics would need to rise to the occasion. OIAA educational materials consistently reveal an underlying investment in having Latin Americans look *to* the United States in order to achieve that progress. For imagined Latin American audiences (Brown, poor, isolated, etc.), social and economic problems were presented as endemic and degenerative. In order for true inter-American understanding to come to fruition, the OIAA presumed, Latin American audiences needed to learn social, cultural, and dietary behaviors sanctioned by the United States. That benevolent, paternalistic figure frequently appeared in OIAA films as a disembodied white hand wielding a corrective paintbrush and chuckling indulgently at Latin American foibles. There was no doubt—for the OIAA or its materials—who needed to be taught and who would do the teaching.

In such contexts, the educational purpose was not to exchange knowledge but to teach "other" Americans the tools for modern life that would allow them to emulate an idealized [US] America. The OIAA's foundational investment in a hemispheric solidarity grounded in US superiority and premised on paternalistic whiteness is inescapable here. Educational work directed toward Latin America, then, offers a particularly obvious place to begin an analysis of the OIAA's effort to shape hemispheric looking through the white-tinged lenses of US preeminence.

During World War II, the OIAA was the primary US office engaged in hemispheric education. Other agencies within the State Department took up "cultural and educational activities," but "while the [State Department's] Division of Cultural Affairs was running a rather timid program that was largely confined to the realms of cultural highbrows and academics, the OIAA's approach to culture and education was brasher, broader, and more openly concerned with foreign-policy objectives."[37] Nothing exemplifies that brash investment in popular education so much as the series of health and literacy films coproduced by the OIAA and the Walt Disney Company at the height of the war. It provides both representative anecdotes and particularly intense examples of OIAA intentions.

When considering the educational purpose of the OIAA-Disney films, it is nearly impossible to separate content learning, matters of bodily comportment, and incorporation of "modern" (read: white, US) values. For OIAA staff, taking up any one of those tasks meant engaging the others. Their consistent discussions of behavior, information, and modernity during the films' production remind us that the OIAA's purpose was never simply to teach literacy or basic hygiene. Those skills were aimed toward another end: one in which

---

37. Cramer and Prutsch, "Nelson A. Rockefeller's Office of Inter-American Affairs," 796.

Latin American (and to some extent Latinx) audiences would remain distinct from the United States but closely affiliated with and dependent upon it. That end required a whole-body education in Americanness. The OIAA relationship with the Walt Disney Company was premised on the understanding that Disney could reach not only hearts and minds but whole bodies in service of specifically *American* aims.

US publics of color, particularly Latinx publics, existed in a sort of limbo for the OIAA. Only rarely do they appear explicitly among potential audiences or representatives in OIAA discussions. However, they played a pivotal role in the development of the health and literacy project, serving as early test subjects for the films. Mexican Americans, especially, were also among the audiences that OIAA leaders imagined might benefit from the films after their use in Latin America. It is telling that Latinx publics in the United States appear as possible audiences in discussions of OIAA remedial educational projects but not in other efforts to promote hemispheric solidarity. The OIAA imagined both US-born Latinxs and Latin American migrants as deficient or incomplete hemispheric subjects rather than as representatives of already existing trans-American solidarity.[38] Their elision from OIAA frameworks makes patently clear the white supremacy infusing the image of the United States as a great, good neighbor.

That OIAA-Disney relationship began in 1941, when the OIAA Communications Committee approved a draft project authorization proposing the creation of a "Walt Disney Productions Film Unit" that might produce up to fifty-two short-subject motion pictures for the US government—the OIAA and beyond.[39] Based on need, those films "would include propaganda, entertainment, documentary, informative and training subjects."[40] The Walt Disney Company had already shown itself capable of these tasks, having produced similar films for the Canadian government.[41] But it wasn't just Disney's past experience that made it a desirable partner. OIAA staff saw animation as a particularly persuasive and appealing medium, a feature essential to the success of any mass education project. While it is unclear whether the Productions Unit was ever approved, at least a reduced version of it was green-lit by the State Department. Disney's subsequent role in the OIAA and across the US government was substantial. They produced training films for the armed services, propaganda films for circulation within the United States and abroad, and edutainment shorts for civilian populations. By 1943, government and

---

38. Flores and Villarreal, "Mobilizing for National Inclusion."
39. "Project Authorization."
40. "Project Authorization."
41. "Project Authorization."

military contracts accounted for 94 percent of Disney's output.[42] Walt Disney himself was a fierce advocate for [US] American values and a savvy businessman. His relationship with the US government served both purposes. Disney films projected "the unmixed blessings of technology, the exceptional status of the United States, the benevolence of authority figures and the virtues of submitting to them."[43] These ideas were "preached, openly and explicitly, in Disney edutainment films."[44] The films thus fit neatly into a hemisphere where US values and US good will were paramount.

Over the next five years, the OIAA's relationship with the Walt Disney Company was extensive, varied, and bureaucratically complex. From it flowed a stream of motion pictures created under at least three separate contracts: NDCar 110 (related to a survey tour of South America undertaken by Disney, which resulted in two feature-length films), OEMcr-108 (for a travelogue depicting the tour undertaken in NDCar 110), and OEMcr 107, which included agricultural films, propaganda, and the health and literacy project.[45] These contracts were frequently revised as circumstances changed. The purpose of the collaboration, however, remained consistent: The OIAA capitalized on Disney's good image in Latin America and the unique combination of propaganda, entertainment, and education that the Disney Studios produced. The "Walt Disney Productions Film Unit" project authorization puts it particularly forcefully: "It is believed that this project would provide a ready instrument for propaganda and instructional activities for the benefit of morale and defense in the Western Hemisphere."[46] Every OIAA-Disney project presumed that the Walt Disney Company, and Disney himself, were particularly adept at the combined affective, cognitive, and bodily education that the OIAA required in its pursuit of Latin American acquiescence to a US-led hemisphere.

In a memo written near the end of the OIAA's existence, the organizers of the health and literacy film project laid out a presumption that had been underlying the project all along: "The films must rate high in entertainment value. Adult illiterates, after a hard day's work, cannot be attracted, and their interest cannot be sustained, unless we offer entertainment as an inducement. This is proven beyond any doubt by the observation of our field parties."[47] Pleasurable vision meant willing bodies and engaged learners—even when their bodies were tired. An educational program that did not take account of

---

42. Roe, "The Canadian Shorts," 15.
43. Van Riper, introduction to *Learning from Mickey*, 2.
44. Van Riper, introduction to *Learning from Mickey*, 2.
45. Niles to McCarthy, August 4, 1942.
46. "Project Authorization."
47. "Adult Literacy Program," 2.

the bodies concerned was doomed from the start. And so, when the OIAA set out to teach literacy in Latin America, they aimed to craft modern, American, invested yet docile bodies that would be amenable to US vision. Ultimately, the Disney-OIAA health and literacy campaign never went beyond the testing phase. However, the testing period's materials, development, and uptake illustrate—robustly and in detail—the OIAA's bodily, affective educational project in Latin America. In all those materials, we see education by motion pictures imagined as urgent, as necessarily visual, and as having implications for individual bodies, national bodies, and the hemispheric body.

The idea for an OIAA literacy program emerged in fall 1942, when Dr. Enrique de Lozada, a special advisor to Rockefeller, suggested a meeting of Latin American and US educators to discuss a "campaign against illiteracy in the other American republics."[48] The OIAA quickly approached Disney, "in view of the high caliber of the training films" Disney had produced for the US Army and Navy.[49] Meanwhile, de Lozada continued to encourage the OIAA to sponsor collaboration among educators, emphasizing the need for adult literacy projects. He recommended projects aimed toward "practical simple improvement in the students' knowledge of living . . . such as health, nutrition, or some other fundamental interest."[50] From early on in the project, literacy, bodily health, and visual stimulus were knit together as essential, co-constitutive elements.

In early 1943, Disney representatives went to Central America and the Caribbean to learn about local educational systems and make plans for a film series that "could be adaptable to current educational methods and systems."[51] Rockefeller's argument to the House of Representatives appropriations committee at the time suggested that addressing illiteracy was crucial to hemispheric quality of life and hemispheric solidarity. He explained that illiteracy "is one of the big barriers to the rising standard of living in these countries" and that the films would be distributed most widely in those places "where illiteracy is holding back the economic development of the country."[52] The United States was, of course, the standard to which those countries were to rise. The Latin American places particularly targeted were invariably imagined as lower-class, darker-skinned, and Indigenous. Though urban working classes were sometimes invoked, the rural poor figured prominently in OIAA plans, the testing process, and the films themselves. US-Mexico borderlands

---

48. de Lozada to Gotaas et al., January 2, 1946, 1.
49. de Lozada to Gotaas et al., January 2, 1946, 1.
50. de Lozada to Gotaas et al., January 2, 1946, 1–2.
51. de Lozada to Gotaas et al., January 2, 1946, 2.
52. de Lozada to Gotaas et al., January 2, 1946, 2–3.

were also sometimes incorporated into this framework. "Holding back" economic development, in other words, was racialized here and in Latin America. It should not be surprising that the films produced to draw those racialized others up toward US standards were ultimately built around US, not Latin American, "current educational methods and systems."[53]

Production of the films began in earnest in fall 1943. At first, the educational advisory team for the films included experts from the United States and Mexico. The US-based experts were mostly university faculty with expertise in education and literacy.[54] The Mexican delegation included three educational experts: Eulalia Guzmán, a teacher who had directed a Mexican Literacy Campaign in 1923; Estella Soní, director of a school in Mexico City; and Guadalupe Cejudo, the Mexico City supervisor of schools. As planning for the films progressed, the Mexican educators argued that teaching Spanish-language literacy required a phonetic system. The US educators, in contrast, advocated for the "so-called global system, in which an entire sentence is presented to begin with."[55] In his report on the exchange, de Lozada succinctly concludes, "The latter system was finally incorporated in the film."[56] He also notes, parenthetically, that Guzman left the project in protest at that time.[57]

The following fall, the literacy and health films were taken to Mexico, Honduras, and Ecuador for field testing. The experts tasked with assessing the films' effectiveness in Latin America quickly reported back that they were a success, encouraging the project to move forward with a larger series of films. In Mexico, though, things did not go entirely smoothly. Guzman took her pedagogical concerns to the press and, in the process, positioned the program as "evidence of 'American Imperialism.'"[58] Though Mexican officials had seemed enthusiastic during the initial planning phase, the testing team arrived in Guadalajara to find that no testing subjects had been recruited. The "Subjective Report" on the field testing, presented soon after return to the United States, offered two explanations for that failure: lack of capacity among local Mexican officials and "the opposition of Miss Eulalia Guzman, which pro-

---

53. de Lozada to Gotaas et al., January 2, 1946, 2.
54. Dr. Mildred Wiese, who played an ongoing role in the project, was an expert in adult education. Dr. George Sanchez, a professor of education at the University of Texas, focused his research and advocacy on the rights of Indigenous and Mexican American students in public education. The group was later joined by Dr. Antonio Rebolledo, professor of education at Highlands University, who espoused more derogatory notions about the language-learning capacities and needs of socially marginal Spanish speakers.
55. de Lozada to Gotaas et al., January 2, 1946, 5.
56. de Lozada to Gotaas et al., January 2, 1946, 6.
57. de Lozada to Gotaas et al., January 2, 1946, 6.
58. de Lozada to Gotaas et al., January 2, 1946, 6.

duced a type of 'passive resistance' to the program."[59] Mexican leaders were, in other words, recalcitrant and lacking capacity—symptomatic of exactly the sort of "holding back" the OIAA aimed to ameliorate.

Despite those logistical issues, OIAA assessments of the testing program were roundly celebratory, describing dramatic uptake from targeted populations. Mexican officials may have been resistant to OIAA purposes, but their people were not. The "Subjective Report" noted that "it was interesting to note a marked change as the program developed. . . . Sullen and discouraged at first, they became cheerful and interested, making many sacrifices to come to class."[60] The final report on the literacy program likewise concluded, "Illiterate adults learn to read from films. Students enjoy this method of learning more than methods previously learned. Students, on finding they are learning to read, gain visibly in self-confidence and ambition."[61] Though the project subsequently went by the wayside as the war ended, this enthusiasm for literacy training through film as a source of dramatic hemispheric development speaks volumes. The leaders of the other American republics had fallen short in their previous efforts, but US pedagogical investment—bright, shining, and modern—produced results.

In the OIAA health and literacy films, "the advantages of knowing how to read and write" were consistently framed in terms of health and prosperity.[62] In total, Disney produced twelve films for two series: "Health for the Americas" and "Reading for the Americas." An English-language brochure introducing the "Health for the Americas" series frames the affective investments of the project in ways equally applicable to both series: The films' "main function is to arouse interest and awareness rather than teach detailed facts."[63] They did not neglect the teaching of facts, but those facts where carefully chosen and couched: "The health facts presented step by step are given factually without foreign symbolism or fantasy. . . . Emphasis throughout is placed on cause and reasons for health measures rather than on methods and procedures."[64] In practice, that focus on cause and effect meant a focus on individual choices: You drink dirty water, you get sick; you learn to read, you become more prosperous. Consistently, those choices aimed to incorporate viewers as healthy

---

59. Clark and Madison, "Subjective Report," 5. The report notes that Guzman had significant influence, having "[written] to the heads of education, State and Federal, in the Guadalajara area, denouncing the program and urging them to have no part in it."
60. Clark and Madison, "Subjective Report," 6.
61. de Lozada to Gotaas et al., January 2, 1946, 7–8.
62. Alstock to Disney, December 7, 1942.
63. "Health for the Americas."
64. "Health for the Americas."

members of a hemispheric whole. The "Subjective Report," for example, celebrates a moment when high school girls in Guadalajara watching a film about tuberculosis breathed in time with the film's instructions, participating in the enactment of healthy American bodies.[65]

It is noteworthy that, by omitting "methods and procedures," the films also omitted systemic and structural causes. The "Health for the Americas" film *Cleanliness Brings Health*, for example, sets an impoverished, struggling family alongside a stable, successful family and proceeds from the assumption that the former would become the latter if only they would change their behavior: raise their cooking surface off the ground, fence their animals, build a latrine, and wash their hands. The film, of course, takes no account of the financial investments necessary to make those changes, let alone the larger social, economic, and political forces that might have led one family to poverty and the other to plenty.

The four "Reading for the Americas" films were created to partner with two specific "Health for the Americas" films, and the six films were shown in conjunction during the testing. Not surprisingly, given that pairing, the "Reading for the Americas" films taught literacy and hygienic behavior in tandem, making bodily health and literate capacity nearly indistinguishable. In the films, reading and health are bodily matters and the health of the individual body and the social body are inextricable. Literacy is about how you look, what you drink, how you work, and how the human body functions. All these sensory engagements were presented as essential for modern life, and they modeled an American life patterned after the United States. The "Reading for the Americas" films taught those lessons of literate bodily comportment through a study in contrasts. A healthy, modern, virile "José" and a perpetually ill, impoverished, and befuddled "Ramón" each made choices around sanitation that had drastic implications for their lives. Learning to read alongside José and Ramón meant learning to read their choices and their bodies.

It will surprise no one that the depictions of "José" and "Ramón" play on the broadest stereotypes of Mexican culture and ethnicity. José, the model citizen, is muscular—Charles Atlas with short, neatly trimmed dark hair and clean, peach-colored skin (figure 4.1). He struts about the fields and house, working hard and eating well. He is active or poised for incipient action, but he is also something of an automaton. His facial expressions rarely change, and at one point he dutifully allows himself to be folded into a chair that magically appears behind him at the invitation of the unseen narrator. José is "un joven sano." He is compliant and literally pliable.

---

65. Clark and Madison, "Subjective Report," 8.

FIGURE 4.1. *Left*, José, still from *La Historia de José*, "Reading for the Americas" series, 1944. Produced by the Walt Disney Company for the Office of the Coordinator of Inter-American Affairs.

FIGURE 4.2. *Right*, Ramón, still from *La Historia de Ramón*, "Reading for the Americas" series, 1944. Produced by the Walt Disney Company for the Office of the Coordinator of Inter-American Affairs.

Ramón, on the other hand, is drawn to embody the "degenerate" Mexican (figure 4.2). His untidy hair and drooping mustache accompany disreputable clothes, light brown skin, a distinctly pear-shaped silhouette, and a befuddled expression. The second film about Ramón opens with him attempting to flee the scene, apparently tired of being the problem character. He is retrieved by the noticeably lighter-skinned fingers of the narrator. Ramón spends a good portion of the films lying in bed, too ill to get up, let alone work. His few trips outside the house take him to the bank of a river where he draws himself a dipper of microbe-infested water to drink. Though Ramón wears more clothing than José, he is repeatedly "undressed" by the films as they go into x-ray mode to show the troubling effects of microbes on his system. By the time the films get around to teaching whole-language sentences, it is already apparent that José is "un joven sano" (modern, ideal, and almost American) and Ramón is defined and confined by his actions: He "drinks bad water," makes bad choices, and embodies everything that holds Latin America back from its American ambitions.

Though pictures alone were not enough to achieve the films' ends, it is still true that what the films brought before their audiences' eyes had designs on not only literate knowledge but bodily comportment. And the ideal bodily comportment was modeled on and consistently served the interests of a US version of America. The "Subjective Report" joyfully shares the story of an Indigenous woman from rural Guadalajara who told the field-testing team,

"You know, I just love Ramon [sic]. I think he's such a dear, sweet, man, but I am very upset because last night I went home and dreamed all night about Jose [sic]. I must be in love with him."[66] If the field-testing team were inclined toward psychoanalysis, this familiar affection for Ramón and desire for José would be precisely what they were hoping for. Who wouldn't want to join José's American family?

The actual language teaching in the films corroborates that visual emphasis on American bodies and American ideals. The "Reading for the Americas" films taught "reading" by inviting their audience to identify, memorize, and repeat the words in a few basic sentences, starting with "José es un joven sano" and "Ramón toma agua mala" ("José is a healthy youth" and "Ramón drinks bad water"). For training films aimed at an illiterate, Spanish-speaking audience, this was a strange choice. There was no effort to introduce audiences to the sounds of the letters, which are always consistent in Spanish and crucial to beginning literacy. Phonetics had been dismissed along with Guzman. Instead, words were taught as isolated figures discernable by shape and size—short words and long words, words that start with curvy or looped letters. Each new vocabulary word stood on its own. Indeed, while teaching "José es un joven sano," the film failed to even note that "José" and "joven" started with the same letter and sound. And yet, one need not know that the "whole word" approach is problematic for teaching Spanish-language literacy to understand that the literacy taught in these films was, ultimately, in service of other ends. Even if an audience member left the hall with new confidence in their ability to recognize words and learn to read, they also left with fewer than a dozen words in their vocabulary—and they had gained no tools for deciphering new words encountered out in the world.

What they did gain, however, was a set of visual and sonic lessons in proper American behavior. The whole segment of "Ramón está enfermo" that is dedicated to identifying who drinks good water is emblematic of this theme. After introducing sentences such as "José toma agua buena" and "José no toma agua mala," the narrator asks the audience to remember first which water is good and which is bad—with pictures showing "agua buena" superimposed over a boiling kettle and "agua mala" across a stream. Then, having established which water is good and which is bad, the narrator shifts to identify which *characters* make good and bad choices, asking, "Who drinks good water?" and then showing the sentence the readers are supposed to be learning, "José toma agua buena," and asking them to read it back. In the film, the voices of a faux

---

66. Clark and Madison, "Subjective Report," 6.

audience respond aloud: "José toma agua buena," then "José come bien," and then "José no está enfermo."

"But Ramón . . . again?" continues the narrator, and Ramón appears, blissfully drinking water from the stream. With that reminder, the scene shifts and "Ramón está enfermo" appears across Ramón lying in bed. The imagined audience, in other words, is learning not only the words, not only the health practices, but also the types of people who do them. The next lesson reinforces this point. It shifts from specifics (José and Ramón) to types. The readers learn the sentence "Un enfermo no come bien." Suddenly, "a sick person" is a category and, quite clearly, a category they should avoid. Literacy, bodily comportment, and productive labor go hand in hand. When Ramón is finally cured, he stands and begins working steadily in his garden. The music and picture then fade out, ending with a drawing of the hemisphere. One last reminder of literacy's American, bodily purpose.

Ultimately, what José, Ramón, and the OIAA-Disney films reveal is that the OIAA's purpose was not to provide access to literacy for Latin American masses but to ensure that learning and progress happened in a particular mode—one modeled on US presumptions about proper bodies and individual choices. Though the United States appeared in the films only at the opening and closing credits, the presumption that health and literacy were valuable because they promoted productivity and progress quite clearly carried US American values, as did the film's emphasis on individual actors gaining individual benefits. The films, in other words, were stories of American magnitude premised on the model of the United States as the proper and preeminent embodiment of America.

Conversations about and reactions to the films corroborate that underlying investment in a hemisphere built on US American terms. Memos exchanged during the production of the films suggest that stakeholders had definite notions of what it meant to look *to* the United States. In one particularly evocative memo about a related project, Disney's agricultural motion picture, *The Soybean,* a consultant drew attention to the difference between looking *at* and looking *to.* Homer N. Calver, invited to comment on the draft film, recognized that it was meant to impart US-based values about farming and nutrition (looking *to*), but, in his estimation, the current version asked Latin American viewers to look *at* the United States as well. That error, he thought, would impede the film's larger goal of influencing agricultural practice. The barn shown early in the film, he wrote, "is a fine looking American barn," but "not typical, I believe of the type of barns which a Latin American farmer would have."[67] Likewise, images of a typical diet received a curt "It is

---

67. Calver to Edwards, July 1, 1943, 1.

doubtful that this is a normal diet in most parts of Latin America," and he inquired, "Why recommend soybeans as a substitute for foods they don't eat, can't get and don't want?"[68] Throughout his review, Calver expressed confidence that Latin Americans needed US agricultural knowledge, but he argued that they had to encounter that knowledge couched in Latin American contexts. In Calvert's assessment, looking to the United States from Latin America meant looking at appropriately Latin American scenes but from a distinctly US perspective. That same presumption infused every educational film made by Disney and the OIAA.

Speaking of the health films before an audience of mostly OIAA staff, Dr. Thomas Mackie made explicit the US values meant to be transmitted through those films. Noting that their Latin American audience would include "skilled urban workers and Indians," Mackie explained that "they have no foundation of scientific facts on which our modern medicine is based."[69] The first of the facts that Mackie presented, however, was only a fact within a Western, individualistic paradigm: "(1) personal responsibility for health: man's share in taking care of himself."[70] The films, in other words, began from—and sought to inculcate—the presumption that the individual was the prime locus of action and interaction. That entirely Euro-US ideological framework promulgated a story of American magnitude founded on the great (white) man achieving great things—the *megethos* of Church and Bingham, not that of the guides who saw them safely to their goals.

Those same individualist American values were equally palpable in the "Reading for the Americas" films. Even the choice to focus on "health" in order to teach literacy signals a US perspective. One group of expert reviewers, for example, pointed out that "health" was a rather abstract concept that might not have much appeal, "especially in countries where there is not the same obsession to be healthy as in the United States."[71] Such criticism did not, however, change the OIAA's direction. The films continued to present abstract values informed by distinctly US ideologies as models for emulation by Latin American audiences. In a memo to Walt Disney offering critical guidance on the proposed literacy program, another advisor noted that, even if literacy was the basic goal of the program, its economic and propaganda benefits merited emphasis.[72] Presenting healthy, virile José as the figure to be emulated meant holding up not only the lighter-skinned and more "modern" character but

---

68. Calver to Edwards, July 1, 1943, 1.
69. "Statements at the Preview of Health Films," 2.
70. "Statements at the Preview of Health Films," 2.
71. Clark to Harrison, May 30, 1945, 4.
72. Cutting to Disney, n.d.

also the character whose underlying values of productivity and bodily health aligned directly with those of the United States. José and those who emulated him looked to the United States.

The insistence on literacy and health in service of economic progress should be unsurprising. After all, in the mid-twentieth century, projects actually seeking to promote literacy and political empowerment among marginalized groups were more likely to be organized by social movements than government agencies. In the United States at that moment, literacy tests disenfranchised African American and Mexican American communities, and literacy campaigns would soon become crucial organizing tools. Across Latin America, likewise, though government agencies offered literacy programs, many republics used literacy requirements to disenfranchise racialized groups, and grassroots literacy campaigns were frequently met with violence.[73] Even if contemporary literacy scholarship shows us that literacy's consequences are limited and highly inflected by state power, these social movements across the Americas wielded literacy training for political effect. They, too, were often invested in ends other than language proficiency, and they were squashed by state power in response.

And so, we return at last to Sodi de Pallares's apparently but not actually isolated voice of critique to acknowledge what she recognized all along: It was not the films' dubious ability to teach literacy that ought to raise Latin American eyebrows but rather the underlying presumptions of what it meant, looked like, and felt like to read as Americans. The project's concern for proper comportment, proper reading, and proper looking invited audiences to look to the United States as exemplar and guide. Its obvious reliance on white, Euro-US preeminence also, however, made space for Latin American audiences to look askance. And many did. Even beyond Guzman's campaign to discredit the films, some of the positive responses appearing in the OIAA files suggest a sidelong sort of participation in hemispheric solidarity, one that refused to fully accept American magnitude on US terms. An article in Quito, Ecuador's conservative newspaper, *El Comercio*, for example, celebrated the OIAA visit but framed it firmly within local successes. Its August 1944 article about the project, "6.500 analfabetos adultos en toda la república aprenden a leer y escribir," asserted that the OIAA chose to conduct tests in Ecuador because local groups had already made significant progress themselves.[74] The "6,500" of the article's title had been taught not by the OIAA, but by the Ecuadorian Union Nacional de Periodistas (UNP; National Journalists' Union). *El Com-*

---

73. For examples from Ecuador, see for example, A. Kim Clark, "Racial Ideologies"; Christa J. Olson, *Constitutive Visions*; Rodas, *Crónica de Un Sueño*.

74. "6.500 Analfabetos."

ercio presented the OIAA representatives as visitors who learned from local literacy experts.[75] In a related article, *El Comercio*'s writer concludes, "Ecuador is the first county to serve as a site for these tests because the Campaign carried out by the UNP is one of the best that has been carried out in any country. If the experience here indicates that the method is effective, then it will be implemented in various countries, including the United States and other hemispheric nations."[76] The OIAA wanted Latin American audiences to watch the literacy and health films and come to behave like a very particular sort of Americans, tacitly acknowledging US dominance. Working askance, some of those audiences—including Eulalia Guzman, María Elena Sodi de Pallares, and the writers at *El Comercio*—recentered American magnitude southward.

Exchanging Glances

Under the auspices of the OIAA, individuals, groups, objects, and ideas were directed back and forth across the hemisphere throughout the war years. *Relationship* was the basic currency of hemispheric solidarity. In line with the Roosevelt administration's position, the OIAA understood the hemisphere to be fundamentally in relation already—sharing histories, beliefs, and values. Hemispheric unity required recognizing and living into that relationship as imagined by the United States.[77] Individuals must be brought to see one another, interact with one another, and recognize one another as sharing American identities.[78] In an interview after his visit to Mexico in conjunction with the OIAA, Walt Disney highlighted precisely this investment when he explained that the "relationship between our peoples will be further improved when they learn more about their mutual culture, art, music, and ways of living generally."[79] Where Bingham had critiqued the Monroe Doctrine largely on the basis that the American nation-states were fundamentally heterogeneous, the OIAA and its affiliates imagined a shared America premised on mutual appreciation and recognition. What they had in common, though, were always those aspects of history, culture, and ways of living that were modeled after the United States.

The OIAA's investment in exchange was also a direct response to its enduring rhetorical problem. If Latin Americans were skeptical of US intentions,

---

75. "6.500 Analfabetos."
76. "Expertos."
77. Rankin, *¡México, La Patria!*, 66.
78. Rankin, *¡México, La Patria!*, 64; "Report on Conference," 3.
79. "Disney Finds US-Mexico Bond Strong."

then building interpersonal connections and staging genuine mutual interest were crucial strategies for shifting Latin American gazes. There is paradox here: Visits by Latin Americans to the United States and by US nationals to Latin America were intended simultaneously to allay Latin American concerns about US arrogance and persuade Latin Americans that the United States was, indeed, preeminently American.

To achieve that end, OIAA staff carefully managed their office's visibility when coordinating exchange. Their funding required that the US government receive some credit, but they were well aware that excessive emphasis on government involvement could taint the apparent authenticity of the relationships built. OIAA staff also recognized, though, that judicious use of prominent US citizens could demonstrate respect and investment. For this reason, the question of how much to say, where to say it, and who should do the saying recurs across OIAA files. At major events, a radio address from Rockefeller or a speech by a US ambassador could set just the right tone.[80] At other times, the OIAA stepped back, allowing visitors to shine on their own. The US ambassador to Mexico, for example, urged the OIAA to walk quietly in promoting Walt Disney's visit in December 1942, commenting that "the connection of the Office of the Coordinator with the trip should not be in any way publicized."[81] Good American relationships meant curating exactly who was understood to be in relationship—and the US government was often not the best choice of partner. This fact can be seen in sharp relief in the Sodi de Pallares editorial that opens the chapter, where Walt Disney's reputation remains above the fray while the meddling of the United States is excoriated. Indeed, Sodi de Pallares seemed quite willing to acquiesce to Disney's American preeminence, celebrating the "technical and artistic potential" of the United States.[82] Much as that interaction caused trouble for them, OIAA staff repeatedly found Disney's untarnishable reputation helpful for promoting its American project.

The education programs discussed above prioritized popular audiences and tended to approach Latin America explicitly in terms of its lack. Most exchange programs, however, imagined a professional, upper-class Latin American audience. Though OIAA-sponsored exchange still promoted hemispheric values from the perspective of the United States, it was typically premised on an encounter among (near) equals. The underlying assumption was that equals would, of course, quickly recognize the value of US leadership. Equality need not stand in the way of preeminence—at least not from the

---

80. See, for example, Braden, "Translation of Speech by the Ambassador"; McCray to Harrison, October 9, 1941; Pierce to Caldwell, May 4, 1944.
81. Messersmith to US Secretary of State, November 28, 1942.
82. Sodi de Pallares, "Genialidad de Walt Disney."

perspective of those declaring themselves preeminent. Thus, when contemporary Latin American art was brought to tour the United States, the OIAA's art world consultants regularly weighed in on aesthetic quality—expressing reservations about popular Latin American artists' caliber or surprise at the overall quality of a given show. After previewing a selection of contemporary Chilean artwork, for example, Blakemore Godwin, director of the Toledo Museum of Art, commented, "They are far better than we had expected. . . . If the rest approach what we have seen, I think we could make a selection that would go over in the US—would not get any more slaps than any other contemporary show."[83]

On the other hand, when the art division sent exhibits of contemporary US art to tour major Latin American cities, their concern was to avoid pictures that would give cultural offense. There was no expectation that Latin American critics might find the art itself lacking. When those critiques did appear, they were uniformly interpreted as political rather than aesthetic in nature.[84] In general, US representatives presumed that the appeal of US art was universal. The US ambassador to Chile commented at the opening for an exhibit there, for example, "In the recent generations some of the greatest painters and sculptors of the world have been North Americans."[85] The ambassador must have been walking on dangerous ground with that claim, yet despite his diplomatic training, he showed no awareness that Chileans might dispute his assumptions about where greatness lay.

Other State Department representatives were more subtle in their approach. In a radio interview given during an exhibit in Peru, Stanton Catlin, the OIAA representative traveling with the show, used his response to the question "How has the exhibition of American painting been received in Lima?" to highlight the kind of engagement he saw as most valuable, framing it as a signal of the high cultural knowledge of their Peruvian hosts. "I have been deeply impressed," he explained, "by the way in which people here have tried to appreciate these works of art of my country not only from their own points of view but by imagining the points of view of the artists who painted them, sensing the life and conditions which influenced them, grasping the ideas and emotions which inspired them."[86] In short, Catlin recognized that local perspectives were different from those of the United States, acknowledged the validity of those perspectives, but marked as particularly valuable

---

83. Godwin to Adams, September 25, 1941.
84. See, for example, Office of the Coordinator of Inter-American Affairs, "The Unpopularity of Modern Art."
85. Bowers to US Secretary of State, October 1, 1941.
86. Catlin, interview by Radio Nacional.

the capacity to look from another's perspective. He invited Peruvian viewers to inhabit US perspectives in order to best understand the art. Such practice in viewing from a US perspective did not negate the Peruvian point of view, but it suggested that US things should be viewed from US perspectives. Given what we know about the OIAA's larger orientation, we can sense an implicit message here: Latin Americans were invited to take up US ways of seeing while viewing an array of matters that "belonged" to the United States, the nature and import of "America" among them.

Later in the interview, Catlin explained the overall purpose of the exhibit in a way that corroborates this implication. The exhibit had been touring major Latin American cities "in order to bring the people and the artists of these countries an impression of the life of the United States as seen by its artists and at the same time to show the styles, techniques, and artistic points of view being developed today in the United States."[87] "It is also hoped," Catlin continued, "that this will be the beginning of broad activities in artistic exchange between my country and yours and other American countries."[88] Mutual respect and recognition were, in other words, the aim. The interviewer immediately picked up on the one-sided nature of the current exhibit, commenting, "May I ask if you think it is possible for an exhibition of Peruvian art to go to the States in the near future in exchange for the present exhibition of United States art?"[89] Catlin had presented the exhibit as a gift from the United States, inviting Peruvians to look at and to the United States. The interviewer reversed Catlin's premise—presenting Peruvian hosts as having given the gift and wondering when the United States would reciprocate and look at and to Peru. This is subtle stuff, but in the interviewer's reversal we can see that they very clearly caught Catlin's message, reading it both in terms of a long history of US presumption and in the less overt but still palpably one-sided terms of the good neighbor. The interviewer, drawing Peruvian gazes back south, deprived US American magnitude of the appreciation it demanded.

If most OIAA exchange programs worked from that tenuous and fraught presumption of being a leader among equals, Walt Disney was a somewhat different case. His visits to Latin America under OIAA auspices were more condensations of OIAA purpose than representative anecdotes for it. No one claimed to be Disney's equal: He was an American paragon. This freed the OIAA to attach their interests to Disney's and not worry as much about accusations of arrogance. Disney was consistently presented in Latin American media as respectful and decorous, an affable visiting noble whose generosity

---

87. Catlin, interview by Radio Nacional.
88. Catlin, interview by Radio Nacional.
89. Catlin, interview by Radio Nacional.

was to be welcomed. His visits to South America included opportunities for Latin American artists to learn from, visit with, and even work alongside Disney's staff, while Disney himself played the role of ambassador par excellence.

Disney's ambassadorial travels in Latin America were crucial to the OIAA. They dramatically expanded the reach and impact of exchange. On one level, exchanges organized around Walt Disney were much like others facilitated by the OIAA: He went, he visited, he met influential people, and his presence was chronicled in local media. Disney drew media attention wherever he went, and his presence and art were widely celebrated. His sponsorship by the OIAA was frequently mentioned, but relegated to later paragraphs. Disney presence, however, consistently advanced OIAA efforts. In a message sent back to the art division in October 1941, Catlin mentioned the salubrious effects of a chance visit by Disney to the exhibit of US contemporary art in Santiago, Chile. He commented, "Walt Disney has been here. He came to the exhibition on Wednesday last, was mobbed by a thousand people, completely delirious, who nevertheless bought slews of catalogues [from the exhibit] for his autograph. He had himself photographed standing by the Dike and Sheets watercolors—two artists who have worked in his studio."[90] Disney's presence, in this case, raised the value of the exhibit for visitors, granting it extra luminescence and encouraging visitors to view the art in light of his admiration for it. Not every visitor who requested Disney's autograph on a copy of the exhibit catalogue would look at the catalog in new ways, but there was, nevertheless, an imprimatur of idealized Americanness brought to it. Likewise, the Mexico City magazine *Población* clearly received (and amplified) that message when it chronicled Disney's visit to Mexico in early 1943. In addition to commenting on the particular glamour of Disney's visit, the article extended the circle of admiration, expressing gratitude to the OIAA, Nelson Rockefeller, and Francis Alstock (director of the motion picture division) and naming such sponsored visits as "an important factor in the growing closeness between our two peoples."[91] Disney was a pivot point for exchange, and the OIAA gladly made use of his particularly grand Americanness.

However, though Disney's in-person appeal was significant and certainly advanced the OIAA's aims, his visits had another benefit that made Disney's Latin American exchanges particularly powerful and wide-ranging: They were reproduced and circulated through film. Not only did news reels capture and distribute Disney's time in Latin America, but Disney himself incorporated the visits into his work. Indeed, his travels in Latin America were

90. Catlin to Lyford, October 3, 1941.
91. "Walt Disney Nos Visita," 37.

always presented as opportunities for gathering new material, not just glad-handing. Part of *Población*'s enthusiasm for Disney's presence was the promise that Disney would be creating a new and authentically Mexican character to appear alongside Donald Duck and José Carioca in the feature-length film that would eventually become *Three Caballeros*.[92] And *Three Caballeros* itself reproduced the theme of exchange, inviting viewers who might never have left their home region or shaken hands with a visiting dignitary to imagine themselves building relationships alongside Donald, José, and the Mexican rooster, Panchito Pistola. In promoting *Three Caballeros*, OIAA staff members were clearly thinking in terms of such virtual exchange. One extensive memo about publicity proposed an essay contest on the theme "Why I like the Three Caballeros" that would extend both imagined and actual hemispheric exchanges. Submitters might, Russell Pierce of the motion picture division mused, be asked to prepare their essays in the languages of all three main characters (English, Spanish, and Portuguese), thus actively participating in virtual exchange through language as well as imagining it by reflecting on the film. The winners would be awarded an actual tour across the three countries.[93] This was a unique and powerful feature of Walt Disney's work for the OIAA—exchange could happen through visual, sonic, and embodied forms even when participants in the exchange remained in their home communities. And those exchanges would be framed in Disney's particularly and enthusiastically [US] American light.

Writing of the Mexican context specifically, Rankin suggests that the OIAA missed an opportunity for successful propaganda because it insisted on a message tied to US-led Pan-Americanism.[94] Appeals to Mexican nationalism, Rankin argues, would have been much more effective.[95] The OIAA files corroborate Rankin's assessment. The OIAA's exchange programs may well have solidified the vision of a US-led hemisphere among white audiences in the United States who viewed art exhibits and saw Disney films.[96] In Latin America, however, we see consistent reassertions of national pride and cultural distinctiveness. Audiences there regularly refused to view the hemisphere entirely on US terms. In addition to explicit objections to the

---

92. "Walt Disney Nos Visita," 36–37.
93. Pierce to Caldwell, April 25, 1944, 6.
94. Rankin, *¡México, La Patria!*, 11.
95. Rankin, *¡México, La Patria!*, 7.
96. Visitors to the OIAA-sponsored exhibit of Chilean contemporary art and another OIAA traveling exhibit of Latin American art in the United States clearly understood hemispheric solidarity through the lens of the "good neighbor" policy, with its equal presumptions of unity and leadership. See, for example, Dings to Godwin, July 15, 1942; Lanier to Rockefeller, June 23, 1942.

exchanges—which the OIAA often explained in terms of Nazi sympathies—OIAA efforts were also met with subtler but equally forceful assertions of distinction. The article in *Población*, mentioned above, celebrates the particularly rich culture and environment of Mexico, suggesting that Disney found there "a vigorous contribution to his art that has been profoundly established in every community around the world."[97] The article, thus, stakes its own claim on Disney rather than encouraging its readers to align themselves with Disney as an exemplar of US values. Likewise, the OIAA files contain two copies of an excerpt from a confidential report in which the author expresses concern that Uruguayans will be disappointed with *Three Caballeros* because it, like *Saludos Amigos,* failed to even mention Uruguay. Though *Saludos* had done well there, "the movie-going public of that small country, now so closely allied to the United States, resented the fact that Uruguay was conspicuous by its absence in *Saludos,* not even mention being made of them, let alone a short pictorial sequence" And, the author continued, "I feel certain that they will resent the fact that again in [*Three Caballeros*] Uruguay is left out entirely."[98] The potential for such resentment signals a presumption of national dignity and pride of place that may accept US leadership as inevitable but remains skeptical of it. These small signs make clear—perhaps even more than the vociferous denunciations offered more rarely—that Latin Americans recognized US purpose and even sometimes accepted it, but also consistently pushed it off-center and out of focus. Latin Americans managed simultaneously to celebrate the connections made, appreciate Disney's films (and the other art, music, and commercial products highlighted by OIAA programs), and recognize that their Northern interlocutors were not particularly good neighbors. The OIAA's underlying presumptions did not go unnoticed and, in response, Latin Americans consistently approached the relationships offered by sidling into them, looking askance.

Entertaining Magnitude

For the OIAA, the appeals of working with Disney were many. The Walt Disney Company brought significant experience, positive global name recognition, exemplary commitment to US values, and, as this section will emphasize, an incredible mass appeal. Disney's films—no matter their purpose—were consistently entertaining, and they always drew eyes. That allure had advan-

---

97. "Walt Disney Nos Visita," 36.
98. "Excerpt from Confidential Report."

tages for Disney's participation in education and exchange projects, of course, but it also became an end in itself for the OIAA. As Cramer and Prutsch note, "Striving to win Latin American hearts and minds on the cultural and spiritual high ground . . . did not prevent the OIAA from simultaneously seeking to exploit the attractions of US popular culture for increasingly broad audiences south of the Rio Grande," promoting a "less serene, or even frolicking, side of US civilization."[99] OIAA staff understood that their American purpose could be achieved through many means. Nearly every project authorization prepared for a contract with the Walt Disney Company invoked this aspect of the company's appeal. Disney's motion pictures were "Ambassador[s] of Good Will" that would "emphasize the unity of our peoples and the common bond existing by virtue of mutual appreciation of the world famous Disney characters."[100] Such projects would "take advantage of Disney's good will and prestige which are unique the world over" and well tuned to draw audiences and approbation.[101] The OIAA was confident that getting eyes on Disney films would create an enormous amount of positive public feeling. And that public feeling would accrue not only to Disney but also to the United States. What Disney brought before their eyes would help Latin Americans look to the United States and appreciate its particular magnitude.

Disney's brand of entertainment filled an essential niche in the OIAA mission: It was readily adapted to persuasive purpose. Disney's "edutainment," even before the term was coined, was essentially an affective theory of persuasion. It presumed that seeing, identifying, understanding, and feeling were deeply connected and that people learned through sensation rather than cognition. Especially when the OIAA considered popular—rather than elite—audiences, full body engagement became essential. As I have already noted, this aspect of mass appeal was discussed explicitly in preparation for the literacy films, where attraction, attention, and sustained engagement were predicated on visceral appeal.[102] But Disney's ability to engage a wide audience in hemispheric understanding was also consistently treated as a matter of sensations and feelings when OIAA staff discussed Disney's OIAA-supported feature films—*Saludos Amigos* and *Three Caballeros*—as well. Russell Pierce's plan for promoting *Three Caballeros* in Latin America, for example, noted that "The Three Caballeros" themselves (meaning Donald, José, and Panchito)

---

99. Cramer and Prutsch, "Nelson A. Rockefeller's Office of Inter-American Affairs," 796–97.
100. "Project Authorization. Disney Trip to Mexico."
101. "Project Authorization. Walt Disney Field Survey."
102. "Adult Literacy Program," 2.

"offer[ed] exceptional opportunity for a human and colorful promotion job."[103] Here, though Pierce had just warned that the OIAA could not sponsor "pure entertainment," it is clear that the motion picture division saw Disney's multi-sensory appeal as essential for establishing the "real hemispheric cooperation" at the heart of the OIAA's mission.[104] Donald, José, and Panchito, embodying American interaction, would also promote [US] American ends.

The need to balance persuasive purpose and entertainment value appears throughout OIAA discussion of its relationship with Disney. A mass audience required entertainment, but the message of hemispheric cooperation had to come through above all else. Ultimately, then, entertainment became a carrier—a rhetorical capsule that would deliver benevolent, desirable, US-led hemispheric solidarity. In this sense, not only was persuasion a visceral phenomenon—made possible through engaging bodies—but hemispheric solidarity was as well. Audiences in Latin America needed to feel close to the United States. They needed to find themselves laughing at the same things as their neighbors throughout Latin America and their neighbors to the north. Pierce's promotion campaign was full of opportunities for audiences to be aware of themselves as hemispheric audiences. Building from a plan to have *Three Caballeros* premiere simultaneously in the United States, Mexico, and Brazil, Pierce recommended a shortwave radio pickup between the three countries "broadcast in three languages simultaneously to all of them" that would generate mutual awareness of watching alongside others.[105] Being engaged as audiences—watching, listening, laughing—and being aware of oneself as part of a larger American audience that was also watching, listening, and laughing, would not just produce hemispheric solidarity, it was hemispheric solidarity enacted.

That sort of extended, shared participation in the hemisphere wasn't the initial plan for the OIAA-Disney collaboration. The OIAA contract that ultimately resulted in *Saludos Amigos* and *Three Caballeros* started off as an agreement for twelve shorts on Latin American themes, emphasizing a US audience over a hemispheric one. Very quickly, however, plans changed and Disney began work on what would become *Saludos Amigos*. The contract was revised in 1943 to stipulate three "packages" rather than twelve shorts. This shift in the plan is important to note on two fronts: (1) It moved the contract's emphasis more toward entertainment than education and (2) it more clearly encompassed a hemispheric audience without decentering US control over American stories.

---

103. Pierce to Caldwell, April 25, 1944, 2.
104. Pierce to Caldwell, April 25, 1944, 1, 6.
105. Pierce to Caldwell, April 25, 1944, 3.

Saludos Amigos and *Three Caballeros* were both released for general audiences in the United States and Latin America, but Disney and the OIAA took care to signal the importance of their Latin American audiences. The project authorization for Disney's December 1942 trip to Mexico notes that while the trip was "designed to promote better relations between Mexico and the United States," the film itself was even more important: "It is contemplated that the motion pictures resulting from this trip will provide a greater understanding between these two countries. It will emphasize the unity of our peoples and the common bond existing by virtue of mutual appreciation of the world-famous Disney characters."[106] Only a limited Latin American audience would encounter Disney's actual visit but, OIAA staff hoped, the film would ensure that the visit's import circulated much more widely in Mexico and beyond. "Mutual appreciation" of Disney-created characters might then extend to mutual appreciation of other US media, culture, and life.

The Latin American distribution of Disney's motion pictures and the OIAA's promotion of them aimed to foster buy-in to the films' ideas through a sense of ownership over the characters. Introducing the Brazilian parrot, José Carioca, was considered a signature success of *Saludos Amigos*. *Three Caballeros* built on that idea. The "American" Donald Duck, the Brazilian José Carioca, and the Mexican rooster Panchito Pistola were a trio of American heroes brought together by Disney (via Donald Duck). Two important Latin American countries thus represented Latin American participation in an America united through friendship with the United States. Individual viewers, the OIAA hoped, might take up that invitation and likewise feel hemispheric solidarity with the United States because they saw themselves in the characters representing their interests. We see evidence of this effort in the *Población* article discussed in the previous section, where the creation of Panchito Pistola is heralded as a key element of Disney's visit to Mexico and a signal of appreciation for Mexican culture, though *Población* notably resisted full acquiescence to the US terms of the exchange.

In this sense, Disney's feature-length OIAA films took a different approach to imagining hemispheric cooperation than did most other OIAA efforts. Typically, OIAA projects aimed at cooperation sought to promote systemic relationships (among institutions, businesses, governments, countries). Individual encounters were, typically, understood as meetings of representatives who stood in for larger agencies. Appreciation for a single artist, even, was meant to promote respect for "our" art or "theirs." Disney's feature-length OIAA films highlighted relationships among individuals more exclusively. Panchito and

---

106. "Project Authorization. Disney Trip to Mexico," 2.

José were markedly Mexican and Brazilian, of course, and meant to signal US recognition of those countries, but the friendships Donald formed with them were not explicitly tied to national identity. Instead, in the films, they were personal relationships—the films were about friends introducing one another to their homes.

Much of the OIAA's work with regard to the films, then, was to clarify and frame the relationships depicted in them as representations of hemispheric solidarity in which the United States was both center and head. In *Saludos Amigos* that message came across most forcefully in the film's last two segments, where Goofy brought the US cowboy spirit to the Argentinian *pampas* and Disney animators met/created José Carioca. US frameworks (the masculine myths of the ever-expanding frontier and the erudite, energetic explorer encountering "natives" that pervade previous chapters) drove Disney's American visions too.[107] In *Three Caballeros,* the hemispheric work was even more palpable thanks to the film's central framing device: the celebration of Donald's birthday. The film's movement across the hemisphere is driven by Donald opening "packages" from his Latin American friends. Those packages draw him into stories about those friends' home countries. He observes and corroborates Brazilian and Mexican scenes, approving their American character. Both films' pioneer nostalgia—with Goofy appearing as a cowboy among *gauchos* and Donald and José taking up Panchito Pistola's gun-toting bravado—invoked a frontier myth shared across the American republics, but treated it very much in US terms. Frontiers, in the films, are spaces of exploration, adventure, and individual freedom. The United States extends them and enforces them through friendly relationships, extending and enforcing the boundaries of American magnitude in the process.

OIAA discussions of how best to promote *Three Caballeros* made explicit this purpose of centering hemispheric cooperation on US terms. A *Three Caballeros*-themed comic book that Disney and the OIAA planned to distribute in Latin America, for example, underwent multiple revisions in the planning stage to ensure that it accomplished hemispheric ends. In July 1944, Pierce wrote to Floyd Gottfredson of Walt Disney Productions to explain that "the strip should have more proganda [sic] on the idea of inter-American cooperation." Though Pierce acknowledged that was "a very high-sounding phrase for an idea like a comic book," the basic point was that the comic needed a narrative through-line that made connections between the individual characters and the countries they represented. So, for example, he asked, "Could Jose (sic) Carioca be made to refer in some natural way to what Brazil

---

107. Greenberg, *Manifest Manhood*; Pratt, *Imperial Eyes.*

has done for the United States?"[108] Three OIAA investments come clear: First, the comic book needed to make explicit gestures toward practical aspects of hemispheric cooperation. Second, the emphasis—for a Latin American audience—needed to be on the active participation of Latin American countries in supporting the war effort. And third, the end goal of such cooperation ought to be investment in US leadership. Brazil and Mexico provided raw materials for the US war effort, making them essential partners in a project headed and defined by the United States. Pierce commented in a later letter that previous OIAA comic books generated significant interest in Latin America, crowing that "in some countries children have actually staged riots to get copies of the booklets," and noting that "the circulation is perhaps the largest of any printed document distributed by the Office."[109] That recognition of popular appeal—the entertainment value of the comic books—placed even more importance on them. They had to be infused with carefully aimed propaganda because they were so ferociously devoured by the children whose investments and values would shape US-Latin American relations for the long haul. The future of US standing in the Americas relied, in part, on teaching children to look to the United States for entertainment and leadership.

Ultimately, what came to matter through the Disney-OIAA feature films and what tied the United States, Mexico, and Brazil (and by extension, the whole continent) together was hemispheric sentiment on US terms. As in the reformatted frontier myth in *Saludos Amigos* and *Three Caballeros,* that included a sense of American greatness that echoed ironically yet palpably with the presumptions of US grandeur and destiny that had exculpated territorial theft from Mexico one hundred years earlier.

And so, it is ironic but perhaps not surprising that one of the great twentieth-century critiques of US imperialism from a Latin American perspective took Disney—and Donald Duck in particular—as its representative anecdote. Ariel Dorfman and Armand Mattelart's *Para Leer al Pato Donald* (*How to Read Donald Duck*), first published in Chile in 1971, focused on Disney's comic books, not its films, and was separated from the OIAA's efforts by a generation (Dorfman was a toddler during World War II). And yet, the message that Disney's characters represented a hemispheric American ideal on US terms and, so, ought to be viewed askance resonates across the decades.

Files in the National Archives include no evidence that there was pushback on *Saludos Amigos* or *Three Caballeros* other than Uruguay's dismay at being left out. This does not mean, however, that there was no skepticism.

---

108. Pierce to Gottfredson, July 19, 1944.
109. Pierce to Caldwell, April 25, 1944, 5.

Indeed, the OIAA files contain a hint of that skepticism's likely character. In a 1942 newspaper article tucked into the records of the motion picture division, filmmaker Julian Bryan contended that Hollywood's "good neighbor films" were a failure. Bryan explained, "On the whole, South Americans like us—and our movies. But they resent Hollywood's inaccuracies and bad taste in representing their countries in the movies."[110] While Bryan exempted Disney from his critique, noting that Disney was wildly popular in South America because he distributed his films with Spanish and Portuguese dubbing, there is no doubt that Latin American skepticism persisted nevertheless. They looked critically at representations of themselves and, equally, at representations of a subordinate relationship with the United States. Though the OIAA clearly sought to incorporate Bryan's criticism into future practice, even collaborating with Bryan on a series of films for US audiences, the reminder that Latin Americans were anything but passive viewers who happily accepted messages of US dominance is resonant. It is possible, even likely, that *Saludos Amigos* and *Three Caballeros* had Latin American viewers who embraced José Carioca, Panchito Pistola, and even Disney himself, but looked sidelong at Donald Duck's blathering, bombastic personification of the United States.

In our analyses, visual rhetoric scholars have a tendency to presume that what was shown is what was seen. In practice, however, we know that is rarely the case. Viewers look on their own terms and bring their own histories and contexts to bear even as they are shaped by what is available to see. Likewise, OIAA staffers labored under the hope—though perhaps not always the certainty—that they could capture Latin American viewers' hearts and minds on US terms just as they aimed to establish Pan-Americanism on US terms. Their mission depended on Latin American viewers acquiescing—at least some of the time—to that presumption of the United States as first among equals. But, we can be sure that when they were confronted with what mattered to Disney and the OIAA, Latin American viewers looked askance as often as they gazed straight ahead with shining eyes and eager hearts.

Conclusion

Megethos pervaded the work of the Office of the Coordinator of Inter-American Affairs throughout its existence. It is there in the presumption that film was a particularly powerful tool for education, exchange, and persuasive entertainment because of the sheer force of moving image and recorded

---

110. "Lecturer Calls."

sound. It is there in the OIAA's concern for establishing US American importance in the form of "looking to." And it is there—in the form of *megethos* deflated—in every Latin American look askance.

The OIAA's ultimate purpose was to secure American magnitude, but its efforts were only ever partly successful. The image-makers and audiences populating previous chapters imagined American magnitude for the sake of US audiences, and they presumed that achieving American magnitude required only US action. However, by the middle of the twentieth century, the rising global power of the United States brought home the realization that American magnitude had to be corroborated from the outside. Ironically, at the cusp of superpower status, US grandeur and self-regard were newly vulnerable. The other American republics were the obvious best witnesses for American magnitude, but they were risky interlocutors. Even the most pro-US Latin American audiences would only be somewhat amenable to the themes of American magnitude as perpetuated by the United States. American magnitude, after all, made troublesome symbolic claims on Latin Americans' own homelands and histories. Of course they looked askance.

The story of the OIAA's effort to secure acquiescent Latin American viewers also, inexorably, draws attention to another fact of public feeling: It is not only Latin Americans who have looked askance at the tropes and practices of American magnitude. American magnitude was and is premised on a normative white, settler vision. Americans in the United States have also sidled up to American magnitude, pulling it off-course and making use of it slantwise. The racist, pro-slavery overtones of the US-Mexican War, the Yankee presumptions of Church and the Hudson River School, and Bingham's quasi-missionary scientific zeal all invited skepticism of American magnitude within and beyond the United States. It comes into particular focus, though, in this chapter's artifacts. I close, therefore, with a return to one of the health and literacy films discussed briefly above, *Cleanliness Brings Health*.

Cleanliness Brings Health features two families, presented as generically Latin American but vaguely Mexican by stereotypical phenotype, dress, and housing. One family, the "clean family," lives comfortably and healthily. The other, the "careless family," is impoverished and sick. No one in either family is named, except the son in the impoverished family—"little Johnny"—who is completely enervated by illness. As I describe in the education section, the short film presents cleanliness and health as matters of simple behavior and choice. If the impoverished family built a latrine, if they washed their hands, if they changed how they cooked, they too would be comfortable and healthy. Instead, though, the impoverished family infects itself. The father goes into the cornfield to relieve himself, touches dirt where he and others have left feces, carries germs—represented as a gray shadow on his hand—into the house, eats without washing his hands, and so spreads those germs to the whole family.

Here's what I didn't mention about *Cleanliness Brings Health*: I am not translating the film's title. I am not translating the son's name. The educational short—the only version of this film available in OIAA files—is in English (the Rockefeller Archives Center holds a Spanish-language version). The pamphlet "Health for the Americas" that lists all nine animated shorts in the series is, likewise, in English, and suggests that those films also are available with English dubbing. The pamphlet invokes a Latin American audience, explaining that the films are "for use in health instruction programs for areas where modern health centers have been newly established by the cooperative health services" and "for use also in schools and for general distribution" with an assumed audience from "urban skilled workers to rural Indians." The English dubbing, however, suggests otherwise. And, as we know, OIAA conversations about using both the health and literacy films included consideration of use in the United States.

As I close this chapter that has focused on efforts to establish American magnitude by inviting Latin Americans to see the United States as the center of the hemisphere, this English-language version of the short emphasizes a crucial point: Under the American vision elaborated by Disney and the OIAA, the Americanness of impoverished Brown, Black, and Spanish-speaking audiences in the United States was as partial and decentered as was that of any Latin American. If you "needed" the *Cleanliness Brings Health* film or the "Reading for the Americas" films, then you were racialized and symbolically deported from the center of America.[111] But those racialized, deportable viewers in the United States, like their counterparts in Latin America, were never content to look, doe-eyed, at American magnitude. Viewers in the United States also sometimes look askance at the magnitude being brought, repeatedly, before their eyes. They, too, sidle along the edges of American magnitude's public feeling or cut their eyes at it.[112] They, too, knock a white, US-led hemisphere off its feet, centering it elsewhere and otherwise.

---

111. For more on rhetorics of deportation, see, for example, Cisneros, *The Border Crossed Us*; DeChaine, *Border Rhetorics*; Flores, "Stoppage and the Racialized Rhetorics of Mobility"; Flores, *Deportable and Disposable*.

112. See, for example, work on "Brownness" and affect in Calafell, "Brownness, Kissing, and US Imperialism"; Muñoz, "Feeling Brown."

CHAPTER 5

Size Matters

In a 2017 *Reading the Pictures* post about the visual politics of the then-new Trump administration, I wrote, "Big crowds (or small), overwhelming chaos (or isolation), and disproportionate representation have become the visual hallmarks of the Trump era so far." I drafted the final words of this monograph from an improvised home office while the United States failed to manage the magnitude of a global pandemic. The lines of that post resonate across time, in the midst of a fragile, fractured political era, and throughout the analyses of this project. Throughout his presidency, Donald Trump wielded *megethos* as his rhetorical figure of choice, and American magnitude loomed large in his presidency. But even if he took American magnitude not just to but beyond its logical conclusions, Trump was not unique in his reliance on *megethos* nor was he uniquely responsible for the United States' late capitalist size obsession. Responses to Trump, likewise, fundamentally relied on magnitude. His opponents carefully calculated the size of protests, declared that "democracy dies in darkness," decried the death of American leadership in the world, and made frequent ableist, body-shaming claims that linked size and importance.

Well beyond the frame of presidential politics and across ideological paradigms, dominant characterizations of the United States of America in the early twenty-first century are all about big consequences in the world. Even US shortcomings are dramatic. And yet, though magnitude remains a remarkably compelling national frame, it is also troubled. As political upheaval, environmental crisis, and unrestrained white supremacist nationalism surge, pundits and scholars have predicted the end of American democracy and American empire.[1] Given the dramatic framings that pervade those predictions, I expect the rhetorical life of American magnitude will endure awhile, at least in popular political heuristics. However, it too may be nearing its end.

Having spent four chapters and almost a decade on magnitude, I know how seductive it is. Once I began noticing magnitude in general and American magnitude in particular, I saw it everywhere, ubiquitously at work in national discourse and visual culture. In her synthesis of the articles in volume 48, issue 4 of *Rhetoric Society Quarterly*, Cara Finnegan points out just how deeply I rely on magnitude to assert the value of my own interventions.[2] This book, likewise, recirculates and centers American magnitude even as I seek to destabilize it.

Despite the ease with which we might dismiss Trumpian orders of magnitude, I suspect that I am not alone among scholars in being tethered to magnitude. Most of us are in debt to it, one way or another. We assert novelty and import in order to make space for our work. We make the case for our disciplines by linking them to consequentiality and value. For those of us working in the United States, such appeals also readily affiliate themselves with American magnitude. Compositionists, rhetoricians, and humanists more broadly regularly invoke [US] American democracy to establish the importance of our disciplines. Even scholars who are skeptical of citizenship frame accounts of its consequential power in terms tightly bound with the presumptions of American magnitude and the white settler model of the US citizen.[3] Magnitude—with all its white, settler-colonial valances—consistently frames what topics scholars and disciplines value and how they ought to be pursued.

In this conclusion, I make two moves in light of that persistent, troubling reliance on magnitude. The first accepts magnitude but grapples with its ubiquity—if magnitude is all around us and essential to any rhetorical effort, then what makes American magnitude particular and, thereby, analytically generative? The second turns away from magnitude's claim to importance, closing a book about grandeur with a case for the small, the quotidian, and the ineffectual. As historical and political events (e.g., the COVID-19 pandemic, political instability, economic decline, environmental collapse) increasingly make clear, US consequence never was quite what its purveyors imagined it to be.

---

1. See, for example, Edsall, "I Fear"; Engelhardt, "The End"; Lachmann, "Life at the End"; Mercieca, *Demagogue for President*; Packer, "America's Plastic Hour."
2. Finnegan, "The Critic as Curator."
3. Karma Chávez, Ersula Ore, and Amy Wan all helpfully illuminate and trouble this tendency. Chávez, "Beyond Inclusion"; Ore, *Lynching*; Wan, "In the Name of Citizenship."

This rhetorical history of American magnitude may well tell its story from the perspective of its twilight days.

The Case for Tracking American Magnitude

Magnitude has been a ubiquitous and driving trope for US national rhetorics. Appeals to greatness—destiny, exception, sublimity, primacy—pervade dominant political discourse and hegemonic depictions of national identity. Take a US American commonplace, scratch its surface, and *megethos* shines through. "Make America Great Again" has acquired a particular meaning since 2016, but it has long been a basic requirement of mainstream public discourse that rhetors acquiesce to the notion that the United States holds a particularly important, millennial place in the world.[4] The basic grammar of patriotic affiliation with the United States is steeped in *megethos*. So are the county's stories of identity and purpose.

But the fact that US public discourse has leaned heavily on appeals to magnitude to establish its place in the world makes it typical, not extraordinary. One of Farrell's main points about magnitude is that it is everywhere. "In ordinary orderly times," he explains, "we have tended to think that things matter first and only then does rhetoric come creeping into the scenario."[5] But, he continues, when things aren't ordinary, we quickly realize "the utter fragility of our customs *and* conventions, as well as their *inadequacy* as resources for explanation."[6] In other words, communities across contexts, places, and times have been persuaded into their customs and conventions by appeals to magnitude. Values, beliefs, attitudes, and presumptions come to be held in common through repeated, persistent, and frequently unnoticed assertions of their importance.[7] If one accepts Farrell's definition of rhetoric as "the art . . . of making things matter" and its presumption that rhetoric creates (as well as circulates) relative importance, then magnitude is a fundamental ingredient in all rhetorical practice and in the production of rhetoricity itself.[8] *Megethos* is in the rhetorical water, and we consume it constantly.

But, Farrell also reminds his readers that magnitude is most notable and most debated in anxious times. Likewise, for those hoping to unsettle its com-

---

4. Ned O'Gorman, "Eisenhower."
5. Farrell, "The Weight of Rhetoric," 470.
6. Farrell, "The Weight of Rhetoric," 470.
7. Rhetoric is, in other words, constitutive. Burke, *A Grammar of Motives*; Charland, "Constitutive Rhetoric"; Christa J. Olson, *Constitutive Visions*.
8. Farrell, "Sizing Things Up," 1.

mon sense, it is useful to start by identifying the presumptions and instabilities of "ordinary, orderly" magnitude.[9] No matter their subject, then, rhetorical scholars have good reason to look for magnitude in moments of upheaval. And, having found it, we have equally good reason to track it back into the mundane in order to find its origins and investments.

Matters of magnitude pervade nationalist discourse—and not just in the United States. Even listing just American examples would fill another book, but here are a few: When Ecuador faced national crisis and diminished borders in the mid-twentieth century, Benjamín Carrión elevated his homeland as a "great, small nation," praising the grandeur of Ecuador's terrain and his compatriots' capacious artistic spirit.[10] Around the same time, José Vasconcelos lauded *la raza cobriza* as the culmination of history and the starting place for a great new Mexico and a great new América.[11] Speaking in Cuba in 1994, Hugo Chávez relied on magnitude to call for a grand "revolutionary and Latin American project" that would tie Central America, South America, and the Caribbean together as their destiny demanded, quoting Simón Bolívar, José Martí, Pablo Neruda, and Eduardo Galeano in the process.[12] Magnitude recurs every time a rhetor lauds their nation-state as it was, is, or could be. Megethos, after all, is really just a means of establishing importance and exigence. Nationalism, by definition, needs it.

But in the texts that I invoke above, Carrión, Vasconcelos, and Chávez were not simply relying on magnitude as a strategy of import—they were relying on (and contrasting) a very particular sort of magnitude. That particular magnitude, they presumed, came into being because of the nature of the place about which they wrote or spoke. Carrión, Vasconcelos, and Chávez, along with many of their compatriots, offered up Américan magnitude. That magnitude, crafted from and for what Martí termed "Nuestra América," was entirely conscious of the other American magnitude, the United States' version of American magnitude. Referring to it and resisting it, Carrión, Vasconcelos, Chávez, and others claimed a teleology of American potential that stood in direct and often explicit contrast to that articulated by the United States. Their arguments were not simply appeals to magnitude in the schoolyard format of "You think you're so great? Well, we're *really* great." They did not simply pit competing claims of magnitude against one another. Instead, such invocations of Américan magnitude presumed that a specific sort of magnitude was at work within America and sought to reclaim if from the United States. They

---

9. Farrell, "The Weight of Rhetoric," 470.
10. Carrión, *Cartas Al Ecuador*.
11. Vasconcelos and Jaén, *The Cosmic Race*.
12. Chávez, "Hugo Chávez Speech in La Habana."

invoked fundamental rhetorics of US commonsense and then they inverted and subverted those rhetorics. Those appeals to Américan magnitude did not, however, overturn the presumption of a magnitude particularly tethered to the hemisphere.

American magnitude is something other—more—than simply a series of exaggerated value claims applied to America (the United States or otherwise). Dominant discourse in the United States has not only made claims about the grandeur of the United States as America, it has consistently asserted that American grandeur itself is what makes the United States great. American exceptionalism—particularly the narrative of the United States as the end of history—fundamentally asserts that US magnitude emerges from a preexisting, constitutive magnitude. The erroneous but powerful impression, then, is that American magnitude must preexist rhetoric. It is not made, but given.

From that presumption of original magnitude emerge the particularly imperial and colonial modes of magnitude that constitute US discourse. If scope, consequence, and size are what make the United States great, then expansion and influence-wielding are endemic national qualities. In order to maintain its American status—its magnitude—the United States must be in others' business, be pressing on boundaries, and be taken into account. A nation whose greatness is grounded in its own magnitude is a nation that can never be a good neighbor. It is too certain of its destiny and too anxious of its own status. Its neighborliness will always be contingent on opportunities to demonstrate superiority, magnanimity, and/or power.

For this reason, the creation of the United States *as* America has historically had a great deal more to do with southward encounters than northward ones. A powerful sense of difference from and superiority over the people and nations of Latin America has, paradoxically, driven dominant rhetors in the United States to more consistently engage that region when elaborating national magnitude via broader American claims. Again and again, US rhetors have had the opportunity to engage northward to establish the magnitude of the United States but have looked southward instead. Constitutive white supremacist frameworks have made Latin America the proving ground for US American magnitude.

In 1845, on the eve of the US-Mexican War, tensions were high between the United States and Britain over the Oregon Territory. Britain was an imperial power on American soil. The principles of the Monroe Doctrine ought to have made its presence the greater threat. Yet the United States chose war with Mexico—its sister republic—instead. Frederic Church traveled into the Arctic just as he traveled to Ecuador and Colombia. His paintings of the far north, like his paintings of the Andes, established American grandeur through scenes of sublime nature. But though Church temporarily named his most famous Arctic painting *The North* in a timely patriotic nod, he more consistently chose the volcanic Andes to reflect the turmoil of the Civil War in his paintings. Seventy-five years later, in the midst of another war, Franklin Roosevelt called for an "arsenal of democracy" that would extend outward from the United States to defend the whole hemisphere, including Canada and South America. However, despite Roosevelt's explicit concern for hemispheric security, there is no direct reference to Canada in his "Arsenal of Democracy" speech. He invoked only threats to US cities and South American countries and anxiety about the Axis establishing a foothold in the South.[13]

Canada could have been part of the United States' demonstration of its particular American magnitude, but it typically hasn't been. The reason is simple: The bad neighborliness inevitable to American magnitude grows out of and leads to racism, colonialism, and imperialism. "Latin" America—racialized, feminized, other—fit the needs of a purified, masculine, self-interested American magnitude. But even as the Latin American anxieties and objects of US American magnitude made possible particularly emphatic claims to grandeur, they also reveal its delicacy.

Whether American magnitude comes into focus through the slow accumulation of objects and feelings, the framing work of stories told and retold across contexts and media, or a dramatic revelation before the eyes of the right viewers, it is a simultaneously sturdy and fragile thing. Driven deep into common sense, it is hard to recognize for what it is and nearly impossible to uproot. And yet, the intensity of feeling it engenders speaks to its own instability and uncertainty. Who but a people profoundly committed to, but utterly unsure of, their own size would need the comfort of a "Make America Great Again" hat and a "big, beautiful wall" on their southern border? It doesn't take a psychoanalytic orientation to look askance at a nation whose story of its own importance relies, tautologically, on its inherent consequentiality. Such a nation is perpetually at risk of following leaders with brittle egos that need constant massaging. By this measure, it is a miracle how much time elapsed between Andrew Jackson and Donald Trump.

Presentations of American magnitude have not always been as swollen as they were in the Trump era. As Farrell predicted, the signs of American magnitude are easy to recognize when they emerge, bloated, in moments

---

13. As a member of the Empire, Canada was already involved in World War II when Roosevelt delivered his "Arsenal of Democracy" fireside chat. Despite that fact, Roosevelt mentions Canada neither as a point of hemispheric strength nor as a point of weakness. Instead, portions of the United States and South America stand in, synecdochically, for hemispheric risk and the United States, alone, figures as the source of hemispheric deliverance.

of intensity. However, such eruptions have their origins in more pervasive practices. American magnitude has many modes. This book has offered some particularly salient examples, aiming to both show the texture of American magnitude and highlight its trans-American constitution. Soldiers' letters and lithographs helped reveal American magnitude at its slowest and subtlest and marked the shift from a grandeur primarily premised on acquiring territory to one primarily premised on acquiring vision and influence. Following Church as he retraced Humboldt's footsteps and painted great American scenes, we mapped some of the stories that perpetuate American magnitude and found them riddled with elisions and wrong turns. American stories, that chapter whispers, can be told otherwise. The Yale Peruvian Expedition's explorations and photographs illuminated American magnitude as a process of appropriation and revelation in which Andean places and Incan achievements were made to reflect US consequence. There too, however, things might have been otherwise. Bingham's wrong turns occluded places and stories that resisted the YPE's brand of discovery, invention, and revelation. Finally, centering those elisions and wrong turns, analysis of the OIAA's "good neighbor" projects allowed us to recognize that American magnitude doesn't just rely on Latin America for sublime visions and scenic backdrops. It also longs for and requires Latin American viewers willing to corroborate the United States' particular and primary place in America.

"American magnitude" names a habitual presumption and a persistent rhetorical strategy. Tracking its invocation across moments, modes, and places has brought to light its constitutive force and its fragility. Looking for consequence that would reflect and corroborate a particular, palpable Americanness, US image-makers and audiences frequently found it. They also found their limits. Premised on grandeur and thirsty for approbation, American magnitude is inevitably insecure and needy. The grand stories and great accomplishments revealed to viewers in the United States were accompanied—persistently and pervasively—by failures and shortcomings that needed to be omitted, obscured, or explained away. Across the chapters of this book, we have followed the paths by which the United States has emerged as America—inevitable, consequential, and profound. We have also come across other paths that can be followed to other conclusions.

Diminishing Returns

"One of the emerging crises for this new century," Ralph Cintrón wrote in 2010, "may be the widening of a disjunction between the limitlessness that democratic subjectivity implies . . . and the limitedness that material life represents (for instance, the sustainability of resources)."[14] Whether we are talking about the extreme version espoused by Trump or the more familiar versions that have accumulated across myriad stories and revelations, American magnitude is unsustainable—environmentally, economically, geopolitically, and morally. It is extractivist, xenophobic, and racist. That reality can't be corrected by shouting it down or making America great. I am also skeptical that the problems of American magnitude can be ameliorated through appeals to other, "better" grand narratives or millennial visions. Ultimately, magnitude will not help us escape the mess that American magnitude makes, indexes, and perpetuates. The either-or, over-and-above frameworks that define magnitude are, themselves, part of the problem. Magnitude, for all that it promises the superlative, will always have diminishing returns.

Having reached the limit of magnitude, it might be tempting to pursue its opposite. However, because magnitude traffics in binaries, magnitude's opposite is still a measure of magnitude: the infinitesimal (instead of the grand), the weak (instead of the powerful), the unimportant (instead of the consequential). Turning to the neglected, less-admired side of magnitude's binaries and investing energy there may provide some relief from its calamity. However, my goal, in closing, is to go half a step further. Though magnitude will always be an available strategy and a pervasive appeal, these last pages reach toward a post-magnitude rhetoric. They imagine—tentatively, imperfectly—pathways toward a rhetorical theory beyond magnitude. Such a theory, I suspect, would be self-consciously flawed and intentionally hazy of telos. It would, like the rhetorical theory elaborated by Felipe Guaman Poma de Ayala, begin from a presumption that "the conditions necessary for being heard and listened to are always tenuous and often untenable."[15] Such a theory would privilege little moves taken with full awareness that their consequences will be limited and contradictory. It would be a rhetorical theory intent on finding neither the middle ground between the poles of magnitude, nor the underside of magnitude, but a multiplicity of directions that can be taken through plural worlds where values proliferate.

I am far from the first to imagine such a rhetorical theory. Guaman Poma, writing a generation after the fall of Tahuantinsuyo, wrote more than a thousand pages in pursuit of it. Rubén Casas and I have argued that his *Primer Nueva Corónica y Buen Gobierno* stumbled toward "a theory of rhetoric in the depths of colonial culture" in which rhetorical practice "is profoundly open-

---

14. Cintrón, "Democracy," 106.
15. Olson and Casas, "Felipe Guaman Poma de Ayala's *Primer Nueva Corónica y Buen Gobierno*," 468.

ended, ... privileges fragmentation, and ... refuses identification" with power.[16] In the centuries since Guaman Poma wrote, decolonial, Indigenous, Black, and feminist theory and practice have, likewise, offered implicit and explicit theories of rhetorics plural and otherwise. Derrick Bell's "racial realism" and critical race theory,[17] Andean plurinational and pluriversal politics,[18] the intersectional praxis of Black Lives Matter,[19] the frameworks of the modernity/coloniality research program,[20] and Indigenous-led scholarship and activism in the face of climate collapse[21] all—to varied extents and in varied ways—offer frameworks for thinking and doing rhetoric that are not entirely premised on appeals to magnitude. Informed by that work, I close by outlining four practices for a post-magnitude rhetorical history, theory, and criticism. These practices amplify the cautions, limitations, and warnings that often accompany the theories invoked above—especially when they speak toward white settler audiences.[22] My hope in outlining them is that those of us steeped in American magnitude might learn to sit with limitedness and do so without equating it with apathy or futility.

Practice 1: Be Partial[23]

Magnitude is dramatic. It traffics in extremes: consequential/inconsequential, momentous/irrelevant, extraordinary/ordinary.[24] Either America becomes "great again" or, as Trump warned in his 2017 inaugural address, it devolves

---

16. Olson and Casas, "Felipe Guaman Poma de Ayala's *Primer Nueva Corónica y Buen Gobierno*," 474.
17. See, for example, Bell, *And We Are Not Saved*; Bell, *Faces at the Bottom of the Well*; Kynard, *Vernacular Insurrections*; Ore, *Lynching*.
18. See, for example, Confederación de Nacionalidades Indígenas del Ecuador, "Declaration of Quito"; Simbaña and Martínez Abarca, *¡Así Encendimos La Mecha!*; Querejazu, "Encountering the Pluriverse"; Yampara Huarachi, "Cosmovivencia Andina."
19. Garza, *The Purpose of Power*; Towns, "Black 'Matter' Lives."
20. See, for example, Escobar, "Worlds and Knowledges Otherwise"; Mignolo, "The Geopolitics of Knowledge."
21. See, for example, Davis and Todd, "On the Importance of a Date"; Whyte, "Our Ancestors' Dystopia Now."
22. The phrase "other possible worlds" here refers to the framework for the first World Social Forum in Porto Alegre, Brazil in 2001: *Otro Mundo es Posible*. Activists and scholars have subsequently taken up the phrase and used it to imagine alternatives to racist, colonial, imperialist, capitalist systems worldwide.
23. I am partially in debt to Haraway for this naming. I had toyed with it and rejected it (going with "adequate" instead), but rereading Haraway's "Situated Knowledges" persuaded me back to the partial. Haraway, "Situated Knowledges."
24. Most of the pairings I offer here come from Farrell, "The Weight of Rhetoric," 471.

into "American carnage." There are only two options and both are exceptional. Academics, and perhaps especially writing teachers, are well aware of the havoc this orientation wreaks on lives, relationships, and institutions. The first practice for rhetoric beyond magnitude invites us to step away from the choice between greatness and failure and instead treasure the partial and the adequate.

Being partial could mean finding a place partway along the line between magnitude's extremes or parsing the Aristotelian mean between perfection and perfidy. In this case, however, I mean something slightly different. Rather than acquiescing to a frame that has two poles but refusing to choose between them, being partial, here, includes a recognition that the poles are illusory. This acknowledgement that ultimate, ideal ends are inaccessible is not an admission of defeat. Instead, as Bell notes with regard to civil rights, "freed from the stifling rigidity" of certain accomplishment (or miserable failure), those pursuing racial justice "are impelled *both* to live each day more fully *and* to examine critically the actual effectiveness" of strategies.[25] Being partial is a call to begin with the resources and skills presently available and turn them toward the tasks at hand. "The world always exceeds our conception of it," Alexis Shotwell notes.[26] Our theories will fall short and our life spans are extraordinarily brief. "Despite this," she continues, "we can still pursue changed worlds."[27] Lacking satisfying solutions to our world's wicked problems doesn't mean abandoning the effort to address them. It means taking up small work for the sake of that small work, not presuming that it will lead, eventually, to greatness. Paraphrasing Haraway, Shotwell aims toward a "real, possible world" that is "partially shared, offers finite freedom, adequate abundance, modest meaning, and limited happiness. Partial, finite, adequate, modest, limited—and yet worth working on, with, and for."[28] It may be difficult to imagine US national rhetorics embracing the "partial, finite, adequate, modest, and limited" in the short term. But in our everyday lives, in our analyses, and in the things we make matter, rhetoricians can choose to value and pursue them. We need, as Haraway says, "the ability partially to translate knowledges among very different—and power-differentiated—communities . . . in order to build meanings and bodies that have a chance for life."[29] Being partial invites us to embrace a principle of diminished position and increased responsibility for those meanings and bodies.

---

25. Bell, *Faces at the Bottom of the Well*, 199.
26. Shotwell, *Against Purity*, 4.
27. Shotwell, *Against Purity*, 4.
28. Shotwell, *Against Purity*, 5; Haraway, "Situated Knowledges," 579.
29. Haraway, "Situated Knowledges," 580.

Practice 2: Keep a Messy Slate

Magnitude is slate clearing. Grandeur intends to wipe away what came before and focus attention on the consequential now. The past might be useful for authorizing present purpose, but it must be sanitized and purified first. Many pundits and critics pondered aloud precisely which previous era Trump meant when he summoned his compatriots to make America great *again*. His supporters, likewise, were entirely vague about when that past greatness was. That lack of specificity isn't surprising. No past moment, faced in its entirety, would fit the bill. But magnitude doesn't need the specific past. The imagined grandeur of the past is only of use so far as it supports the clean slate of a great present and future.

Moving beyond magnitude, in contrast, requires working with a messy, full, and obviously overwritten slate. As, Shotwell writes, "The slate has never been clean, and we can't wipe off the surface to start fresh—there is no 'fresh' to start."[30] New beginnings are appealing but treacherous and, ultimately, illusory. In this sense (and at the risk of reopening an old argument), in a rhetorical theory beyond magnitude all rhetorical theory and criticism are also rhetorical history.

In *Planting the Anthropocene,* Jennifer Clary-Lemon invites her readers to see ourselves "exist[ing] in the long tail of an ongoing decision about the trouble we are in."[31] The trouble we are in is, in large part, caused by the practices and presumptions of white settler American magnitude. Any rhetorical theory beyond magnitude has to keep track of that fact. It must account for past choices that don't merely haunt the present, but continue to live on in it. Magnitude would draw distinctions and lines between the past and the present. The desire to start from a blank slate, Clary-Lemon suggests, is a markedly Western urge, relying on a linear notion of time. She recommends that we instead "gather [before] different ancestors . . . who may help us think through time as something that *cannot* restart because time itself is cyclical, seasonal, spatial—a coil, triangle, branch, or double spiral as easily as a line."[32] Beyond magnitude, the eventful and the mundane coexist, the past and present imbricate each other. The "trouble we're in" is a simultaneously past, present, and future trouble, marking every available slate and embedded in every page. This inherently messy slate should not come as a surprise to anyone who has sat with the lessons offered by scholars in racial rhetorical criticism, feminist and

---

30. Shotwell, *Against Purity,* 4.
31. Clary-Lemon, *Planting the Anthropocene,* 168.
32. Clary-Lemon, "Gifts, Ancestors, and Relations," para. 22.

queer rhetorics, and cultural rhetorics (among others).[33] Yet many scholars continue to act as though novelty and newness were uncontested values while simultaneously relying on the same old, white, masculine, Western scholarly genealogies to authorize their innovations.[34] Rhetorical theory and practice, in other words, remain invested in the clean slate that magnitude promises.

Undermining those persistent values and practices likely requires unsettling the equally persistent "modern Western myth" of the universe. As Amaya Querejazu explains, "This myth has separation as its core feature, it is the main rule to see and understand the cosmos."[35] In that myth, time moves forward, separating past from present. Binaries split nature from culture and self from other. The new replaces the old. A rhetorical theory beyond magnitude will recognize—with Querejazu, Mignolo, and many others—that such lines are *options* for explaining experience, not accurate representations of a singular universe.[36] It will recognize, as well, how often those lines inform (and derail) dominant US American rhetorical practice. And then, it will seek out and learn from practices otherwise.

In a rhetorical theory beyond magnitude, every slate is messy and multiple. While rhetors and rhetoricians operate in many different worlds, enact many different epistemologies, and participate in many different ontologies, those worlds, epistemologies, and ontologies overlap and interweave.[37] Slates, lands, and lives are marked by these overlappings and interweavings. As the next practice emphasizes, that mutual marking requires rhetoricians who are accountable to and for multiple communities.

Practice 3: Do the Hard Work of Connection

Magnitude is isolated and confident. The city on a hill is an example to all. Good or ill, it stands alone.[38] American magnitude is particularly steeped in this aspect of magnitude. Nearly every US American myth enshrines it: exceptionalism, the frontier, the rugged individual, and so on. And, as others have repeatedly pointed out, this practice of magnitude also infuses aca-

---

33. See, for example, Karma Chávez, *Queer Migration Politics*; Davis, "A Black Woman as Rhetorical Critic"; Flores, "Between Abundance and Marginalization"; Powell et al., "Our Story Begins Here"; Washington, "Woke Skin, White Masks."
34. Wanzer-Serrano, "#RhetoricSoWhite."
35. Querejazu, "Encountering the Pluriverse," 6.
36. Querejazu, "Encountering the Pluriverse"; Mignolo, *The Darker Side*; Escobar, "Worlds and Knowledges Otherwise"; Wanzer, "Delinking Rhetoric."
37. Watson and Huntington, "They're *Here*—I Can *Feel* Them," 275.
38. Cotton, "Gods Promise to His Plantation."

demic norms (see, e.g., the comfort with analyzing the work of a single great rhetor and the privileging of single-author publication).[39] Despite protestations of rigor, those moves toward magnitude are also, often, moves toward (imagined) safety. They evince a desire for invulnerability and a need to evade responsibility.

Moving beyond magnitude, in contrast, requires risking community. Malea Powell and scholars across cultural rhetorics and Indigenous studies have repeatedly invited rhetoricians to attend to our relations and replace magnitude with accountability.[40] Andrea Riley-Mukavetz, for example, calls rhetorical scholarship to invest in "the communal, the collective, and relational" instead of pursuing the new, eventful, and dramatic.[41] Such invitations ask rhetoricians to recognize how thoroughly enmeshed we are in communities, contexts, and places and to see that enmeshing as requiring accountability.

White settler rhetoricians have sometimes treated the invocation of relations and the use of story as soft, fuzzy, or lacking rigor, dismissing them in the process. Collaboration, likewise, loses prestige because it is associated with feminized relations and decreased effort. Both these knee-jerk reactions are grounded in a fundamental misunderstanding of community. They treat relationships as sites of ease, escape, and safety, not as sites of accountability, labor, and responsibility. Moving beyond magnitude requires doing the hard work of community—building relationships and accountability. It also requires making conscious choices about which communities we will be responsible to.

The histories and practices of American magnitude leave those of us who benefit from it in debt. American magnitude is what Clary-Lemon terms a "terrible gift"—toxic, infesting, and harmful.[42] In America, white settlers have given that terrible gift and have received it. Rhetorical scholars, too, have given and received that terrible gift. Habitually privileging the singular (white, masculine, settler) scholar, disciplinary investment in what Lisa Corrigan and Anjali Vats term the "pathological economy" of "academic shareholder whiteness" has created noxious relations and accountability practices.[43] Changing those habits, as the final practice suggests, requires recognizing them and then building other mechanisms.

---

39. For two different instantiations of this well-established argument, see Corrigan and Vats, "The Structural Whiteness"; Lunsford and Ede, *Writing Together*.

40. See, for example, Powell, "Down by the River"; Powell, "Stories Take Place"; Powell et al., "Our Story Begins Here"; Arola, "My Pink Powwow Shawl"; Justice, "Go Away, Water!"

41. Riley-Mukavetz, "On Working from or with Anger," sec. 4, para. 1.

42. Clary-Lemon, "Gifts, Ancestors, and Relations," para. 16.

43. Corrigan and Vats, "The Structural Whiteness," 221–22.

Practice 4: Care

Magnitude is extractivist and competitive. It takes, appropriates, and hoards. Under the frame of magnitude, one either wins or loses. Moving beyond magnitude means moving away from zero-sum, winner-take-all orientations. Accomplishing that shift involves attending to another aspect of relation and community: the value of care. Davis and Todd theorize relation as an alternative to the teleological, magnitude-infused, urge for "salvation" from the disaster of the Anthropocene. Instead, they write, "We call here for a tending once again to relations to kin, to life, longing, and care. . . . This commitment to tenderness and relationships is one necessary and lasting refraction of the violence and unjust worlds set in motion by the imperialist white supremacist capitalist [hetero]patriarchy . . . and the beginning of the colonial moment."[44] Care, in this sense, offers an entirely different orientation to the work of mattering than magnitude does. That orientation takes shape in feminist, intersectional, Indigenous, and anti-racist practice and scholarship, not as an empty expression of affection but as a critical investment in worlds otherwise.[45]

I introduce "care" as the final practice for a rhetorical theory beyond magnitude, feeling equal parts confidence and caution. "Care," especially when advocated by a professional class white settler woman such as myself, has frequently come as a steamroller, not a critical practice. My people have used it to demand gentle handling and ensure that our white feelings and intentions matter more than legacies of racist harm and present-day aggressions (micro and macro). But the invocations of care that I cite here reject that white fragility. The care that they, and I, invoke is fierce, risky, and demanding of commitment. It is, as Karma Chávez might put it, a practice of fugitivity, not of sanctuary.[46] This care is expressly enacted at the margins, by the marginalized, and for the marginalized.[47] In place of "'niceness,'" "familial affection,'" and "civility,'" Corrigan and Vats call for "models of decolonized radical care where collaboration is prioritized and where growth is modeled and nurtured through intimate networks of collective solidarity and mutuality."[48] Those models and networks must be built and sustained; they are not made to order. But they are possible.

---

44. Davis and Todd, "On the Importance of a Date," 775.
45. See, for example, Blankenship, *Changing the Subject*; Davis, "In the Kitchen"; Corrigan and Vats, "The Structural Whiteness"; Querejazu, "Encountering the Pluriverse"; Restaino, *Surrender*.
46. Karma Chávez, "From Sanctuary."
47. See, for example, Davis, "In the Kitchen"; Piepzna-Samarasinha, *Care Work*.
48. Corrigan and Vats, "The Structural Whiteness," 225.

Pursuing care, however, is a practice of the imperfect. "Sometimes," writes Riley-Mukavetz, "you'll fuck it up."[49] Clary-Lemon asks, "What might it look like if every . . . scholar, as a matter of etiquette and decorum . . . allowed the possibility to see themselves as mistaken?"[50] Arola calls for scholars to "tak[e] the time to acknowledge your own limitations" and recognize that "we aren't the center. There are relations beyond our understanding."[51] Emphasizing care, in other words, directs us back to matters of accountability and relationship, to our messy slates, and to being partial. Worlds and rhetorical theories beyond magnitude are gifts we don't deserve, responsibilities we can't evade, and practices we'll never fully achieve.

"All there is," Shotwell writes, "is the possibility of acting from where we are."[52] We live in a world shaped by investments in magnitude in general and American magnitude in particular. But, as Kyle Powys Whyte suggests, actions of protest, restoration, and relationship-building offer essential ways forward.[53] The magnitude of colonialism, white supremacy, and imperialism threaten to overwhelm. Small steps, partial acts, and fugitive care are all we have available to us. They may also be precisely what we need.

---

49. Riley-Mukavetz, "On Working from or with Anger," sec. 4, para. 1.
50. Clary-Lemon, "Gifts, Ancestors, and Relations," para. 25.
51. Jordan et al., "Continuing the Conversation," 395; Arola, "My Pink Powwow Shawl," 389.
52. Shotwell, *Against Purity*, 4.
53. Whyte, "Our Ancestors' Dystopia Now," 213.

BIBLIOGRAPHY

Archival Sources

"6.500 Analfabetos Adultos en Toda La República Aprenden a Leer y Escribir. Comisionados Por Oficina del Coordinador Para Ensayar Nuevo Método de Alfabetización Visitaron Ayer La U. N. P." *El Comercio.* August 9, 1944. US National Archives. RG 229 Entry 77 Box 959. Folder: Literacy Program * Miscellaneous OEMcr-107–305.

"Adult Literacy Program (Basic Adult Education)," March 12, 1945. US National Archives. RG 229 Entry 77 Box 960. Folder: Health and Literacy Program.

Allerton, Mary. "Church's 'Heart of the Andes.'" *New Hampshire Statesman,* February 18, 1860.

Alstock, Francis. Letter to Roy Disney, December 7, 1942. US National Archives. RG 229 Entry 77 Box 958. Folder: Disney Trip to Mexico.

"Ancient Incas of Peru." *Daily People,* December 23, 1912.

"Ancient Incas Ruined City." *Los Angeles Times,* January 7, 1912.

"The Annual Pictorial Herald. Illustrated History of the Mexican War." *New York Herald,* December 22, 1847.

"Army of the Centre. Letter from a Correspondent of the National Intelligencer. Camp Crockett, (near the Alamo,) San Antonio de Bexar, Texas, Sept. 1, 1846." *Niles' National Register,* October 10, 1846.

"Art Matters—'Heart of the Andes' in Cincinnati." *Cincinnati Daily Commercial,* November 28, 1860.

Benjamin, Samuel Greene Wheeler. "Fifty Years of American Art. 1828–1878 (II)." *Harper's Monthly Magazine,* September 1879.

"Bingham Back with Pre-Incas' Skulls." *New York Times,* December 20, 1912.

Bingham, Hiram. "Assignment of Photographic Negatives and Numbers." Instructions for Staff, 1914–15, n.d. Yale Peruvian Expedition Papers, Group 664. Series I. Box 1. Folder 1–18 "Instructions for Staff, 1914–15." Sterling Memorial Library Manuscripts and Archives. Yale University.

———. "Circulars of the Peruvian Expedition of 1912. No. 1. Suggestions for the Work of Assistants," 1912. Yale Peruvian Expedition Papers, Group 664. Series I. Box 1. Folder 1–15 "Instructions for Staff, 1912." Sterling Memorial Library Manuscripts and Archives. Yale University.

———. "The Discovery of Machu Picchu." *Harper's Monthly Magazine,* April 1913.

———. "The first point of attack for the Expedition . . . ," n.d. Yale Peruvian Expedition Papers, Group 664. Series I. Box 1. Folder 1–3 "Plans for Expedition, 1914–15." Sterling Memorial Library Manuscripts and Archives. Yale University.

———. "General Instructions," 1912. Yale Peruvian Expedition Papers, Group 664. Series I. Box 1. Folder 1–15 "Instructions for Staff, 1912." Sterling Memorial Library Manuscripts and Archives. Yale University.

———. "In the Wonderland of Peru." *The National Geographic Magazine* 24, no. 4 (April 1913): 387–573.

———. Letter to Manager, Associated Press, New Haven, CT, May 14, 1912.

———. *The Monroe Doctrine: An Obsolete Shibboleth.* New Haven/London: Yale University Press/Humphrey Milford Oxford University Press, 1913.

———. "The New Peruvian Expedition under the Auspices of Yale University and the National Geographic Society," 1914. Yale Peruvian Expedition Papers, Group 664, Series 1, Box 1, Folder 1–5, Press Releases and Reports, 1912, 1914–15. Sterling Memorial Library, Yale University.

———. "No. 19. Directions for Using Color Chart," n.d. Yale Peruvian Expedition Papers, Group 664, Series 1, Box 1, Folder 1–15, Instructions for Staff, 1912. Sterling Memorial Library, Yale University.

———. "Official Circulars of the Peruvian Expedition of 1912. No. 9," n.d. Yale Peruvian Expedition Papers, Group 664. Series I. Box 1. Folder 1–15 "Instructions for Staff, 1912." Sterling Memorial Library Manuscripts and Archives. Yale University.

———. "Official Circulars of the Peruvian Expedition of 1912. No. 13. Collection of Archeological and Osteological Material," n.d. Yale Peruvian Expedition Papers, Group 664. Series I. Box 1. Folder 1–15 "Instructions for Staff, 1912." Sterling Memorial Library Manuscripts and Archives. Yale University.

———. "The Peruvian Expedition of 1912," 1913. Yale Peruvian Expedition Papers, Group 664. Series I. Box 1. Folder 1–5 "Press releases and reports, 1912, 1914–15." Sterling Memorial Library Manuscripts and Archives. Yale University.

———. "The Peruvian Expedition of 1912." Report. New Haven, CT, March 1913. Yale Peruvian Expedition Papers, Group 664. Series I. Box 1. Folder 1–5 "Press releases and reports, 1912, 1914–15." Sterling Memorial Library Manuscripts and Archives. Yale University.

———. "Peruvian Expedition of 1914–15. Official Circular #10. The Daily Journal," n.d. Yale Peruvian Expedition Papers, Group 664. Series I. Box 1. Folder 1–18 "Instructions for Staff, 1914–15." Sterling Memorial Library Manuscripts and Archives. Yale University.

———. "Peruvian Expedition of 1914–15. Official Circular #20, Revised. Assignment of Photographic Negatives and Numbers," n.d. Yale Peruvian Expedition Papers, Group 664. Series I. Box 1. Folder 1–18 "Instructions for Staff, 1914–15." Sterling Memorial Library Manuscripts and Archives. Yale University.

———. "Peruvian Expedition of 1915 (Copy for Yale Catalogue)," 1915. Yale Peruvian Expedition Papers, Group 664. Series I. Box 1. Folder 1–5 "Press releases and reports, 1912, 1914–15." Sterling Memorial Library Manuscripts and Archives. Yale University.

———. "Peruvian Expeditions. Summary of the Work of 1915," 1915. Yale Peruvian Expedition Papers, Group 664. Series I. Box 1. Folder 1–5 "Press releases and reports, 1912, 1914–15." Sterling Memorial Library Manuscripts and Archives. Yale University.

———. "Plan for 1912," n.d. Yale Peruvian Expedition Papers, Group 664. Series I. Box 1. Folder 1–2 "Plans for Expedition, 1912." Sterling Memorial Library Manuscripts and Archives. Yale University.

———. "Plan for the Peruvian Expedition of 1914–15, under the Auspices of Yale University and the National Geographic Society," 1914. Yale Peruvian Expedition Papers, Group 664. Series I. Box 1. Folder 1–4 "Plans for expedition, 1914–15." Sterling Memorial Library Manuscripts and Archives. Yale University.

———. "Table of Contents," n.d. Yale Peruvian Expedition Papers, Group 664. Series I. Box 1. Folder 1–18 "Instructions for Staff, 1914–15." Sterling Memorial Library Manuscripts and Archives. Yale University.

Bowers, Charles. Letter to US Secretary of State, October 1, 1941. RG 229 Entry 90 Box 1209 Office of Inter-American Affairs, Records of the Department of Information, Education Division, Records Concerning Exhibits and Related Projects (E-90) Art. Folder: ART 1941 Latin American Exhibitions of Contemporary Painting NDCar—14 $50,100.

Braden, Spruille. "Translation of Speech by the Ambassador of the United States of America at the Opening of the Exhibition of Contemporary American Art at the National Library, on the Afternoon of July 19, 1941," July 19, 1941. US National Archives. RG 229 Entry 90 Box 1209 Office of Inter-American Affairs, Records of the Department of Information, Education Division, Records Concerning Exhibits and Related Projects (E-90) Art. Folder: ART 1941 Latin American Exhibitions of Contemporary Painting NDCar—14 $50,100.

"Braved Perils in Peru." *New York Tribune*, December 20, 1912.

Butler, B. F., and C. Lewis. *Death of Lieut. Col. Henry Clay Jr.* 1847. Lithograph.

Calver, Homer N. Letter to Thomas C. Edwards. "Comments on the Motion Picture 'The Soybean,'" July 1, 1943. US National Archives. RG 229 Entry 77 Box 959. Folder: Walt Disney Productions Film Unit OEMcr-107.

Carrión, Benjamín. *Cartas Al Ecuador*. Quito: Editorial Gutenberg, 1943.

Catlin, Stanton. Interview by Radio Nacional. Radio, December 1, 1941. RG 229 Entry 90 Box 1209 Office of Inter-American Affairs, Records of the Department of Information, Education Division, Records Concerning Exhibits and Related Projects (E-90) Art. Folder: ART 1941 Latin American Exhibitions of Contemporary Painting NDCar—14 $50,100.

———. Letter to Olive M. Lyford, October 3, 1941. US National Archives. RG 229 Entry 90 Box 1209 Office of Inter-American Affairs, Records of the Department of Information, Education Division, Records Concerning Exhibits and Related Projects (E-90) Art. Folder: ART 1941 Latin American Exhibitions of Contemporary Painting NDCar—14 $50,100.

Church, Frederic Edwin. "Sangay Diary 1857," n.d. Olana New York State Historical Site Archives. OL.1980.28 Sangay Diary 1857.

———. "A Trip to the Volcano Sangai in Equador. F. E. Church's Diary," n.d. Olana New York State Historical Site Archives. OL.2001.4567.A-M.

"Church's Heart of the Andes." Unknown Publication, St. Louis, MO, 1861. Olana New York State Historical Site Archives. Research Collection.

"Church's 'Heart of the Andes' (Correspondence of the Philadelphia Press)." *Chicago Press and Tribune,* May 28, 1859.

Clark, Eleanor F. Letter to Wallace K. Harrison. "Literacy Film Showings, University of Chicago, May 17, 1945," May 30, 1945. US National Archives. RG 229 Entry 77 Box 959. Folder: Literacy Program * Miscellaneous OEMcr-107-305.

Clark, Eleanor F., and Ryland R. Madison. "Subjective Report on Health and Literacy Film Testing Trip," January 1, 1945. US National Archives. RG 229 Entry 77 Box 959. Folder: Motion Picture Division Project Files OEMcr107 to OEMCR-5230.

Confederación de Nacionalidades Indígenas del Ecuador. "Declaration of Quito." *Native Web* (blog), July 1990. http://www.nativeweb.org/papers/statements/quincentennial/quito.php.

Conze, Alexander. Letter. Camp Crockett near St. Antonio de Bexar, September 10, 1846. Chronological File 1846, June 28—1847 October 26 Conze, Alexander. Wisconsin Historical Society Archives.

Cotton, John. "Gods Promise to His Plantation." In *The Kingdom, the Power & the Glory: The Millennial Impulse in Early American Literature,* edited by Reiner Smolinski, 11–19. Dubuque, IA: Kendall/Hunt Pub. Co, 1998.

Crockett, John. Letter to Andrew Crockett, January 23, 1847. Abraham Lincoln Presidential Library, Small Collection 356—Crockett, John M.

Crooker, Turner. Letter to Marry Crooker, April 8, 1847. Wisconsin Historical Society Archives, Crooker Family Papers, Letters of Turner Crooker, 1846–1847.

Crooker, Turner. Letter to Mary Crooker, April 27, 1847. Wisconsin Historical Society Archives, Crooker Family Papers, Letters of Turner Crooker, 1846–1847.

Cutting, John. Letter to Walt Disney. "Memo," n.d. US National Archives. RG 229 Entry 77 Box 959. Folder: Literacy Program * Miscellaneous OEMcr-107-305.

Dings, Mrs. Percy J. Letter to Blakemore Godwin, July 15, 1942. US National Archives. RG 229 Entry 90 Box 1209.

"Discover Lost City of the Andes." *The American Architect,* July 9, 1913.

"Disney Finds US-Mexico Bond Strong. Mickey Mouse Creator Home from Southern Country; Declares Nation behind Allies." *Los Angeles Examiner,* December 24, 1942. US National Archives. RG 229 Entry 77 Box 958. Folder: Disney Trip to Mexico.

Douglass, Frederick. "The American Apocalypse: An Address Delivered in Rochester, New York, on 16 June 1861." In *The Frederick Douglass Papers,* vol. 3: 1855–1863: 435–45. Series One: Speeches, Debates, and Interviews, n.d. https://frederickdouglass.infoset.io/islandora/object/islandora%3A995.

Emmerson, James. Letter to Jonathan Emmerson, November 8, 1847. Abraham Lincoln Presidential Library, Small Collection 457—Emmerson, James W.

Engelmann, Adolph. "The Second Illinois in the Mexican War. Mexican War Letters of Adolph Engelmann, 1846–1847." Translated by Otto B. Engelmann. *Journal of the Illinois State Historical Society* 26, no. 4 (January 1934): 357–452.

"Evening Star Washington, DC." Newspaper Clipping, January 16, 1916. Yale Peruvian Expedition Papers, Group 664 Series VI Box 35A, "Photographs, Maps and Scrapbooks."

"Excerpt from Confidential Report Dated 5/25/43; Country—B. S. Argentina; Number-MI-260837; Doc. Date-5/6/43; Subject: PEOPLE OF URUGUAY RESENT EXCLUSION FROM DISNEY MOTION PICTURES ON SOUTH AMERICA," May 25, 1943. US National Archives. RG 229 Entry 77 Box 959. Folder: Walt Disney Field Survey and Short Subjects on the Other American Republics NDCas-110.

"Expertos en Campañas de Desanalfabetización de EE.UU. y Puerto Rico se Allan en Esta Ciudad. Observarán La Campaña Que Realiza la Unión Nacional de Periodistas." *El Comercio.* August 9, 1944. US National Archives. RG 229 Entry 77 Box 959. Folder: Literacy Program * Miscellaneous OEMcr-107–305.

"Finds Bones of Ancient Man." *New York Times,* January 21, 1912.

"Fine Arts." *New York Herald,* April 4, 1867. America's Historical Newspapers.

"Fine Arts—View of the Battle of Buena Vista." *New York Herald,* September 7, 1847.

"From the New York Sun. The Demonstration Yesterday." *Hillsdale Whig Standard,* May 18, 1847.

Godwin, Blakemore. Letter to Philip Adams, September 25, 1941. RG 229 Entry 90 Box 1209 Office of Inter-American Affairs, Records of the Department of Information, Education Division, Records Concerning Exhibits and Related Projects (E-90) Art. Folder: Art 1942 Toledo Museum of Art-Chile Survey Trip (Major US Museum Relations with Individual Countries in L. A. #1) $1654.72.

Harris, Thomas L. Letter to A. K. Riggins, October 24, 1846. Abraham Lincoln Presidential Library, "Harris, Thomas L. (Maj. Petersburg, IL) Letters, 1846–47 (Mexican War) Photostats."

"'Health for the Americas' Films Produced for the Office of Inter-American Affairs By Walt Disney Studios," 1945. US National Archives. RG 229 Entry 77 Box 959. Folder: Literacy Program * Miscellaneous OEMcr-107–305.

"The Heart of the Andes." *The Atlantic Monthly,* July 1859. 128–29. Olana New York State Historical Site Archives. Research Collection.

"The Heart of the Andes." *Chicago Tribune,* January 17, 1861.

"Heart of the Andes." *Chicago Tribune,* February 13, 1861.

"The Heart of the Andes." *Evening Post,* April 30, 1859.

"The Illumination." *Sunbury American and Shamokin Journal,* April 24, 1847.

"The Illumination in Philadelphia." *The Richmond Enquirer,* April 24, 1847.

"Important Pre-Inca Finds." *Chicago Defender,* February 10, 1912, Big Weekend edition, sec. Prominent People.

"Instructions for Topographers, 1915," n.d. Yale Peruvian Expedition Papers, Group 664, Series 1, Box 1, Folder 1–19, "Instructions for Staff, 1914–15" Sterling Memorial Library Archives and Manuscripts. Yale University.

J. M. S. "Church's Heart of the Andes." *North American and United States Gazette,* February 27, 1860.

King, John Nevin. Letter to James King, August 22, 1846. Abraham Lincoln Presidential Library. King Family Papers, Box 3, Folder 39: John Nevin King Letters 1847–1848.

King, John Nevin. Letter to Eliza Dunustan, November 28, 1846. Abraham Lincoln Presidential Library. King Family Papers, Box 3, Folder 39: John Nevin King Letters 1847–1848.

King, John Nevin. Letter to Charles King, February 3, 1847. Abraham Lincoln Presidential Library. King Family Papers, Box 3, Folder 39: John Nevin King Letters 1847–1848.

Koerner, Gustave. *Memoirs of Gustave Koerner, 1809–1896: Life-Sketches Written at the Suggestion of His Children.* Edited by Thomas J. McCormack. Vol. 1. Cedar Rapids, IA: Torch Press, 1909.

Lanier, R. O'Hara. Letter to Nelson Rockefeller, June 23, 1942. US National Archives. RG 229 Entry 90 Box 1209 Folder: Traveling Exhibitions Publicity.

"Lecturer Calls Good Neighbor Films Failure," April 11, 1942. US National Archives. RG 229 Entry 77 Box 944. Folder: Three Descriptive Films by Julien Bryan on the Other American Republics MP-1302.

"Literary Notes." *Trenton Evening Times,* January 6, 1912.

"Lost City in the Clouds Found after Centuries. Prof. Hiram Bingham of Yale Makes the Greatest Archaeological Discovery of the Age by Locating and Excavating Ruins of Machu Picchu on a Peak of the Andes in Peru." *New York Times,* June 15, 1913, sec. Sunday Magazine.

de Lozada, Enrique. Letter to Harold B. Gotaas, Halfdan Gregerson, Francis Alstock, and Kenneth R. Iverson. "Adult Literacy Program," January 2, 1946. US National Archives. RG 229 Entry 77 Box 959. Folder: Literacy Program * Miscellaneous OEMcr-107–305.

"The Man about Town." *Harper's Weekly,* May 30, 1857.

"Marvelous Lost City Found by Yale Men." *Lexington Herald,* December 26, 1911.

McCray, Porter A. Letter to Wallace K. Harrison, October 9, 1941. US National Archives. RG 229 Entry 90 Box 1209 Folder: Art 1941 US Exhibitions at Guatemala.

McGinnis, Theodore. Letter to William Beal, February 23, 1847. Wisconsin Historical Society Archives, Genealogical Items, 1847, 1890, and 1932.

"Memorandum of Agreement between the National Geographic Society on the One Hand and Yale University and Hiram Bingham, Director of the Peruvian Expedition of 1912 on the Other." Memorandum, May 2, 1912. Yale Peruvian Expedition Papers, Group 664. Series I. Box 2. Folder 2–24 "Official Documents and Legal Papers, 1912." Sterling Memorial Library Manuscripts and Archives. Yale University.

"Memorandum of Agreement . . . between the United States of America . . . and the Museum of Modern Art." Memorandum, October 16, 1941. US National Archives. RG 229 Entry 90 Box 1209. Folder: ART 1941 Travelling Exhibitions of LA Art for Smaller Centers of US.

Messersmith, George. Letter to US Secretary of State, November 28, 1942. US National Archives. RG 229 Entry 77 Box 958. Folder: Disney Trip to Mexico.

"Mr. Church's New Picture." *New York Times,* April 28, 1859.

"Mystery and Romance of 'Lost City of the Incas' Revealed in Ruins Unearthed by Professor Bingham." *New York Herald,* January 18, 1914. Yale Peruvian Expedition Papers, Group 664, Series 6, Box 35A. Sterling Memorial Library, Yale University.

"Newspaper Clipping," January 16, 1916. Yale Peruvian Expedition Papers, Group 664, Series VI, Box 35A. Sterling Memorial Library, Yale University.

Niles, Donald M. Letter to Charles E. McCarthy, August 4, 1942. US National Archives. RG 229 Entry 77 Box 959. Folder: Walt Disney Field Survey and Short Subjects on the Other American Republics NDCas-110.

Noble, Rev. Louis L. *Church's Painting. The Heart of the Andes.* New York: D. Appleton and Company, 1859.

———. "Cotopaxi. A Picture by Frederic E. Church Painted from Studies Made in the Summer of 1857." In *Creation & Renewal: Views of Cotopaxi by Frederic Edwin Church,* by Katherine Manthorne, 61–64. Washington, DC: Smithsonian Institution Press, 1863/1985.

Office of the Coordinator of Inter-American Affairs, trans. "The Unpopularity of Modern Art." *Gazeta de Noticias,* November 29, 1941. RG 229 Entry 90 Box 1209 Office of Inter-American Affairs, Records of the Department of Information, Education Division, Records Concerning Exhibits and Related Projects (E-90) Art. Folder: ART 1941 Latin American Exhibitions of Contemporary Painting NDCar—14 $50,100.

"Older Than the Incas." *Anaconda Standard,* August 29, 1912.

Ozburn, Lindorf. Letter to Diza Ozburn, July 14, 1847. Abraham Lincoln Presidential Library. Small Collection 1130–Ozburn, Lindorf.

"Peru Report Is Awaited." *Grand Forks Daily Herald,* December 28, 1911.

"Peruvian Ruins." *Montgomery Advertiser,* December 20, 1912.

Pierce, Russell. Letter to Vern Caldwell, April 25, 1944. US National Archives. RG 229 Entry 77 Box 959. Folder: Walt Disney Field Survey and Short Subjects on the Other American Republics NDCas-110.

———. Letter to Vern Caldwell, May 4, 1944. US National Archives. RG 229 Entry 77 Box 959. Folder: Walt Disney Field Survey and Short Subjects on the Other American Republics NDCar-110.

———. Letter to Floyd Gottfredson, July 19, 1944. US National Archives. RG 229 Entry 77 Box 959. Folder: Walt Disney Field Survey and Short Subjects on the Other American Republics NDCas-110.

"Prof. Hiram Bingham of Yale Makes the Greatest Archaeological Discovery of the Age . . . ." *New York Times,* June 15, 1913.

"Project Authorization," December 12, 1941. US National Archives. RG 229 Entry 77 Box 959. Folder: Walt Disney Productions Film Unit OEMcr-107.

"Project Authorization. Disney Trip to Mexico. Identification No. B-MP-1537," December 22, 1942. US National Archives. RG 229 Entry 77 Box 958. Folder: Disney Trip to Mexico.

"Project Authorization. Identification No. MP-1302," June 13, 1942. US National Archives. RG 229 Entry 77 Box 944. Folder: Three Descriptive Films by Julien Bryan on the Other American Republics MP-1302.

"Project Authorization. Walt Disney Field Survey and Short Subjects on the Other American Republics. Contract NCCAR-110," June 16, 1941.

Ralston, James. Letter to A. Wheat, March 22, 1848. Abraham Lincoln Presidential Library, Small Collection 1228—Ralston, James H.

"Renewing Interest in Geography." *Pittsburgh Post,* January 31, 1915. Yale Peruvian Expedition Papers, Group 664, Series 6, Box 35A. Sterling Memorial Library, Yale University.

"Report on Conference of Leaders of Inter-American Activities in the United States," November 1944. Rockefeller Archives Center. Nelson A. Rockefeller personal papers, Washington, DC, Series O (FA350). Volume 80 (bound volume).

"The Research Com of the Nat Geog Soc . . ." Memo, n.d. Yale Peruvian Expedition Papers, Group 664. Series I. Box 1. Folder 1–2 "Plans for Expedition, 1912" Sterling Memorial Library Manuscripts and Archives. Yale University.

Rockefeller, Nelson. "Chapter II ('The US in the World')," 1949. Rockefeller Archives Center. Nelson A. Rockefeller personal papers, Activities, series A (FA338) Box 24, Folder 153. Reference File No. 9—Part 2, 1949.

———. Letter to US Secretary of State, September 7, 1944. Series A. NAR Personal Activities—FA338—Box 24. Folder 155. Rockefeller Archives Center.

———. Letter to US Under Secretary of State, October 31, 1944. Series A. NAR Personal Activities—FA338—Box 24. Folder 155. Rockefeller Archives Center.

Roosevelt, Theodore. "Corollary to the Monroe Doctrine." December 6, 1904. Our Documents. https://www.ourdocuments.gov/doc.php?flash=true&doc=56&page=transcript.

"Seek Lost Inca Cities." *Los Angeles Times,* May 17, 1911.

"Sees Old Peruvian City." *New York Tribune,* December 22, 1911.

Snyder, Frederick. Letter to John F. Snyder, July 1, 1847. Abraham Lincoln Presidential Library, John F. Snyder Collection, Box 1, Folder: "Correspondence 1847."

———. Letter to John F. Snyder, July 4, 1847. Abraham Lincoln Presidential Library, John F. Snyder Collection, Box 1, Folder: "Correspondence 1847."

———. Letter to John F. Snyder, July 27, 1847. Abraham Lincoln Presidential Latina Library, John F. Snyder Collection, Box 1, Folder: "Correspondence 1847."

———. Letter to John F. Snyder, August 10, 1847. Abraham Lincoln Presidential Library, John F. Snyder Collection, Box 1, Folder: "Correspondence 1847."

———. Letter to John F. Snyder, August 16, 1847. Abraham Lincoln Presidential Library, John F. Snyder Collection, Box 1, Folder: "Correspondence 1847."

Snyder, John F. Letter to Frederick Snyder, May 6, 1847. Abraham Lincoln Presidential Library, John F. Snyder Collection, Box 1, Folder: "Correspondence 1847."

———. Letter to Frederick Snyder, July 15, 1847. Abraham Lincoln Presidential Library, John F. Snyder Collection, Box 1, Folder: "Correspondence 1847."

Sodi de Pallares, María Elena. "Genialidad de Walt Disney Desvirtuada por Extraños," n.d. US National Archives. RG 229 Entry 77 Box 959. Folder: Literacy Program * Miscellaneous OEMcr-107-305.

"Statements at the Preview of Health Films," June 22, 1945. US National Archives. RG 229 Entry 77 Box 959. Folder: Literacy Program * Miscellaneous OEMcr-107-305.

"Translation of an Item Published by Ultimas Noticias September 13, 1944. Diary of a Newspaper Reporter by Carlos Denegri," October 2, 1944. US National Archives. RG 229 Entry 77 Box 959. Folder: Literacy Program * Miscellaneous OEMcr-107–305.

Untitled article. *Duluth News-Tribune,* June 23, 1912.

"Walt Disney Nos Visita." *Población,* February 1943. US National Archives. RG 229 Entry 77 Box 958. Folder: Disney Trip to Mexico.

"Will Seek Lost Cities." *Los Angeles Times,* June 12, 1911.

Winthrop, Theodore. *A Companion to The Heart of the Andes.* New York: D. Appleton and Company, 1859.

"Yale Expedition Back from Peru." *New York Times,* December 22, 1911.

"Young Americans Seek to Erase 'Black Spots' off Map." *New York Times,* June 2, 1912. SM 14.

Secondary Sources

Adams, Mark. "Discover 10 Secrets of Machu Picchu." National Geographic. Accessed September 20, 2020. https://www.nationalgeographic.com/travel/top-10/peru/machu-picchu/secrets/.

Agnew, Lois. "The Civic Function of Taste: A Re-Assessment of Hugh Blair's Rhetorical Theory." *Rhetoric Society Quarterly* 28, no. 2 (Spring 1998): 25–36.

Ahmed, Sara. "Happy Objects." In *The Affect Theory Reader,* edited by Melissa Gregg and Gregory J. Seigworth, 29–51. Durham, NC: Duke University Press, 2010.

Alberto, Lourdes. "Coming Out as Indian: On Being an Indigenous Latina in the US." *Latino Studies* 15, no. 2 (July 2017): 247–53.

Amon Carter Museum of Western Art, Martha A. Sandweiss, Rick Stewart, and Ben W. Huseman, eds. *Eyewitness to War: Prints and Daguerreotypes of the Mexican War, 1846–1848.* Fort Worth, TX / Washington, DC: Amon Carter Museum / Smithsonian Institution Press, 1989.

Andrade, Susana. *Protestantismo Indígena: Procesos de Conversión Religiosa En La Provincia de Chimborazo*. Quito / Lima: Abya-Yala / FLACSO, Sede Ecuador / IFEA, 2004.

Anthony, Edwin D., ed. *Records of the Office of Inter-American Affairs. Inventory of Record Group 229*. Washington, DC: National Archives and Records Service, General Services Administration, 1973.

Aristotle. *On Rhetoric: A Theory of Civic Discourse*. Translated by George A. Kennedy. 2nd ed. Oxford: Oxford University Press, 2007.

Arola, Kristin L. "My Pink Powwow Shawl, Relationality, and Posthumanism." *Rhetoric Review* 38, no. 4 (October 2, 2019): 386–90.

Avery, Kevin J. *Church's Great Picture: The Heart of the Andes*. New York: The Metropolitan Museum of Art, 1993.

———. "'The Heart of the Andes' Exhibited: Frederic E. Church's Window on the Equatorial World." *The American Art Journal* 18, no. 1 (1986): 52–72.

Balzotti, Jonathan Mark, and Richard Benjamin Crosby. "Diocletian's Victory Column: Megethos and the Rhetoric of Spectacular Disruption." *Rhetoric Society Quarterly* 44, no. 4 (August 8, 2014): 323–42.

Bauer, Brian S. *Ancient Cuzco: Heartland of the Inca*. Austin: University of Texas Press, 2004.

Bayers, Peter L. *Imperial Ascent: Mountaineering, Masculinity, and Empire*. Boulder: University Press of Colorado, 2003.

Bell, Derrick A. *And We Are Not Saved: The Elusive Quest for Racial Justice; with a New Appendix for Classroom Discussion*. San Francisco: Basic Books, 1989.

———. *Faces at the Bottom of the Well: The Permanence of Racism*. New York: Basic Books, 1992.

Berlant, Lauren Gail. *Cruel Optimism*. Durham, NC: Duke University Press, 2011.

Bingham, Alfred M. *Explorer of Machu Picchu: Portrait of Hiram Bingham*. Greenwich, CT: Triune Books, 2000.

Blair, Hugh. *Lectures on Rhetoric and Belles Lettres*. Eighteenth Century Collections Online Text Creation Partnership. Ann Arbor, MI / Dublin: University of Michigan Library / Messrs. Whitestone, Colles, Burnet, Moncrieffe, Gilbert, etc., 2009. http://name.umdl.umich.edu/004786433.0001.001.

Blankenship, Lisa. *Changing the Subject: A Theory of Rhetorical Empathy*. Logan: Utah State University Press, 2019.

Botero V., Luis Fernando. *Indios, Tierra y Cultura*. Quito: Ediciones ABYA-YALA, 1992.

Brandt, Deborah. *The Rise of Writing: Redefining Mass Literacy*. Cambridge: Cambridge University Press, 2015.

Broaddus, Dottie. "Authoring Elitism: Francis Hutcheson and Hugh Blair in Scotland and America." *Rhetoric Society Quarterly* 24, no. 3/4 (Summer–Autumn 1994): 39–52.

Burger, Richard L., and Lucy Salazar Burger. "Machu Picchu Rediscovered: The Royal Estate in the Cloud Forest." *Discovery* 24, no. 2 (1993): 20–25.

Burke, Kenneth. *A Rhetoric of Motives*. Berkeley: University of California Press, 2013.

Cadena, Marisol de la. *Earth Beings: Ecologies of Practice across Andean Worlds*. Durham, NC: Duke University Press, 2015.

———. *Indigenous Mestizos: The Politics of Race and Culture in Cuzo, 1919-1991*. Durham, NC: Duke University Press, 2000.

Calafell, Bernadette Marie. "Brownness, Kissing, and US Imperialism: Contextualizing the Orlando Massacre." *Communication and Critical/Cultural Studies* 14, no. 2 (April 3, 2017): 198–202.

Camp, Stephanie M. H. *Closer to Freedom: Enslaved Women and Everyday Resistance in the Plantation South.* Chapel Hill: University of North Carolina Press, 2004.

Campt, Tina. *Listening to Images.* Durham, NC: Duke University Press, 2017.

Carey, M. "Mountaineers and Engineers: The Politics of International Science, Recreation, and Environmental Change in Twentieth-Century Peru." *Hispanic American Historical Review* 92, no. 1 (January 1, 2012): 107–41.

Carillo Rowe, Aime, and Sheena Malhotra. "(Un)Hinging Whiteness." In *International and Intercultural Communication Annual. The Same and Different: Acknowledging the Diversity Within and Between Cultural Groups,* edited by Mark P. Orbe, Brenda J. Allen, and Lisa A. Flores, XXIX:166–92. Washington, DC: National Communication Association, 2006.

Carr, Stephen L. "The Circulation of Blair's 'Lectures.'" *Rhetoric Society Quarterly* 32, no. 4 (Autumn 2002): 75–104.

Casey, Edward S. "Attending and Glancing." *Continental Philosophy Review* 37 (2004): 83–126.

———. *The World at a Glance.* Bloomington: Indiana University Press, 2007.

Cedillo, Christina. "Unruly Borders, Bodies, and Blood: Mexican 'Mongrels' and the Eugenics of Empire." *Journal for the History of Rhetoric* 24, no. 1 (2021): 7–23.

Charland, Maurice. "Constitutive Rhetoric: The Case of the Peuple Québécois." *Quarterly Journal of Speech* 73, no. 2 (May 1987): 133–50.

Chávez, Hugo. "Hugo Chávez Speech in La Habana. 1994." TeleSUR English. Posted December 12, 2014. YouTube video. https://www.youtube.com/watch?v=lFzbqFcePp8.

Chávez, Karma R. "Beyond Inclusion: Rethinking Rhetoric's Historical Narrative." *Quarterly Journal of Speech* 101, no. 1 (January 2, 2015): 162–72.

———. "The Body: An Abstract and Actual Rhetorical Concept." *Rhetoric Society Quarterly* 48, no. 3 (May 27, 2018): 242–50.

———. "From Sanctuary to a Queer Politics of Fugitivity." *QED: A Journal in GLBTQ Worldmaking* 4, no. 2 (Summer 2017): 63–70.

———. *Queer Migration Politics: Activist Rhetoric and Coalitional Possibilities.* Urbana: University of Illinois Press, 2013.

Cifor, Marika. "Affecting Relations: Introducing Affect Theory to Archival Discourse." *Archives & Museum Informatics* 16, no. 1 (2015): 7–31.

Cintrón, Ralph. "Democracy and Its Limitations." In *The Public Work of Rhetoric: Citizen-Scholars and Civic Engagement,* edited by John M. Ackerman and David J. Coogan, 98–116. Columbia: University of South Carolina Press, 2010.

Cisneros, Josue David. *The Border Crossed Us: Rhetorics of Borders, Citizenship, and Latina/o Identity.* Tuscaloosa: The University of Alabama Press, 2014.

Clark, A. Kim. "Racial Ideologies and the Quest for National Development: Debating the Agrarian Problem in Ecuador (1930–50)." *Journal of Latin American Studies* 30, no. 2 (May 1998): 373–93.

Clark, Gregory. "The Oratorical Poetic of Timothy Dwight." In *Oratorical Culture in Nineteenth-Century America: Transformations in the Theory and Practice of Rhetoric,* 57–77. Carbondale: Southern Illinois University Press, 1993.

———. *Rhetorical Landscapes in America: Variations on a Theme from Kenneth Burke.* Columbia: University of South Carolina Press, 2004.

Clary, David A. *Eagles and Empire: The United States, Mexico, and the Struggle for a Continent.* New York: Bantam Dell, 2009.

Clary-Lemon, Jennifer. "Gifts, Ancestors, and Relations: Notes toward an Indigenous New Materialism." *Enculturation,* November 12, 2019.

———. *Planting the Anthropocene: Rhetorics of Natureculture.* Logan: Utah State University Press, 2019.

Cloud, Dana L. "'To Veil the Threat of Terror': Afghan Women and the (Clash of Civilizations) in the Imagery of the US War on Terrorism." *Quarterly Journal of Speech* 90, no. 3 (August 2004): 285–306.

Clyde, Wanett. "The (Unexpected) Emotional Impact of Archiving." *WITNESS.Org | Archiving Human Rights* (blog), August 2015. https://archiving.witness.org/2015/08/the-unexpected-emotional-impact-of-archiving/.

Condit, Celeste Michelle. "The Functions of Epideictic: The Boston Massacre Orations as Exemplar." *Communication Quarterly* 33, no. 4 (Fall 1985): 284–99.

Corrigan, Lisa M., and Anjali Vats. "The Structural Whiteness of Academic Patronage." *Communication and Critical/Cultural Studies* 17, no. 2 (April 2, 2020): 220–27.

Cramer, Gisela, and Ursula Prutsch. "Nelson A. Rockefeller's Office of Inter-American Affairs (1940–1946) and Record Group 229." *Hispanic American Historical Review* 86, no. 4 (November 1, 2006): 785–806.

Cushman, Ellen. "Wampum, Sequoyan, and Story: Decolonizing the Digital Archive." *College English* 76, no. 2 (November 2013): 115–35.

Cvetkovich, Ann. *Depression: A Public Feeling.* Durham, NC: Duke University Press, 2012.

Davis, Heather, and Zoe Todd. "On the Importance of a Date, or Decolonizing the Anthropocene." *ACME: An International Journal for Critical Geographers* 16, no. 4 (2017): 761–80.

Davis, Olga Idriss. "A Black Woman as Rhetorical Critic: Validating Self and Violating the Space of Otherness." *Women's Studies in Communication* 21, no. 1 (1998).

———. "In the Kitchen: Transforming the Academy through Safe Spaces of Resistance." *Western Journal of Communication* 63, no. 3 (September 1999): 364–81.

DeBruyne, Nese F. "American War and Military Operations Casualties: Lists and Statistics." Congressional Research Service, April 26, 2017. https://fas.org/sgp/crs/natsec/RL32492.pdf.

DeChaine, D. Robert, ed. *Border Rhetorics: Citizenship and Identity on the US-Mexico Frontier.* Tuscaloosa: University of Alabama Press, 2012.

Delgado, Richard. "Storytelling for Oppositionists and Others: A Plea for Narrative." *Michigan Law Review* 87, no. 8 (August 1989): 2411–41.

Doss, Erika. *Memorial Mania: Public Feeling in America.* Chicago: University of Chicago Press, 2010.

Dougherty, Timothy R. "Knowing (Y)Our Story: Practicing Decolonial Rhetorical History." *Enculturation,* no. 21: Cultural Rhetorics (2016).

Druschke, Caroline Gottschalk. "A Trophic Future for Rhetorical Ecologies." *Enculturation,* no. 28 (2019). http://enculturation.net/a-trophic-future.

Earle, Chris S. "Dispossessed: Prisoner Response-Ability and Resistance at the Limits of Subjectivity." *Rhetoric Society Quarterly* 46 no. 1 (2016): 47–65.

Edbauer, Jenny. "Unframing Models of Public Distribution: From Rhetorical Situation to Rhetorical Ecologies." *Rhetoric Society Quarterly* 35, no. 4 (Fall 2005): 5–24.

Edsall, Thomas B. "I Fear That We Are Witnessing the End of American Democracy." *The New York Times.* August 26, 2020, sec. Opinion. https://www.nytimes.com/2020/08/26/opinion/trump-republican-convention-racism.html.

Engelhardt, Tom. "The End of the American Century." *The Nation,* June 19, 2020. https://www.thenation.com/article/world/trump-empire-decline/.

Escobar, Arturo. "Worlds and Knowledges Otherwise: The Latin American Modernity/Coloniality Research Program." *Cultural Studies* 21, no. 2–3 (March 2007): 179–210.

Espinosa, Mariola. *Epidemic Invasions: Yellow Fever and the Limits of Cuban Independence, 1878–1930*. Chicago: The University of Chicago Press, 2009.

Farrell, Thomas B. "Sizing Things Up: Colloquial Reflections as Practical Wisdom." *Argumentation* 12 (1998): 1–14.

———. "The Weight of Rhetoric: Studies in Cultural Delirium." *Philosophy and Rhetoric* 41, no. 4 (2008): 467–87.

Finnegan, Cara A. "The Critic as Curator." *Rhetoric Society Quarterly* 48, no. 4 (August 8, 2018): 405–10.

———. *Making Photography Matter: A Viewer's History from the Civil War to the Great Depression*. Urbana: University of Illinois Press, 2015.

———. *Picturing Poverty: Print Culture and FSA Photographs*. Washington, DC: Smithsonian Institution Press, 2003.

———. "Recognizing Lincoln: Image Vernaculars in Nineteenth-Century Visual Culture." *Rhetoric & Public Affairs* 8, no. 1 (2005): 31–58.

Finnegan, Cara A., and Jiyeon Kang. "'Sighting' the Public: Iconoclasm and Public Sphere Theory." *Quarterly Journal of Speech* 90, no. 4 (November 2004): 377–402.

Flores, Lisa A. "Between Abundance and Marginalization: The Imperative of Racial Rhetorical Criticism." *Review of Communication* 16, no. 1 (January 2, 2016): 4–24.

———. *Deportable and Disposable: Public Rhetoric and the Making of the "Illegal" Immigrant*. University Park: The Pennsylvania State University Press, 2020.

———. "Stoppage and the Racialized Rhetorics of Mobility." *Western Journal of Communication* (October 16, 2019): 1–17.

Flores, Lisa A., and Mary Ann Villarreal. "Mobilizing for National Inclusion: The Discursivity of Whiteness among Texas Mexicans' Arguments for Desegregation." In *Border Rhetorics: Citizenship and Identity on the US-Mexico Frontier*, edited by D. Robert Dechaine, 86–100. Tuscaloosa: University of Alabama Press, 2012.

Foos, Paul. *A Short, Offhand, Killing Affair: Soldiers and Social Conflict during the Mexican-American War*. Chapel Hill: University of North Carolina Press, 2002.

García, Romeo. "Creating Presence from Absence and Sound from Silence." *Community Literacy Journal* 13, no. 1 (2018): 7–15.

Garland-Thomson, Rosemarie. *Staring: How We Look*. Oxford: Oxford University Press, 2009.

Garza, Alicia. *The Purpose of Power: How to Build Movements for the 21st Century*. New York: One World, 2020.

Goldberg, David Theo. *The Threat of Race: Reflections on Racial Neoliberalism*. Malden, MA: Wiley-Blackwell, 2009.

Gómez, Leila. "Machu Picchu Reclamada. Viajes y Fotografías de Hiram Bingham, Abraham Guillén y Martín Chambi." *Revista Iberoamericana* 73, no. 220 (September 2007): 497–513.

Gómez-Barris, Macarena. "Andean Gateways: Transnational Healing and Spiritual Tourism in the Sacred Valley, Peru." In *Re-Framing the Transnational Turn in American Studies*, edited by Winifried Fluck, Donald E. Pease, and John Carlos Rowe, 337–55. Hanover, NH: Dartmouth College Press, 2011.

Greenberg, Amy S. *Manifest Manhood and the Antebellum American Empire*. Cambridge: Cambridge University Press, 2005.

———. *A Wicked War: Polk, Clay, Lincoln, and the 1846 US Invasion of Mexico*. New York: Vintage Books, 2013.

Gries, Laurie E. *Still Life with Rhetoric: A New Materialist Approach for Visual Rhetorics.* Logan: Utah State University Press, 2015.

Gruesz, Kirsten Silva. "America." In *Keywords for American Cultural Studies,* edited by Bruch Burgett and Glenn Hendler, 16–22. New York: New York University Press, 2007.

Guardino, Peter F. *The Dead March: A History of the Mexican-American War.* Cambridge, MA: Harvard University Press, 2017.

Hall, Amy Cox. "Collecting a 'Lost City' for Science: Huaquero Vision and the Yale Peruvian Expeditions to Machu Picchu, 1911, 1912, and 1914–15." *Ethnohistory* 59, no. 2 (April 1, 2012): 293–321.

———. *Framing a Lost City: Science, Photography, and the Making of Machu Picchu.* Austin: University of Texas Press, 2017.

Hallenbeck, Sarah. "Toward a Posthuman Perspective: Feminist Rhetorical Methodologies and Everyday Practices." *Advances in the History of Rhetoric* 15, no. 1 (January 2012): 9–27.

Halloran, S. Michael, and Gregory Clark. "National Park Landscapes and the Rhetorical Display of a Civic Religion." In *Rhetorics of Display,* edited by Lawrence Prelli, 141–56. Columbia: University of South Carolina Press, 2006.

Haraway, Donna. "Situated Knowledges: The Science Question in Feminism and the Privilege of Partial Perspective." *Feminist Studies* 14, no. 3 (Autumn 1988): 575–99.

Hartelius, E. Johanna, and Jennifer Asenas. "Citational Epideixis and a 'Thinking of Community': The Case of the Minuteman Project." *Rhetoric Society Quarterly* 40, no. 4 (2010): 360–84.

Harter, Jim. *World Railways of the Nineteenth Century: A Pictorial History in Victorian Engravings.* Baltimore: Johns Hopkins University Press, 2005.

Hartman, Saidiya. "Venus in Two Acts." *Small Axe* 12, no. 2 (June 2008): 1–14.

Harvey, Eleanor Jones. "America's Moral Volcano." *New York Times,* February 5, 2013, sec. Opinion. https://opinionator.blogs.nytimes.com/2013/02/05/americas-moral-volcano/.

———. *The Civil War and American Art.* Washington, DC / New Haven, CT: Smithsonian American Art Museum / Yale University Press, 2012.

Hawhee, Debra. "Looking into Aristotle's Eyes: Toward a Theory of Rhetorical Vision." *Advances in the History of Rhetoric* 14, no. 2 (July 2011): 139–65.

———. *Rhetoric in Tooth and Claw: Animals, Language, Sensation.* Chicago: The University of Chicago Press, 2016.

———. "Rhetoric's Sensorium." *Quarterly Journal of Speech* 101, no. 1 (January 2, 2015): 2–17.

Hawhee, Debra, and Christa J. Olson. "Pan-Historiography: The Challenge of Writing History across Time and Space." In *Theorizing Histories of Rhetoric,* edited by Michelle Ballif, 90–105. Carbondale: Southern Illinois University Press, 2013.

Heaney, Christopher. *Cradle of Gold: The Story of Hiram Bingham, a Real-Life Indiana Jones and the Search for Machu Picchu.* New York: MacMillan, 2011.

Henderson, Timothy J. *A Glorious Defeat: Mexico and Its War with the United States.* New York: Hill and Wang, 2007.

Henkin, David M. *The Postal Age: The Emergence of Modern Communications in Nineteenth-Century America.* Chicago: University of Chicago Press, 2006.

Hilfrich, Fabian. *Debating American Exceptionalism: Empire and Democracy in the Wake of the Spanish-American War.* New York: Palgrave Macmillan, 2012.

Holmes, David G. "Say What? Rediscovering Hugh Blair and the Racialization of Language, Culture, and Pedagogy in Eighteenth-Century Rhetoric." In *Calling Cards: Theory and Practice in the Study of Race, Gender, and Culture,* edited by Jacqueline Jones Royster and Ann Marie Mann Simpkins, 203–13. New York: State University of New York Press, 2005.

Horner, Winifred Bryan. *Nineteenth-Century Scottish Rhetoric: The American Connection.* Carbondale: Southern Illinois University Press, 1993.

Howat, John K. *Frederic Church.* New Haven, CT: Yale University Press, 2005.

Huntington, David C. "Landscapes and Diaries: The South American Trips of F. E. Church." *Brooklyn Museum Annual* 5 (1965): 65–98.

Jack, Jordynn. "A Pedagogy of Sight: Microscopic Vision in Robert Hooke's *Micrographia.*" *Quarterly Journal of Speech* 95, no. 2 (May 2009): 192–209.

Jackson, Rachel C. "Resisting Relocation: Placing Leadership on Decolonized Indigenous Landscapes." *College English* 79, no. 5 (May 2017): 495–511.

Jackson, Rachel C., and Dorothy M. Whitehorse DeLaune. "Decolonizing Community Writing with Community Listening: Story, Transrhetorical Resistance, and Indigenous Cultural Literacy Activism." *Community Literacy Journal* 13, no. 1 (2018): 37–54.

Johannsen, Robert Walter. *To the Halls of the Montezumas: The Mexican War in the American Imagination.* New York: Oxford University Press, 1985.

Johnson, Jenell. "'A Man's Mouth Is His Castle': The Midcentury Fluoridation Controversy and the Visceral Public." *Quarterly Journal of Speech* 102, no. 1 (January 2, 2016): 1–20.

Johnson, Nan. *Nineteenth-Century Rhetoric in North America.* Carbondale: Southern Illinois University Press, 1991.

Jordan, Jay, Kristin L. Arola, Casey Boyle, Gabriela Raquel Ríos, Donnie Johnson Sackey, Julie Jung, Scot Barnett, Mai Nou Xiong, Timothy R. Dougherty, and Lauren Cagle. "Continuing the Conversation: Perspectives on Cultural and Posthumanist Rhetorics." *Rhetoric Review* 38, no. 4 (October 2, 2019): 394–99.

Justice, Daniel Heath. "'Go Away, Water!': Kinship Criticism and the Decolonization Imperative." In *Reasoning Together: The Native Critics Collection,* 147–68. Norman: University of Oklahoma Press, 2008.

Kaplan, Amy. *The Anarchy of Empire in the Making of US Culture.* Cambridge, MA: Harvard University Press, 2005.

Keeling, Diane M., and Jennifer C. Prairie. "Trophic and Tropic Dynamics: An Ecological Perspective of Tropes." In *Tracing Rhetoric and Material Life: Ecological Approaches,* edited by Bridie McGreavy, Justine Wells, George F. McHendry Jr., and Samantha Senda-Cook, 39–58. New York: Palgrave Macmillan, 2018.

Kelly, Franklin. *Frederic Edwin Church and the National Landscape.* Washington, DC: Smithsonian Institution Press, 1988.

———. "A Passion for Landscape: The Paintings of Frederic Edwin Church." In *Frederic Edwin Church,* edited by Franklin Kelly, 32–75. Washington, DC: National Gallery of Art, 1989.

Kennedy Troya, Alexandra. "Artistas y Científicos: Naturaleza Independiente en el Siglo XIX en Ecuador (Rafael Troya y Joaquín Pinto)." *Estudios de Arte y Estético* 37 (1994): 223–41.

———. "La Percepción de lo Propio: Paisajistas y Científicos Ecuatorianos del Siglo XIX." In *El Regreso de Humboldt. Exposición En El Museo de La Ciudad de Quito, Junio-Agosto Del 2001,* edited by Frank Holl, 113–27. Quito: Museo de la Ciudad de Quito, 2001.

Kramer, Paul A. *The Blood of Government: Race, Empire, the United States, & the Philippines.* Chapel Hill: University of North Carolina Press, 2006.

Kynard, Carmen. *Vernacular Insurrections: Race, Black Protest, and the New Century in Composition-Literacies Studies.* New York: State University of New York Press, 2014.

Lachmann, Richard. "Life at the End of American Empire." *Lit Hub,* January 14, 2020. https://lithub.com/life-at-the-end-of-american-empire/.

Larson, Stephanie R. "'Just Let This Sink In': Feminist *Megethos* and the Role of Lists in #MeToo." *Rhetoric Review* 38, no. 4 (October 2, 2019): 432–44.

LaWare, Margaret R. "Encountering Visions of Aztlan: Arguments for Ethnic Pride, Community Activism and Cultural Revitalization in Chicano Murals." *Argumentation and Advocacy* 34 (Winter 1998): 140–53.

Leary, John Patrick. *A Cultural History of Underdevelopment: Latin America in the US Imagination.* Charlottesville: University of Virginia Press, 2016.

Levander, Caroline Field, and Robert S. Levine. "Introduction: Essays beyond the Nation." In *Hemispheric American Studies,* edited by Caroline Field Levander and Robert S. Levine, 1–17. New Brunswick, NJ: Rutgers University Press, 2008.

Lewis, Martin W., and Kären Wigen. *The Myth of Continents: A Critique of Metageography.* Berkeley: University of California Press, 1997.

Lowry, Elizabeth. "The Flower of Cuba: Rhetoric, Representation, and Circulation at the Outbreak of the Spanish-American War." *Rhetoric Review* 32, no. 2 (April 2013): 174–90.

Lunsford, Andrea A., and Lisa S. Ede. *Writing Together: Collaboration in Theory and Practice, a Critical Sourcebook.* Boston, MA: Bedford/St. Martins, 2012.

Malin, Brenton J. "Looking White and Middle-Class: Stereoscopic Imagery and Technology in the Early Twentieth-Century United States." *Quarterly Journal of Speech* 93, no. 4 (November 2007): 403–24.

Manthorne, Katherine. *Creation & Renewal: Views of Cotopaxi by Frederic Edwin Church.* Washington, DC: Smithsonian Institution Press, 1985.

Martinez, Aja Y. *Counterstory: The Rhetoric and Writing of Critical Race Theory.* Champaign, IL: Conference on College Composition and Communication, National Council of Teachers of English, 2020.

———. "A Plea for Critical Race Theory Counterstory: Dialogues Concerning Alejandra's 'Fit' in the Academy." *Composition Studies* 42, no. 2 (2014): 33–55.

———. "The Responsibility of Privilege: A Critical Race Counterstory Conversation." *Peitho* 21, no. 1 (2018): 212–33.

Maxwell, Keely. "Tourism, Environment, and Development on the Inca Trail." *Hispanic American Historical Review* 92, no. 1 (January 1, 2012): 143–71.

McKeon, Richard. "Creativity and the Commonplace." *Philosophy and Rhetoric* 6, no. 4 (Fall 1973): 199–210.

Mercieca, Jennifer R. *Demagogue for President: The Rhetorical Genius of Donald Trump.* College Station: Texas A&M University Press, 2020.

Mignolo, Walter. *The Darker Side of Western Modernity: Global Futures, Decolonial Options.* Durham, NC: Duke University Press, 2011.

———. "The Geopolitics of Knowledge and the Colonial Difference." *South Atlantic Quarterly* 101, no. 1 (Winter 2002): 57–96.

Miller, Bonnie M. *From Liberation to Conquest: The Visual and Popular Cultures of the Spanish-American War of 1898.* Amherst: University of Massachusetts Press, 2011.

Miller, Carolyn R. "The Aristotelian Topos: Hunting for Novelty." In *Rereading Aristotle's Rhetoric,* 130–46. Carbondale: Southern Illinois University Press, 2000.

Mirzoeff, Nicholas. *The Right to Look: A Counterhistory of Visuality.* Durham, NC: Duke University Press, 2011.

Mould de Pease, Mariana. "Un Día en la Vida Peruana de Machu Picchu: Avance de Historia Intercultural." *Revista Compultense de Historia de América* 27 (2001): 257–79.

Muñoz, José Esteban. "Feeling Brown: Ethnicity and Affect in Ricardo Bracho's *The Sweetest Hangover (and Other STDs)*." *Theatre Journal* 52 (2000): 67–79.

Murphy, Gretchen. *Hemispheric Imaginings: The Monroe Doctrine and Narratives of US Empire*. Durham, NC: Duke University Press, 2005.

———. *Shadowing the White Man's Burden: US Imperialism and the Problem of the Color Line*. New York: New York University Press, 2010.

Na'puti, Tiara R. "Archipelagic Rhetoric: Remapping the Marianas and Challenging Militarization from 'A Stirring Place.'" *Communication and Critical/Cultural Studies* 16, no. 1 (January 2, 2019): 4–25.

Navarro, José Gabriel. *La Pintura en el Ecuador del XVI al XIX*. Quito: Dinediciones, 1991.

Navas Sanz de Santamaría, Pablo, and Frederic Edwin Church. *The Journey of Frederic Edwin Church through Colombia and Ecuador, April–October 1853*. Bogotá: Villegas Editores / Universidad de los Andes / Thomas Greg & Sons, 2008.

Nevins, Allan. Introduction to *Polk: The Diary of a President 1845–1849*, by James K. Polk, xi–xxii. London: Longmans, Green, and Co., 1952.

Novak, Barbara. "American Landscape: Changing Concepts of the Sublime." *The American Art Journal* 4, no. 1 (1972): 36–42.

O'Gorman, Edmundo. *The Invention of America: An Inquiry into the Historical Nature of the New World and the Meaning of Its History*. Bloomington: Indiana University Press, 1961.

O'Gorman, Ned. "Eisenhower and the American Sublime." *Quarterly Journal of Speech* 94, no. 1 (February 2008): 44–72.

———. "Longinus's Sublime Rhetoric, or How Rhetoric Came into Its Own." *Rhetoric Society Quarterly* 34, no. 2 (March 2004): 71–89.

Olson, Christa J. "American Magnitude: Frederic Church, Hiram Bingham, and Hemispheric Vision." *Rhetoric Society Quarterly*, September 15, 2017, 1–25.

———. "'But in Regard to These (the American) Continents': US National Rhetorics and the Figure of Latin America." *Rhetoric Society Quarterly* 45, no. 3 (May 27, 2015): 264–77.

———. *Constitutive Visions: Indigeneity and Commonplaces of National Identity in Republican Ecuador*. University Park: The Pennsylvania State University Press, 2014.

Olson, Christa J. "The Democratic Hemisphere" in *Rhetorics of Democracy in the Americas*, edited by Adriana Angel, Michael L. Butterworth, and Nancy R. Gómez, 23–38. University Park: The Pennsylvania State University Press, 2021.

Olson, Christa J., and Rubén Casas. "Felipe Guaman Poma de Ayala's *Primer Nueva Corónica y Buen Gobierno* and the Practice of Rhetorical Theory in Colonial Peru." *Quarterly Journal of Speech* 101, no. 3 (July 3, 2015): 459–84.

Olson, Lester C. *Emblems of American Community in the Revolutionary Era: A Study in Rhetorical Iconology*. Washington, DC: Smithsonian Institution Press, 1991.

———. "Pictorial Representations of British America Resisting Rape: Rhetorical Re-Circulation of a Print Series Portraying the Boston Port Bill of 1774." *Rhetoric & Public Affairs* 12, no. 1 (2009): 1–36.

Ore, Ersula J. *Lynching: Violence, Rhetoric, and American Identity*. Jackson: University Press of Mississippi, 2019.

Packer, George. "America's Plastic Hour Is upon Us." *The Atlantic*, October 2020. https://www.theatlantic.com/magazine/archive/2020/10/make-america-again/615478/.

Panagia, Davide. *The Political Life of Sensation*. Durham, NC: Duke University Press, 2009.

Patterson, Thomas C. *The Inca Empire: The Formation and Disintegration of a Pre-Capitalist State.* New York: Berg / St. Martin's Press, 1991.

Peeples, Jennifer. "Toxic Sublime: Imaging Contaminated Landscapes." *Environmental Communication* 5, no. 4 (December 2011): 373–92.

Pérez, Emma. *The Decolonial Imaginary: Writing Chicanas into History.* Bloomington: Indiana University Press, 1999.

Pérez, Louis A. *Cuba in the American Imagination: Metaphor and the Imperial Ethos.* Chapel Hill: University of North Carolina Press, 2008.

Piepzna-Samarasinha, Leah Lakshmi. *Care Work: Dreaming Disability Justice.* Vancouver: Arsenal Pulp Press, 2018.

Pividal, Francisco. *Bolívar: Pensamiento Precursor del Antimperialismo.* Mérida, Venezuela: Impr. de Mérida, 2005.

Polk, James K. *Polk: The Diary of a President.* Edited by Allan Nevins. London: Longmans, Green, and Co., 1952.

Poole, Deborah. *Vision, Race, and Modernity: A Visual Economy of the Andean Image World.* Princeton, NJ: Princeton University Press, 1997.

Powell, Malea. "Down by the River, or How Susan La Flesche Picotte Can Teach Us about Alliance as a Practice of Survivance." *College English* 67, no. 1 (September 2004): 38–60.

———. "Dreaming Charles Eastman: Cultural Memory, Autobiography, and Geography in Indigenous Rhetorical Histories." In *Beyond the Archives: Research as a Lived Process,* edited by Gesa Kirsch and Liz Rohan, 115–27. Carbondale: Southern Illinois University Press, 2008.

———. "Rhetorics of Survivance: How American Indians Use Writing." *College Composition and Communication* 53, no. 3 (February 2002): 396–434.

———. "Stories Take Place: A Performance in One Act." *College Composition and Communication* 64, no. 2 (December 2012): 383–406.

Powell, Malea, Daisy Levy, Andrea Riley-Mukavetz, Marilee Brooks-Gillies, Maria Novotny, and Jennifer Fisch-Ferguson. "Our Story Begins Here: Constellating Cultural Rhetorics." *Enculturation,* no. 18 (2014). http://enculturation.net/our-story-begins-here.

Pratt, Mary Louise. *Imperial Eyes: Travel Writing and Transculturation.* 2nd ed. London: Routledge, 2008.

Querejazu, Amaya. "Encountering the Pluriverse: Looking for Alternatives in Other Worlds." *Revista Brasileira de Política Internacional* 59, no. 2 (2016): 1–16.

Quijano, Anibal. "Coloniality of Power, Eurocentrism, and Latin America." *Nepantla: Views from South* 1, no. 3 (2000): 533–80.

Quijano, Anibal, and Immanuel Wallerstein. "Americanity as a Concept, or the Americas in the Modern World-System." *International Social Science Journal* 29 (1992): 549–57.

Raab, Jennifer. *Frederic Church: The Art and Science of Detail.* New Haven, CT: Yale University Press, 2015.

———. "Landscape and the Risk of Metaphor." *American Art* 31, no. 2 (Summer 2017): 56–58.

———. "'Precisely These Objects': Frederic Church and the Culture of Detail." *The Art Bulletin* 95, no. 4 (December 2013): 578–96.

Rama, Angel. *La Ciudad Letrada.* Hanover, NH: Ediciones del Norte, 1984.

Ramírez Novoa, Ezequiel. *Monroismo y Bolivarismo en América Latina.* Lima: Amaru Editores, 1984.

Rankin, Monica A. *¡México, La Patria! Propaganda and Production during World War II.* Lincoln: University of Nebraska Press, 2009.

Rappaport, Joanne, and Thomas B. F. Cummins. *Beyond the Lettered City: Indigenous Literacies in the Andes.* Durham, NC: Duke University Press, 2012.

Reilly, Tom, and Manley Witten. *War with Mexico!: America's Reporters Cover the Battlefront.* Lawrence: University Press of Kansas, 2010.

Rendahl, Stephen. "The Rhetoric of Imperialism: William Jennings Bryan and Theodore Roosevelt on the Philippine War." *North Dakota Journal of Speech & Theatre* 12 (1999): 57–64.

Restaino, Jessica. *Surrender: Feminist Rhetoric and Ethics in Love and Illness.* Carbondale: Southern Illinois University Press, 2019.

Rice, Jenny. *Distant Publics: Development Rhetoric and the Subject of Crisis.* Pittsburgh, PA: University of Pittsburgh Press, 2012.

———. "The Rhetorical Aesthetics of More: On Archival Magnitude." *Philosophy and Rhetoric* 50, no. 1 (2017): 26–49.

Rifkin, Mark. *Manifesting America: The Imperial Construction of US National Space.* Oxford: Oxford University Press, 2009.

———. "Settler States of Feeling: National Belonging and the Erasure of Native American Presence." In *A Companion to American Literary Studies*, edited by Caroline F. Levander and Robert S. Levine, 342–55. Malden, MA: Blackwell Publishing, 2011.

Riley-Mukavetz, Andrea. "On Working from or with Anger: Or How I Learned to Listen to My Relatives and Practice All Our Relations." *Enculturation*, no. 21 (2016).

Ríos, Gabriela Raquel. "Cultivating Land-Based Literacies and Rhetorics." *Literacy in Composition Studies* 3, no. 1 (March 2015): 60–70.

———. "Mestizaje." In *Decolonizing Rhetoric and Composition Studies*, edited by Iris D. Ruiz and Raúl Sánchez, 109–24. New York: Palgrave Macmillan US, 2016.

Rodas, Raquel. *Crónica de Un Sueño: Las Escuelas Indígenas de Dolores Cacuango, Una Experiencia de Educación Bilingüe en Cayambe.* Quito: Proyecto de Educación Bilingüe Intercultural, 1989.

Roe, Bella Honess. "The Canadian Shorts: Establishing Disney's Wartime Style." In *Learning from Mickey, Donald and Walt: Essays on Disney's Edutainment Films*, edited by A. Bowdoin Van Riper, 15–26. Jefferson, NC: McFarland, 2011.

Romanski, Fred J. "The Fast Mail: A History of the US Railway Mail Service." *Prologue Magazine*, Fall 2005. https://www.archives.gov/publications/prologue/2005/fall/fast-mail-1.html.

Rosenbaum, Julia B. "Frederic Edwin Church in an Era of Expedition." *American Art* 29, no. 2 (Summer 2015): 26–34.

Roth, Mitchel. "Journalism and the US-Mexican War." In *Dueling Eagles: Reinterpreting the US-Mexican War, 1846–1848*, edited by Richard W. Francaviglia and Douglas W. Richmond, 103–26. Fort Worth: Texas Christian University Press, 2000.

Rowe, John Carlos. "Areas of Concern: Area Studies and the New American Studies." In *Re-Framing the Transnational Turn in American Studies*, edited by Winifried Fluck, Donald E. Pease, and John Carlos Rowem 321–36. Hanover, NH: Dartmouth College Press, 2011.

Rowe, John H. "Machu Picchu a La Luz de Documentos de Siglo XVI." *Historica* 14, no. 1 (July 1990): 139–54.

Royster, Jacqueline Jones, and Gesa Kirsch. *Feminist Rhetorical Practices: New Horizons for Rhetoric, Composition, and Literacy Studies.* Carbondale: Southern Illinois University Press, 2012.

Sadowski-Smith, Claudia. *Border Fictions: Globalization, Empire, and Writing at the Boundaries of the United States.* Charlottesville: University of Virginia Press, 2008.

Saldívar, José David. *Trans-Americanity: Subaltern Modernities, Global Coloniality, and the Cultures of Greater Mexico.* Durham, NC: Duke University Press, 2012.

Salomon, Frank, and Mercedes Niño-Murcia. *The Lettered Mountain: A Peruvian Village's Way with Writing*. Durham, NC: Duke University Press, 2011.

Salvatore, Ricardo Donato. "Local versus Imperial Knowledge: Reflections on Hiram Bingham and the Yale Peruvian Expedition." *Nepantla: Views from South* 4, no. 1 (2003): 67–80.

Schroeder, John H. *Mr. Polk's War: American Opposition and Dissent, 1846–1848*. Madison: University of Wisconsin Press, 1973.

Selzer, Jack. "Rhetorical Analysis: Understanding How Texts Persuade Readers." In *What Writing Does and How It Does It: An Introduction to Analyzing Texts and Textual Practices*, edited by Charles Bazerman and Paul Prior, 279–307. Mahwah, NJ: Lawrence Erlbaum Associates, 2004.

Shapiro, Michael J. *The Political Sublime*. Durham, NC: Duke University Press, 2018.

Sharpe, Christina Elizabeth. *In the Wake: On Blackness and Being*. Durham, NC: Duke University Press, 2016.

Shepley, Genoa. "By Which Melancholy Occurrence: The Disaster Prints of Nathaniel Currier, 1835–1840." *Panorama: Journal of the Association of Historians of American Art* 1, no. 2 (Fall 2015): n.p.

Shotwell, Alexis. *Against Purity: Living Ethically in Compromised Times*. Minneapolis: University of Minnesota Press, 2016.

Simbaña, Floresmilo, Adriana Rodríguez Caquana, and Mateo Martínez Abarca, eds. *¡Así Encendimos la Mecha! Treinta Años de Levantamiento Indígena en Ecuador: Una Historia Permanente*. Quito, Ecuador: Abya Yala, 2020.

Smith, Ephraim Kirby. *To Mexico with Scott: Letters of Captain E. Kirby Smith to His Wife*. Edited by Emma Jerome Blackwood. Cambridge, MA: Harvard University Press, 1917.

Soltow, Lee, and Edward Stevens. *The Rise of Literacy and the Common School in the United States: A Socioeconomic Analysis to 1870*. Chicago: University of Chicago Press, 1981.

Soto Vega, Karrieann, and Karma R. Chávez. "Latinx Rhetoric and Intersectionality in Racial Rhetorical Criticism." *Communication and Critical/Cultural Studies* 15, no. 4 (October 2, 2018): 319–25.

Spillers, Hortense J. "Mama's Baby, Papa's Maybe: An American Grammar Book." *Diacrticis* 17, no. 2 (Summer 1987): 64–81.

Spivak, Gayatri Chakravorty. *A Critique of Postcolonial Reason*. Cambridge, MA: Harvard University Press, 1999.

Stern, Steve J. "The Decentered Center and the Expansionist Periphery." In *Close Encounters of Empire: Writing the Cultural History of US–Latin American Relations*, edited by M. Joseph Gilbert, Catherine LeGrand, and Ricardo Donato Salvatore, 47–68. Durham, NC: Duke University Press, 1998.

Stewart, Rick. "Artists and Printmakers of the Mexican War." In *Eyewitness to War: Prints and Daguerreotypes of the Mexican War, 1846–1848*, edited by Martha A. Sandweiss, Rick Stewart, and Ben W. Huseman, 4–43. Fort Worth, TX / Washington, DC: Amon Carter Museum / Smithsonian Institution Press, 1989.

Storm, Jane McManus. "Annexation." Edited by John O'Sullivan. *United States Magazine and Democratic Review* 17, no. 1 (August 1845): 5–10.

Stuckey, Mary E. *The Good Neighbor: Franklin D. Roosevelt and the Rhetoric of American Power*. East Lansing: Michigan State University Press, 2013.

Tell, Dave. "Critique and Investigation." *Journal for the History of Rhetoric* 23, no. 1 (January 2, 2020): 117–18.

Towns, Armond R. "Black 'Matter' Lives." *Women's Studies in Communication* 41, no. 4 (October 2, 2018): 349–58.

Tuck, Eve, and K. Wayne Yang. "Decolonization Is Not a Metaphor." *Decolonization: Indigeneity, Education & Society* 1, no. 1 (2012): 1–40.

Tucker, Spencer, James R. Arnold, Roberta Wiener, Paul G. Pierpaoli, Thomas W. Cutrer, and Pedro Santoni, eds. *The Encyclopedia of the Mexican-American War: A Political, Social, and Military History.* Vol. 1, A–L. Santa Barbara, CA: ABC-CLIO, 2013.

UNESCO World Heritage Centre. "Historic Sanctuary of Machu Picchu." Accessed September 20, 2020. https://whc.unesco.org/en/list/274/.

Valcárcel, Luís E. *De La Vida Inkaica. Algunas Captaciones del Espiritu Que La Animó.* Lima: Editorial Garcilaso, 1925.

———. *Machu Picchu. El Más Famoso Monumento Arqueológico del Perú.* Buenos Aires: Editorial Universitaria de Buenos Aires, 1964.

Van Riper, A. Bowdoin. Introduction to *Learning from Mickey, Donald and Walt: Essays on Disney's Edutainment Films,* edited by A. Bowdoin Van Riper, 1–13. Jefferson, NC: McFarland, 2011.

Vasconcelos, José. *The Cosmic Race: A Bilingual Edition.* Translated by Didier Tisdel Jaén. Baltimore: Johns Hopkins University Press, 1997.

Vertesi, Janet. *Seeing like a Rover: How Robots, Teams, and Images Craft Knowledge of Mars.* Chicago: The University of Chicago Press, 2015.

Vieira, Kate. *American by Paper: How Documents Matter in Immigrant Literacy.* Minneapolis: University of Minnesota Press, 2016.

Vizenor, Gerald Robert. *Manifest Manners: Postindian Warriors of Survivance.* Hanover, NH: Wesleyan University Press, 1994.

Wan, Amy J. "In the Name of Citizenship: The Writing Classroom and the Promise of Citizenship." *College English* 74, no. 1 (September 2011): 28–49.

Wanzer, Darrel Allen. "Delinking Rhetoric, or Revisiting McGee's Fragmentation Thesis through Decoloniality." *Rhetoric & Public Affairs* 15, no. 4 (2012): 647–58.

Wanzer-Serrano, Darrel, ed. "#RhetoricSoWhite." *Quarterly Journal of Speech* 105, no. 4 (2019).

Warner, Michael. "Publics and Counterpublics." *Public Culture* 14, no. 1 (Winter 2002): 49–89.

Washington, Myra. "Woke Skin, White Masks: Race and Communication Studies." *Communication and Critical/Cultural Studies* 17, no. 2 (April 2, 2020): 261–66.

Watson, Annette, and Orville H. Huntington. "They're *Here*—I Can *Feel* Them: The Epistemic Spaces of Indigenous and Western Knowledges." *Social & Cultural Geography* 9, no. 3 (May 2008): 257–81.

Weheliye, Alexander G. *Habeas Viscus: Racializing Assemblages, Biopolitics, and Black Feminist Theories of the Human.* Durham, NC: Duke University Press, 2014.

Wheelan, Joseph. *Invading Mexico: America's Continental Dream and the Mexican War, 1846–1848.* New York: Carroll & Graf, 2007.

Whyte, Kyle Powys. "Our Ancestors' Dystopia Now: Indigenous Conservation and the Anthropocene." In *The Routledge Companion to the Environmental Humanities,* edited by Ursula K. Heise, Jon Christensen, and Michelle Niemann, 206–15. London: Routledge, Taylor & Francis Group, 2017.

Wikipedia. "Machu Picchu." Accessed September 20, 2020. https://en.wikipedia.org/wiki/Machu_Picchu.

Wilmerding, John. "Church, Cotopaxi, and Country." *American Art* 20, no. 2 (2006): 17–21.

Winders, Richard Bruce. "'Will the Regiment Stand It?' The 1st North Carolina Mutinies at Buena Vista." In *Dueling Eagles: Reinterpreting the US-Mexican War, 1846–1848,* edited by

Richard W. Francaviglia and Douglas W. Richmond, 67–90. Fort Worth: Texas Christian University Press, 2000.

Wittenberg, Hermann. "Alan Paton's Sublime: Race, Landscape and the Transcendence of the Liberal Imagination." *Current Writing: Text and Reception in Southern Africa* 17, no. 2 (2005): 3–23.

Wooten, Cecil W. III. *Hermogenes' On Types of Style*. Chapel Hill: The University of North Carolina Press, 1987.

Wynter, Sylvia. "Unsettling the Coloniality of Being/Power/Truth/Freedom: Towards the Human, after Man, Its Overrepresentation—An Argument." *CR: The New Centennial Review* 3, no. 3 (2003): 257–337.

Yampara Huarachi, Simón. "Cosmovivencia Andina. Vivir y Convivir en Armonía Integral—Suma Qamaña." *Bolivian Studies Journal/Revista de Estudios Bolivianos* 18 (November 1, 2011): 1–22.

Yosso, Tara J. *Critical Race Counterstories along the Chicana/Chicano Educational Pipeline*. New York: Routledge, 2006.

Zulli, Diana. "Capitalizing on the Look: Insights into the Glance, Attention Economy, and Instagram." *Critical Studies in Media Communication* 35, no. 2 (March 15, 2018): 137–50.

INDEX

accumulation, 25, 27, 31, 71; Bingham's investment in, 110; circulation and, 33, 43; of documentary material, 32; of feelings, 32–33, 64; magnitude and, 42, 43, 114; *megethos* and, 67; precipitation, 43, 45–46, 64–68, 71; proliferation, 43, 44, 46–50; rhetorical vs. physical, 66; sedimentation, 33, 43, 44–45, 46, 50–63; of territory, 32; theorizing, 42–46; tracking, 43; of US-Mexican War documentation, 39–42, 66. *See also* artifacts; Mexican territory; US-Mexican War (1846–48)

acquisition, 110. *See also* Mexican territory; US-Mexican War (1846–48)

adequate, 189

affect, 21n94. *See also* feeling; sensation

affective turn, 20

African Americans, 8

Ahmed, Sara, 65

air, tropical, 85–88

Alberto, Lourdes, 7, 8

Allerton, Mary, 86

Alvarez, Anacleto, 108, 117, 139, 140

America: as geosocial construct, 5–6; invention of, 4, 5, 10, 108; in maps, 4; United States as, 7, 12, 184; use of term, 3n5

American, 3n5; becoming, 6; feeling, 26; looking, 19–20

American Dream, territory worthy of, 73

Americanness: as category of whiteness, 8–9; feeling and, 19; learning important elements of, 6; performance of, 22; presumption of in Church's paintings, 70; relation to other Americas, 9; of United States, 2

amplification, 13–14

Andean landscape paintings, 25, 137. *See also* Church, Frederic Edwin; Church's paintings

Andes, 79–80, 89. *See also* Church's paintings; Machu Picchu

animation, 154. *See also* OIAA-Disney films

Aristotle, 13–14

art: science and, 83, 100. *See also* Church, Frederic Edwin; Church's paintings

art exhibits, 148, 167–68, 169, 170n96

Arteaga, Melchor, 103, 111

artifacts, 104–5, 110, 111, 112–14, 115–21
artistic travel, 73
artists, Ecuadorian, 98. *See also* Salas, Rafael
Asháninka, 139
Atahualpa, 101
audience, of OIAA, 153, 166–67, 172, 174, 176
Avery, Kevin, 81

Balzotti, Jonathan, 15
Battle of Buena Vista (Robinson), 54 fig. 1.2
Bell, Derrick, 188, 189
Bingham, Hiram, 20, 25, 102, 103, 178, 186; detail and, 114, 134; diary, 111n34; Latin American response to, 144–45; *megethos* and, 121; Monroe Doctrine and, 136, 145, 165; Peruvian government and, 136; presumptions of American magnitude, 114; pursuit of magnitude, 110; questionable methods of, 104; scientific credibility of, 115. *See also* discovery; Machu Picchu; Yale Peruvian Expedition (YPE)
Blackness, 16–17
Blair, Hugh, 16, 17, 23–24
Bolívar, Simón, 146
border crossings, 7
border wall, 67, 185
boundaries, US: acquiescence to, 65–68; glance and, 1–2; "Map of the Western Coast of America," xvi fig. 0.1. *See also* Mexican territory; US-Mexican War (1846–48)
Bragg, Braxton, 46, 55, 57
Brazil, 175–76
Bryan, Julian, 177
Buchanan, James, 34
Buena Vista, battle of, 29, 46, 53–58. *See also* US-Mexican War (1846–48)
buildup of material. *See* accumulation; sedimentation
burial sites, 116, 117
Burke, Edmund, 16
Butler, J., 55 fig. 1.3, 56

Calafell, Bernadette, 22
Calhoun, John C., 36
California, 34, 62n101, 63

Calver, Homer N., 162–63
Cameron, John, 56 fig. 1.4
Campt, Tina, 21
Canada, 185
care, 193–94
Carey, M., 137
Carrión, Benjamín, 183
cartography, 50. *See also* maps
Casas, Rubén, 187
Catlin, Stanton, 167–68, 169
Cedillo, Christina, 33
Cejudo, Guadalupe, 157
Chávez, Hugo, 183
Chávez, Karma R., 9, 23, 193
Chicago Tribune, 80
Church, Frederic Edwin, 25, 69, 135, 137, 178, 186; American magnitude and, 99; Arctic paintings, 184–85; choice to paint Cotopaxi, 76; diary of, 89–90, 91, 92–93; interest in South America, 83–85; as interpreter of Andes, 102; Kichwa people and, 89–94, 145; majoritarian narratives of, 97; masculinity and, 72, 87, 89, 100; orientation toward painting, 72–73; prioritization of achievements, 88–89, 91; promotion by, 78; Sangay and, 90–94; science and, 72, 87, 89, 96, 97, 100; status of, 98, 99–100; trips to South America, 98; view of North American scenes, 98; visual strategies of, 131. *See also* story/stories
Church's paintings: air in, 85–88; *Cotopaxi* (1855), 73 fig. 2.1, 77; *Cotopaxi* (1862), 74–75, 76, 85; depiction of tropics in, 97; detail in, 96; expansionist vision and, 76; *The Heart of the Andes*, 71, 76 fig. 2.4, 77–82, 85–86, 98, 131, 145; as index of US public feeling, 73–77; investment in larger narrative, 72; knowledge making by, 99; misrepresentation of Andean scenes, 96; *The North*, 185; presumption in, 70, 73; review of *The Andes of Ecuador*, 86; storying work of, 89; *View of Cotopaxi*, 75–76. *See also* Church, Frederic Edwin; story/stories
Cincinnati Daily Commercial, 98
Cintrón, Ralph, 186
circulation, 33, 42–43, 44, 45, 46
civil rights, 189

Civil War, US, 25, 76, 185
Clary-Lemon, Jennifer, 190, 194
Clay, Henry, 45
Clay, Henry, Jr., 20, 54–55, 56
Cleanliness Brings Health, 159, 178–79
Cole, Thomas, 72
collaboration, 191–92, 193
Colombia. *See* Andean landscape paintings; Church, Frederic Edwin; Latin America; South America
colonial theft, 110. *See also* artifacts
colonialism, 5, 11, 67, 85; America created through, 8; hemispheres and, 10–12; painting as, 99; racism and, 9; US-Latin American relations and, 185. *See also* US-Mexican War (1846–48)
Columbus, Christopher, 107–8
Comercio, El, 164–65
common sense, 23
community, 191–92, 193
Companion to The Heart of the Andes, A (Winthrop), 78–80
concatenation of texts, 42
confirmation, 1
connection, 28, 191–92
conquest, 51, 52, 58, 63, 67. *See also* Mexican territory; US-Mexican War (1846–48)
consequence, presumption of, 110–11
contemplation, strategic, 97–98
continents, 2n4
cooperation, hemispheric, 174–75. *See also* hemispheric solidarity
core attachments, 15, 47, 65
"Corollary to the Monroe Doctrine," 136
Corrigan, Lisa, 192, 193
Cosmos (Humboldt), 72, 83
Cotopaxi, 69, 72–76. *See also* Andean landscape paintings; Church, Frederic Edwin; Church's paintings
counterstories, 85
covering-over, 42
Cramer, Gisela, 148, 172
critical race theory, 70, 71, 188
criticism, 17
Crooker, Turner, 49

Crosby, Richard, 15
Cuba, 183
cultural distinctiveness, 170–71
cultural forms, 8
Currier, Nathaniel, 40–41, 52, 53 fig. 1.1, 56 fig. 1.4, 57
Cushman, Ellen, 99

daguerreotypes, 30
Darwin, Charles, 76, 83, 96
Davis, Heather, 193
de Lozada, Enrique, 156, 157
Death of Lieut. Col. Henry Clay Jr. (Butler and Lewis), 55 fig. 1.3, 56
debt peonage, 104n6
decolonization, 11
Delgado, Richard, 70
democracy, 150
Democrats, US-Mexican War and, 36, 39
destiny, 71. *See also* manifest destiny
detail, 96, 114, 134–35
differentiation, 12n42, 14
discovery: Columbus and, 107–8; definitions of, 137; Machu Picchu and, 103, 105, 106, 107–10, 114, 126, 130; magnitude and, 109; object of, 121; opacity and, 137–40. *See also* Bingham, Hiram; Machu Picchu; Yale Peruvian Expedition (YPE)
Disney, Roy, 143
Disney, Walt, 142, 155, 166, 168–70, 174, 177
Walt Disney Company, 26, 141; appeal of working with, 171–72; *The Soybean*, 162; during World War II, 154–55. *See also* OIAA-Disney films
Distant Publics (Rice), 64
documentation, 32, 66. *See also* letters, soldiers'; lithography; newspapers
Donald Duck, 176. *See also* OIAA-Disney films
Dorfman, Ariel, 176
double take, 1n2
Douglass, Frederick, 75

Earle, Chris, 48, 49
Eaton, George F., 114

Eaton, Joseph H., 54
economic progress, 157, 164
Ecuador, 69, 183; landscape painting in, 94–98; reaction to OIAA-Disney films in, 164–65. *See also* Andean landscape paintings; Church, Frederic Edwin; Church's paintings; Latin America; South America
Ecuadorian *indigenismo*, 104n7
Edbauer, Jenny, 42
Eden, 81
education, 152–65, 172. *See also* Office of the Coordinator of Inter-American Affairs, US (OIAA); OIAA-Disney films
Engelmann, Adolph, 49, 61, 63
engravings, in newspapers, 41
enslaved Black people, 8
entertainment, 152, 171–77. *See also* OIAA-Disney films
enthymeme, 133–34
equator, 10n28
Erdis, Ellwood C., 113, 114
Espiritu Pampa, 138–39
ethnicity, 6, 8
ethnocentrism, 6; acquisition of Mexican territory and, 52; in Bingham's work, 138
evidence. *See* artifacts
exceptionalism, 71, 82, 184, 191–92
exchange, 152, 165–71. *See also* Office of the Coordinator of Inter-American Affairs, US (OIAA)
exertion, 73. *See also* masculinity
expansionism, 31, 32, 67, 110. *See also* accumulation; US-Mexican War (1846–48)
exploration, 73, 83–85, 136–37. *See also* masculinity
extremes, 188–89

Farrell, Thomas, 15, 19, 32, 47, 65, 109, 134, 182, 185
feeling, 17, 21n94; accumulation of, 32–33, 64; *megethos* and, 13, 14; [US] Americanness and, 19. *See also* sensation; vision
feeling, public, 22; about US-Mexican War, 46, 64–68; Church's painting as index of, 73–77; letters and, 28; *megethos* and, 16; public in, 23

"Feeling Brown" (Muñoz), 22
"felt," use of term, 21n94
Field, Cyrus, 84, 145
films: Disney's visits to Latin America in, 169–70; education by, 143, 156. *See also* OIAA-Disney films
Finnegan, Cara A., 18, 42, 181
Flight of the Mexican Army (Currier), 57
Flores, Lisa A., 9, 13, 14
Foote, Harry, 112
forgetfulness, 31, 32, 33, 66
free press, 47
free speech, 47
Fuentes, Tomas, 108, 117, 139, 140
fugitivity, 193

Gadsden Purchase, 39n40
Gallant Charge of the Kentucky Cavalry Under Col. Marshall, The (Currier), 57 fig. 1.5, 57
García, Romeo, 71
gender, 18, 22. *See also* masculinity
Giant Dinosaurs of the Jurassic, 4–5
glances, 1–2, 51, 60
Godwin, Blakemore, 167
Goldberg, David Theo, 15
Gómez, Leila, 137
Gómez-Barris, Macarena, 106
good neighbor policy, 5, 149–50, 170n96
Grand Forks Daily Herald, 127
grandeur, 14, 17, 18, 80, 186
greed, acquisition of Mexican territory and, 52
Greenberg, Amy, 72, 82
Gries, Laurie, 42, 44
Gruesz, Kirsten Silva, 6
Guadalupe Hidalgo, Treaty of, 25, 34, 39, 51. *See also* US-Mexican War (1846–48)
Guam, 67
Guaman Poma de Ayala, Felipe, 187–88
Guantanamo Bay, 67
Guzmán, Eulalia, 157, 161, 164, 165

Haas, P., xvi fig.0.1

Hall, Amy Cox, 107, 110, 114, 123
Haraway, Donna, 189
Hardin, John, 55
Harper's, 127-30
Harvey, Eleanor Jones, 75, 76
Hassaurek, Friedrich, 96
Hawaii, 67
Hawhee, Debra, 19
health: US values and, 163-64. *See also* OIAA-Disney films
Heaney, Christopher, 109, 139
Heart of the Andes, The (Church), 71, 76 fig.2.4, 76-82, 85-86, 98, 131, 145
hemisphere, American, 7, 11-12
hemispheres, 10-12
hemispheric solidarity, 149, 152, 153, 156, 170-71, 173, 174-75. *See also* Office of the Coordinator of Inter-American Affairs, US (OIAA); US-Latin American relations
hemispheric vision, 22
Henkin, David, 41
Hermogenes of Tarsus, 14
hiding, by revelation, 137-40
Holmes, David G., 24
Howat, John, 96
Humboldt, Alexander von, 72, 80, 82, 83, 84, 92, 96, 97, 100, 186
Huntington, Orville H., 137
hypsos, 16

illiteracy, 155-56. *See also* OIAA-Disney films
image-makers, 12, 20, 24, 145. *See also* Bingham, Hiram; Church, Frederic Edwin; letters, soldiers'; newspapers; Office of the Coordinator of Inter-American Affairs, US (OIAA); OIAA-Disney films
image-making, civic, 8
immigrants, 37
imperial presumption, response to, 144. *See also* OIAA-Disney films
imperialism, 7, 8, 126; racism and, 9; scientific sovereignty and, 110; US-Latin American relations and, 185. *See also* colonialism; settlers
imperialism, US, 7, 67, 146

importance: establishing, 14-15, 183; size and, 180
Incas, 26, 106; burial sites, 116, 117; Manco Capac, 112, 125n82, 138-39; Pachakuti Inka Yupanki, 101, 102, 105n12; YPE's connection with, 124. *See also* Machu Picchu; Quechua people
independence movements, Latin American, 83, 146
indigenismo, Ecuadorian, 104n7
indigenismo, Peruvian, 104
Indigenous peoples: Columbus and, 107n19; excluded from American magnitude, 17; excluded from American sublime, 16-17; as target of OIAA-Disney films, 143. *See also* Quechua people
Indigenous rhetorics, 70, 71
individual, 191-92
influence, US, 68, 136
Inka: use of term, 102n2. *See also* Machu Picchu
intervention, US, 150, 151. *See also* US-Latin American relations
invention, 6; of America, 108; of American magnitude, 122; of Machu Picchu, 107, 108-9, 115, 122; magnitude and, 109
isolation, 191-92

Jackson, Rachel, 11
James, Emmerson, 60
James, Henry, 100
Johnson, Jenell, 23, 64
journalism, popular, 39n41. *See also* newspapers
journalists, 40, 47

Kang, Jiyeon, 42
Kant, Immanuel, 16, 17
Kellogg brothers, 56
Kelly, Franklin, 85, 87, 98
Kendall, George Wilkins, 57
Kennedy Troya, Alexandra, 96, 97
Kichwa people, 89-94, 145
King, John Nevin, 49, 61
Kirsch, Gesa, 85, 97
knowledge, 153. *See also* education

knowledge making, 99

Koerner, Gustav, 1, 2, 46, 51, 60

landscape painting, 25, 72, 137. *See also* Church's paintings

landscapes: photographs of, 120. *See also* Church's paintings; landscape painting

Latin America: Américan magnitude and, 183–84; American magnitude and, 15, 144; Disney's visits to, 168–70, 174; feeling [US] American and, 26; independence movements in, 83, 146; national pride in, 170–71; OIAA's goals and, 148; Panama Canal Zone, 135; reclaiming of magnitude from US, 183–84; response to imperial presumption, 144; Roosevelt's concern for, 185; sense of difference and, 12n42; US influence in, 136; view of OIAA in, 171; World War II and, 146–47. *See also* Office of the Coordinator of Inter-American Affairs, US (OIAA); OIAA-Disney films; South America; US–Latin American relations; *and individual countries*

Latinx Indigenous presence, 7

Leary, John, 82

letters, soldiers,' 27–30, 41, 43, 45, 46–50, 59–63, 186. *See also* US-Mexican War (1846–48)

Lewis, C., 55 fig. 1.3, 56

limitedness, learning to sit with, 188. *See also* post-magnitude rhetoric

Lincoln, Abraham, 45, 55

Abraham Lincoln Presidential Library and Archive, 27

Listening to Images (Campt), 21

literacy, 40, 142, 156, 157, 161, 164. *See also* OIAA-Disney films

lithography, 40–41, 46, 186; "Map of the Western Coast of America," xvi fig. 0.1, 1, 4; public feeling and, 52; US-Mexican War and, 39n41, 40–41, 51, 52–60. *See also* pictures

"A little more grape, Capt. Bragg" (Currier and Cameron), 56 fig. 1.5

Longinus, 16, 19

look, right to, 144

looking to, vs. looking at, 162–63

"Looking White and Middle Class" (Malin), 19

Los Angeles Times, 123

Machu Picchu, 25–26; access to, 123–24; accounts of, 121–36; American magnitude and, 105, 106, 128; American status of, 126; articulation of US hegemony and, 105; artifacts from, 104–5, 110, 111, 112–14, 115–21; conflicting stories about, 105; "discovery" of, 103, 105, 106, 107–10, 114, 126, 130; Indigenous people and, 102, 103, 104n6, 108, 111, 117, 118, 124, 125, 133, 136, 137, 138, 139–40; invention of, 107, 108–9, 115, 122; as "lost city," 123; nationalism and, 106; newspapers and, 122–25, 127–28; origins of, 105n12; Peruvian scholarship and, 104, 105; photography and, 109–10, 119–21, 127–35; presentation of, 106, 107–10; responsibility for ruin of, 125; revelation and, 107, 115, 122, 130, 136, 137, 139–40; sense of affiliation with, 135–36; as site of global heritage, 103; as site of national heritage, 105; Spaniards and, 125–26; tourists to, 104, 105; US civilization and, 133; as [US] American accomplishment, 129. *See also* Bingham, Hiram; Incas; Inka; Quechua people; South America; Yale Peruvian Expedition (YPE)

Mackie, Thomas, 163

magnitude: limit of, 187; opposite of, 187; reliance on, 181; as rhetorical feature, 13; ubiquity of, 182–86. *See also* *megethos*

magnitude, Américan, 183–84

magnitude, American, 2; reserved for white Euro-American colonizers, 16–17; resistance to, 144; skepticism of, 178; tracking, 2, 182–86

mail. *See* letters, soldiers'

majoritarian narratives, 70–71, 85, 97

"Make America Great Again," 8, 182, 185, 190

Malin, Brenton J., 19

Manco Capac, 112, 125n82, 138–39

manifest destiny, 5, 66, 71; as benevolent, 62; expansionism and, 32; recipients of, 9; support for, 34; US-Mexican War and, 31

Manthorne, Katherine, 83, 84

"Map of the Western Coast of America," xvi fig. 0.1, 1, 4

mapmakers, 10

maps: annexation of Mexican territory and, 51; in *Giant Dinosaurs of the Jurassic,* 4–5; inevitable shape of United States and, 3; "Map of the Western Coast of America," xvi fig. 0.1, 1, 4; naming America, 3; "Universalis Cosmographia Secundum Ptholomaei Traditionem et Americi Vespucii Alioru[m]que Lustrationes [St. Dié]," 3 fig. 0.2, 4, 10

masculine presumption, 110

masculinity: Church and, 72, 87, 89, 100; in OIAA-Disney films, 175; [US] American characteristics and, 82; white, 22–23

Mattelart, Armand, 176

Matteson, Tompkins Harrison 56

McClure, John, 78

megethos, 13–19, 163, 182; accumulation and, 67; Bingham's assertion of, 121; epideictic discourse and, 14; establishing importance and, 183; feeling and, 13, 14; OIAA and, 177–78; public feeling and, 16; sensation and, 17–19; sublime linked to, 16–17; Trump's use of, 180; vision in, 18; YPE's use of, 107. *See also* magnitude

Merritt Ives, James, 40, 52

Mexican citizens, 39

Mexican territory: acquiescence to, 33, 46, 52, 67; acquisition of, 25, 31, 51; claimed by US, 34, 35; racism and, 62; US public and, 59–60; US soldiers' relationship to, 61–62, 63; in US-Mexican War lithographs, 56, 57. *See also* accumulation; Texas; US-Mexican War (1846–48)

Mexico, 176, 183; pedagogy in, 142; reaction to OIAA-Disney films in, 141–42. *See also* Latin America; Office of the Coordinator of Inter-American Affairs, US (OIAA); US-Mexican War (1846–48)

Monroe, James, 5

Monroe Doctrine, 67, 80, 136, 165, 184; resistance to, 145, 146

Montgomery, Cora (Jane McManus Storm), 5

Morrison Formation, 4–5

movements, 7, 8

Muñoz, José, 22

Murphy, Gretchen, 8

myth, modern Western, 191

narratives, majoritarian, 70–71, 85, 97

National Geographic Magazine, 127–30, 134

National Geographic Society, 112–13, 129, 134

National Intelligencer, 47

national pride, 47, 170–71

nationalism, 183; Machu Picchu and, 106; US-Mexican War lithographs and, 58–59

Navarro, José Gabriel, 94

Navas Sanz de Santamaría, Pablo, 73, 86, 87

navigation, 10

Nebel, Carl, 57

"New World," 5–6

New York Herald, 41, 54, 127

New York Times, 125, 127, 128, 129

New York Tribune, 125

newness, 6, 191

news, 27–30, 33, 51

newspapers, 29, 39–41; Machu Picchu and, 122–25, 127–28; pictures in, 40–41; US-Mexican War and, 40, 47

Noble, Louis Legrand, 78, 80, 81, 85

normalcy, production of, 52–53

normative, 22

novelty, 191

O'Brien, John P., 57

objects, happy, 65

observation, 73. *See also* masculinity

Office of the Coordinator of Inter-American Affairs, US (OIAA), 26, 141, 186; art exhibits, 148, 167–68, 169, 170n96; audience of, 153, 166–67, 172, 174, 176; entertainment and, 152, 171–77; exchange and, 148, 152, 165–71; imagined Latin American audiences of, 153; Latin American view of, 171; *megethos* and, 177–78; purpose of, 143, 144, 147–48, 151, 162, 178; resistance to, 158; rhetorical problem of, 151, 165–66; visibility of, 166; vision and, 151, 155–56. *See also* OIAA-Disney films

O'Gorman, Edmundo, 5, 16, 19, 108

OIAA (US Office of the Coordinator of Inter-American Affairs). *See* Office of the Coordinator of Inter-American Affairs, US (OIAA)

OIAA-Disney films, 153; audiences of, 154, 172, 174, 176; critiques of, 141–43; educational purpose of, 153; ending of, 142; field testing of, 157–58, 160–61; health and literacy films, 141, 153, 158–59, 161, 178–79; language of, 178–79; language teaching in, 161–62; Mexican consultants for, 142, 143n7, 157; pedagogy of, 142; reception of, 176–77; relationships in, 174–75; *Saludos Amigos*, 171, 172, 173–77; stereotypes in, 159–60; as stories of American magnitude, 162; *Three Caballeros*, 170, 171, 172–77; US values in, 163–64. *See also* literacy

Olson, Lester, 44

On the Sublime (Longinus), 16

On Types of Style (Hermogenes of Tarsus), 14

opacity, 137–40

Oregon Territory, 34, 184

O'Sullivan, John, 5

ownership, claims to, 84

Ozburn, Lindorf, 49

Pachakuti Inka Yupanki, 101, 102, 105n12

painting, 25, 69, 72, 99, 137. *See also* Church's paintings

Palmer, Frances Flora Bond, 54

Panagia, Davide, 23

Panama Canal Zone, 135

Para Leer al Pato Donald (Dorfman and Mattelart), 176

para-coloniality, 85

partial, being, 188–89

particulates, 43

patriotic stances, 78

pauses, 43, 46

pedagogy, 142, 152

penny papers, 39, 40

persuasion, 16, 45, 52n85, 172–73

Peru: artifacts and, 111, 112–14; debt peonage in, 104n6; scholarship in, 104, 105; US art exhibit in, 167–68. *See also* Machu Picchu; Quechua people

Peruvian *indigenismo*, 104

Philippines, 67

phonetics, 161

photography: Machu Picchu and, 109–10, 119–21, 127–35; rise of, 100; scientific practice and, 120

pictorial turn, 20

pictures: art exhibits, 167–68; criteria for inclusion, 24; feeling, 21–22; magnitude and, 18; in newspapers, 40–41; in OIAA-Disney films, 159–60; treated in terms of interpretation, 20–21; US-Mexican War and, 40–41, 46–50, 51. *See also* Church's paintings; lithography; Office of the Coordinator of Inter-American Affairs, US (OIAA); OIAA-Disney films; painting; photography; vision

Pierce, Russell, 170, 172, 173, 175

Planting the Anthropocene (Clary-Lemon), 190

Población, 169, 171, 174

policy. *See* US-Latin American relations

Polk, James K., 34, 35, 36, 39, 51, 65

position, awareness of, 22

Post (Pittsburgh), 127

postal service, 41. *See also* letters, soldiers'

post-magnitude rhetoric, 187–94

Powell, Malea, 71, 192

precipitation, 43, 45–46, 64–68, 71

presumption, 1, 5, 12

Prime Meridian, 10

Primer Nueva Corónica y Buen Gobierno (Guaman Poma), 187–88

prints. *See* lithography

prison writing, 48

proliferation, 43, 44, 46–50

propaganda, 148. *See also* Office of the Coordinator of Inter-American Affairs, US (OIAA); OIAA-Disney films

proprietorship, 83, 84

proprioception, communal, 22

Prutsch, Ursula, 148, 172

public, visceral, 23, 64

public feeling. *See* feeling, public

publics, Latinx, 154

publics, US: Mexican territory and, 59–60; sense of proper boundaries, 64; South American grandeur and, 80

publics of color, US, 154

Puerto Rico, 67
Puracé, 88, 91

Quechua people, 101; labor at Machu Picchu, 104n6, 117, 118, 133; at Machu Picchu, 102, 103, 108, 111, 124, 138, 140; observation by, 144; revelation of Machu Picchu and, 125, 133, 136, 138, 139–40; treatment of, 105. *See also* Incas; Machu Picchu
Querejazu, Amaya, 191
Quijano, Anibal, 5, 7
Quipo (guide), 90, 91, 92–93

Raab, Jennifer, 72, 77, 82, 98
race: American magnitude and, 13, 14, 22; capacity for refined perception and, 18; economic development and, 157; national vision and, 9. *See also* superiority/supremacy
racial justice, 189
racial rhetorical criticism, 13, 14
racism, 6; acquisition of Mexican territory and, 52; America created through, 8; in Bingham's work, 104n9, 138; colonialism and, 9; US-Latin American relations and, 185; US-Mexican War and, 36, 58–59, 62
Ralston, James, 62
Rankin, Monica A., 147, 150, 170
reading, 161. *See also* literacy; OIAA-Disney films
Reading the Pictures, 180
realism, 87
relation, 193; in magnitude, 32
relationship, 165, 174–75. *See also* US-Latin American relations
revelation, 110; discovery and, 106, 108–9; hiding and, 137–40; Machu Picchu and, 107, 115, 122, 130, 136, 137, 139–40; magnitude and, 109
rhetoric: definitions of, 70n2, 182; magnitude and, 13, 15
Rhetoric (Aristotle), 13–14
rhetoric, post-magnitude, 187–94
rhetoric, visual, 20–21
Rhetoric Society Quarterly, 181
rhetorics, Indigenous, 70, 71

Rice, Jenny, 19, 43, 44, 64
Richarte, Torvis, 108, 117, 139, 140
Rifkin, Mark, 33
Riley-Mukavetz, Andrea, 192, 194
Rio Grande, as US's natural boundary, 1
Ríos, Gabriela Raquel, 11
Risso, Charles, 59 fig. 1.6
Robinson, Henry R., 54 fig. 1.2, 54
Rockefeller, Nelson D., 147
Roosevelt, Franklin Delano, 5, 146, 149–50, 185
Roosevelt, Theodore, 136, 146
Rosenbaum, Julia B., 81, 83
Rough and Ready as He Is (Risso), 59 fig. 1.6
Rowe, John Carlos, 10
Royster, Jacqueline Jones, 85, 97

Sadd, Henry S. 56
Salas, Rafael, 94, 96, 98, 137
Saludos Amigos, 171, 172, 173–77
Sangay, 90–94
science: American magnitude and, 100; art and, 83, 100; Church and, 72, 87, 88, 89, 96, 97, 100; photography and, 120
scientific sovereignty, 110
Scott, Winfield, 35, 38, 39
sedimentation, 33, 43, 44–45, 46, 50–63
self-regard, excessive, 141, 142. *See also* OIAA-Disney films
sensation: common sense and, 23; magnitude and, 9–10, 16; *megethos* and, 17–19; OIAA and, 151; sublime and, 17–18. *See also* feeling; vision
settlers, 9, 11, 181. *See also* colonialism; imperialism
Shapiro, Michael J., 16–17
Shotwell, Alexis, 189, 190, 194
sight. *See* vision
size, importance and, 180
slate, messy, 190–91
slave trade, Atlantic, 8
slavery, 35, 75
Smith, Ephraim, 62
Smith, J. H. William, 59 fig. 1.6

Snyder, Frederick, 27–30, 45, 46, 62. *See also* US-Mexican War (1846–48)

Snyder, John, 27–30, 45. *See also* US-Mexican War (1846–48)

Sodi de Pallares, María Elena, 141–42, 143, 164, 165, 166

soldiers, letters from, 27–30, 41, 43, 45, 46–50, 59–63, 186. *See also* US-Mexican War (1846–48)

Soldier's Return, The (Currier), 53 fig. 1.1

Soní, Estella, 157

Soto Vega, Karrieann, 9

South America: climate in, 86–88; US interest in, 83–84; in Waldseemüller's map, 4. *See also* Latin America; Machu Picchu; individual countries

sovereignty: decolonization and, 11; scientific, 110; US's claims of, 12

Spanish language, 142, 143, 157, 161. *See also* OIAA-Disney films

Spanish-American War, 67

Spivak, Gayatri Chakravorty, 16, 17

State Department, US. *See* Office of the Coordinator of Inter-American Affairs, US (OIAA)

stereoscopes, 19

Stewart, Rick, 41, 58

Storm, Jane McManus (Cora Montgomery), 5

story theory, 70

story/stories: of Church and Andean Climate, 85–89; of Church bringing landscape painting to Ecuador, 94–98; of Church's Cotopaxi paintings, 71; of *The Heart of the Andes* as spectacular magnitude, 77–82; knowledge making and, 99; magnitude as, 71, 121–36; of Sangay, 90–94; told by ingroup, 70

strategic contemplation, 97–98

Stuckey, Mary, 149, 150

sublime, 16–18

superiority/supremacy: arguments of, expansionism and, 31; exploration and, 136–37; in image of US, 154; presumptions of, 150

Tahuantinsuyo, 102n2

taste, 23–24

Taylor, Zachary, 29, 30n10, 35, 38, 57, 58, 59 fig. 1.6, 66

telegraph, 40

telluric spirit, 2

territory: accumulation of, 32; worthy of American Dream, 73. *See also* Mexican territory

Texas, 35; annexation of, 5, 34; descriptions of, 61. *See also* US-Mexican War (1846–48)

textual stare, 23

Three Caballeros, 170, 171, 173–77

Todd, Zoe, 193

topography, 53–54, 58–59, 60, 61

transparencies, 29, 41

travel, artistic, 73

travelers, 7, 8, 12. *See also* exchange

traveler-scientists, 96

Trist, Nicolas, 39

tropical climate, in Church's paintings, 85–87

Trump, Donald, 67, 180, 185, 187, 188, 190

Tuck, Eve, 11

Tupac Amaru, 112

UNESCO, 121

United States: as America, 7, 12, 184; Americanness of, 2; inevitable shape of, 3, 5; presumed white settler character of, 9; sense of global consequence, 25; use of term, 3n5

United States Magazine and Democratic Review, 5

Universal, El, 141

"Universalis Cosmographia Secundum Ptholomaei Traditionem et Americi Vespucii Aliou[m]que Lustrationes [St. Dié]," 3 fig. 0.2, 4, 10

Uruguay, 171, 176

US-Latin American relations, 146–47, 185; good neighbor policy, 5, 149–50, 170n96; looking to vs. looking at US, 162–63; presumption of whiteness in, 153. *See also* Office of the Coordinator of Inter-American Affairs, US (OIAA)

US-Mexican War (1846–48), 5, 6, 25, 145, 178, 184, 186; accumulation of documentary material from, 39–42, 66; accumulation of feelings and, 64; Army during, 37–38, 42, 48; Buena Vista, battle of, 29, 46, 53–58; conquest and, 51, 52, 58, 63, 67; deaths in, 34n18, 35, 37; described,

34; documentation of, 27–31, 32, 33, 39n41, 66; forgetfulness and, 31, 32, 33, 66; length of, 35; letters from, 27–30, 41, 43, 45, 46–50, 59–63, 186; lithography and, 39n41, 40–41, 51, 52–60; magnitude and, 31, 46; Mexican citizens in US after, 39; news of, 27–31, 33; newspapers and, 40, 47; opposition to, 39, 45, 48n72, 58; pictures and, 40–41, 46–50, 51; precipitation, 45–46, 64–68; proliferation of documents about, 46–50; public celebration during, 29, 41; public feeling about, 46, 64–68; racism and, 36, 58–59, 62; resistance to American magnitude and, 146; sedimentation, 33, 45, 46, 50–63; sense of proper boundaries and, 64; sentiment about, 35–36; Treaty of Guadalupe Hidalgo, 25, 34, 39, 51; US audiences' experience of, 52; visibility of, 39–42. *See also* accumulation; Mexican territory

usurpation, 110

Valcárce, Luís, 105n12
values, US, 163–64
Vasconcelos, José, 183
Vats, Anjali, 192, 193
Vertesi, Janet, 21
Vespucci, Amerigo, 4
viewers, 177
virility, 87, 88. *See also* masculinity
vision, 9, 13; American magnitude and, 18; in *megethos*, 18; multisensory nature of, 21; OIAA and, 151, 155–56; as sense, 20–21; sublime and, 17. *See also* feeling; sensation
visuality, American, 148. *See also* Office of the Coordinator of Inter-American Affairs, US (OIAA)
Vitcos, 138–39
volcanoes: Puracé, 88; Sangay, 90–94. *See also* Church, Frederic Edwin; Church's paintings

Waldseemüller, Martin, 3 fig. 0.2, 4, 10
war documentation/letters, 27–30, 41, 43, 45, 46–50, 59–63, 186

Warner, Michael, 42, 44
Watson, Annette, 137
Webster, Frances, 50
"Weight of Rhetoric, The" (Farrell), 32
white settler character of US, 9, 181
white supremacy. *See* superiority/supremacy
whiteness: Church's paintings and, 70; normative, 22–23; performance of, 22; [US] Americanness as category of, 8–9; US-Latin American relations and, 153
Whyte, Kyle Powys, 194
Wilmerding, John, 73–74, 76
Winthrop, Theodore, 77, 78, 81, 89, 92, 102, 135, 145
Wittenberg, Hermann, 16, 17
World War II, 146–47, 151; Canada and, 185. *See also* Walt Disney Company; Office of the Coordinator of Inter-American Affairs, US (OIAA); OIAA-Disney films; US-Latin American relations
writing: constitutive purpose of, 47. *See also* letters, soldiers'; newspapers; proliferation
writing, prison, 48

xenophobia, 52

Yale Peruvian Expedition (YPE), 25, 103, 110, 186; artifacts and, 111, 112–14, 115–21; connection with Incas, 124; doctrines of American discovery and, 106; expeditions, 111–13, 124, 126; instructions for, 117, 118, 119–21; *megethos* and, 107; Peruvian resistance to, 126; Peruvian scholars and, 104; presumptions of American magnitude, 114; results of, 121; scientific work by, 117, 118. *See also* Bingham, Hiram; Machu Picchu
Yang, K. Wayne, 11
Yosso, Tara, 70
YPE (Yale Peruvian Expedition). *See* Bingham, Hiram; Machu Picchu; Yale Peruvian Expedition (YPE)